.ock should

CLE

branch of the
the dat

Thomas Cromwell

To Mark Carnes,
Scholar, Teacher, Visionary, and Academic
Entrepreneur Extraordinaire

Thomas Cromwell

Henry VIII's Henchman

J. PATRICK COBY

AMBERLEY

This edition first published in 2012

Amberley Publishing
The Hill, Stroud
Gloucestershire, GL5 4EP

www.amberley-books.com

This edition was published by arrangement with
Lexington Books. © J. Patrick Coby, 2009, 2012

The right of J. Patrick Coby to be identified as
the Author of this work has been asserted in
accordance with the Copyrights, Designs and
Patents Act 1988.

ISBN 978 1 4456 0775 7

British Library Cataloguing in Publication Data.
A catalogue record for this book is available
from the British Library.

Typeset in 11pt on 16pt Palatino.
Typesetting and Origination by Amberley Publishing
Printed in the UK.

Contents

Preface

Thomas Cromwell, principal secretary to Henry VIII, has been the subject of numerous biographies, all of which, until recently, were decades old and long out of print. That now has changed with the appearance of three new biographies, including this one, first published in 2009.

This particular history is both of the man and of the period, since persons other than Cromwell sometimes occupy center stage. Its intended readers are college students and the general public, not experts in the field. It accepts, with qualifications, the still regnant interpretation that Cromwell was a leading figure in Reformation politics. The biographer's bias mandates no less. But it is respectful of dissenting views and tries to give notice of current scholarship, even without the instrumentality of footnotes. Any argument of its own, such as Cromwell's indebtedness to Machiavelli, is entirely subordinate to the narrative of events. (Parenthetical references to Machiavelli's *Prince* and *Discourses on Livy* scattered throughout the book are meant to suggest possible points of influence.) Chronology is maintained wherever possible.

Sixteenth-century spelling – comically phonetic, inventive, idiosyncratic, and unstable – is modernised. Unsourced quotations in the body of the text are mostly from Cromwell's letters or from the *Calendar of Letters and Papers* (see Bibliographical Note).

My thanks to Smith College for the sabbatical leave during which I wrote this book.

Cromwell Timeline

1485? Birth at Putney (Surrey)

1503–12 Travel and work in Italy and the Netherlands

1513? Marriage to Elizabeth Wykys

1514 Trip to Rome

1516 Possible start of association with Cardinal Wolsey

1517–18 Trip to Rome

1523 Election to parliament

1524 Member of Wolsey household; admittance to Gray's Inn

1525–29 Wolsey secretary supervising dissolution of monasteries

1529 Election to parliament as burgess for Taunton

1530 King's servant

1531 Privy councilor

1532 Master of the Jewels; Master of the King's Wards; Clerk of the Hanaper of Chancery

1533 Chancellor of the Exchequer

1534 Principal secretary; Master of the Rolls

1535 Vicegerent of Spirituals; Chancellor of Cambridge

1536 Lord Privy Seal; Baron Okeham

1537 Knight of the Garter

1540, April Earl of Essex; Lord Great Chamberlain

1540, June Arrest for treason and heresy

1540, July Execution

1
Introduction: Thomas Cromwell and the Sixteenth Century

The sixteenth century, as is often said, was a transitional age, a renascence and beginning, but also a continuation of the immediate past, if not a throwback to an earlier time. The chief issue then was the place of the church in civil society. That same issue had preoccupied authorities throughout the Middle Ages, with dramatic church-state clashes erupting at regular intervals. But in the sixteenth century conclusive action was finally taken. The principalities of Europe – some of them at least – moved to terminate interference from papal Rome, to replace the one universal church of Christendom with multiple national churches, and to subordinate these ecclesiastical establishments to the territorial, temporal power.

The territorial state, striving toward sovereignty, was another development of the period. Spain and France began the movement in the fifteenth century; England followed suit in the sixteenth, centralizing power in the monarchy and unifying the island (partially). Feudalism thus evolved into statehood, and magnates ceded influence to bureaucrats. Contrarily, whole provinces changed their rulers, appeared and disappeared, on the basis of marriage alliances between princely households, as if statehood were an article of private property subject to laws of inheritance. An emerging national consciousness did work to undermine

Christian universalism, allowing proud Englishmen to spurn the commands of the Roman pope; but the king of England thought nothing of calling himself the king of France, and the German emperor was simultaneously the king of Spain, the Netherlands, and southern Italy.

In fact, along with the first stirrings of nationhood, an empire, the likes of which Europe had not seen since the days of Charlemagne, was again in the making. Technically confined to the German territories, the Netherlands, and northwestern Italy, the Holy Roman Empire under Charles V was in actuality almost continent-wide. The Habsburgs of Austria had wedded their way to such greatness, acquiring the Netherlands through the marriage of Maximilian and Mary of Burgundy (1477); and then, the *coup de grâce*, acquiring Spain through the marriage of their son Philip to Joanna, the daughter of Ferdinand and Isabella (1496). However, this *coup de grâce* was not quite that, as the project of unifying Europe through royal marriage was not quite complete. France stood between the Spanish and German possessions of Charles (son of Philip and Joanna); accordingly, France was targeted for absorption, either by marriage or by conquest. The territorial integrity of France, much less its independence as an equal sovereign power, was barely a consideration. In the event, France survived the half-century of war with the Empire (which France also helped to cause), because a rival empire in the east, that of the Turks, was expanding westward and threatening Charles' German domains; and because religious reform, started by Martin Luther, was attacking the Empire from within.

This reform, which had many of the markings of religious revivals of previous centuries, represented a partial retreat from the secular humanism of the Italian Renaissance. Instead of reclaiming the lost literatures of Greece and Rome, learning from the ancients so as to build a better world in the present, Protestant Europe sought to connect with primitive Christianity and escape from the world altogether. Translating Scripture, publishing its texts, and submitting their interpretation to the consciences of individuals became the consuming passions of the age. The religious wars which marred the latter half of the century were the product of this intensity of conviction, combined with corrupt and discredited ecclesiastical authorities unable to provide leadership and maintain order. The sixteenth-century papacy was a temporal power like the kingdoms of northern Europe, except that like the Empire it pretended to universality. It governed the Papal States of central Italy, a possession of the popes since before Charlemagne. But only lately, with the outbreak of the French invasions (1494), had the popes become completely enmeshed in worldly affairs. As the governing body of the center-most Italian province, the papacy was needed to organise a defense of the peninsula against the foreign invaders (though just as often it was in league with them). There even was a pope (Julius II) who led forces into battle. Preoccupied thus with war and its expense, this secularised papacy was in no position to respond to the reform demands of Luther and his disciples, nor was it in a position to censure princes whose conduct of state affairs ignored the requirements of Scripture and natural law. The sixteenth century saw the triumph of a style of governance which more closely followed the teachings of Machiavelli than the teachings of classical authors, the humanists, or the Holy Bible. Princes set scruples aside and adopted an 'ends justify-means' philosophy. With the map of Europe subject to alteration by brute force and sharp bargaining, it seemed to many that the world belonged to the audacious and the cunning.

The bloodshed and destruction of the sixteenth century resulted then from two peculiar causes: the religious fervor captivating the populace; and the *raison d'etat* tactics practiced by the rulers. Rebellion was a common occurrence, and tyrannicide a common theme, because in some quarters government was expected to represent 'true faith' and threatened with overthrow if it failed to measure up; and because hereditary right could scarce withstand the momentum of armies in the field and the duplicity of rulers in their courts. But the sanguinary character of the century produced in other quarters an appetite for quiet at any price and a longing for a hereditary principle made unassailable by its association with the divine. The 'divine right of kings' was (re)discovered and solemnised by century's end, both to secure the peace and to elevate the temporal authority to a perch higher than the spiritual. But temporal authority presuming to be the consecrated agent of God was a notion frightening and blasphemous to the minds of some, who looked about for a countervailing force and a countervailing idea to serve as a check upon the absolutism of kings. Parliament was that force, and toleration was that idea.

Because of his early involvement with many of the major actors, events, and controversies of the century, Thomas Cromwell is deserving of the close attention which a biography affords. To be sure, he had no direct dealings with the Turkish empire – though that empire figured in his diplomatic calculations; he did not quite use the language of divine right – though the idea was implicit in the supremacy, and his opponents judged the augmented monarchy of Henry VIII to be a caesaropapist despotism; and he died before religious toleration had acquired much purchase – though his church of the 'middle way' tried to mitigate oppression by allowing for diversity in minor things. But aside from caveats such as these (to which New World exploration might be added), it can be fairly said that the leading issues of the age were presaged in, and perhaps influenced by, Cromwell's short career. Cromwell was in the forefront of the movement to liberate kings from papal control and feudal subservience, to make kings the heads of local churches and central governments, and to free kings from the moral imperatives of religion and philosophy, while tying kings to parliaments and to law. Cromwell's importance and emblematic status derives from his work as architect of the English Reformation in its opening phase. In that capacity and to that end, Cromwell devised the plan that divorced Henry from his wife Catherine, emancipated England from dependency on Rome, delivered supremacy to the monarchy and subordination to the clergy and nobility, rationalised the operations of government and staffed it with 'new men' like himself, financed the nation's wars with the confiscated wealth of the dissolved monasteries, partnered the monarchy with the parliament, subdued Ireland, and absorbed Wales into England. Moreover, his execution of the plan, called initially the king's 'great matter', was an exercise in Machiavellian statecraft, albeit an exercise less than textbook perfect.

Cromwell served a king who disliked him personally and abused him repeatedly (in the words of William Paulet: 'the king beknaves him twice a week and sometimes knocks him well about the pate'); a king who was self-righteous, temperamental, and hard to please; who, though capaciously talented, was lazy and indecisive and yet capable of bursts of overawing energy and self-assurance. It is still a disputed question whether Cromwell managed and manipulated Henry or Henry instructed and commanded Cromwell. The description of Henry as explosive and unpredictable does suggest a preference for the former view; but mainly that debate will not be entered into, much less settled to the satisfaction of all, because the assumption here made is that Cromwell, whatever his relationship with Henry, was a material factor in the transformation of England into a modern state. Few would say otherwise, even if some would argue about degree. Much more than mere servant and something less than effective king, Cromwell, it is supposed, was consequential enough to be worth the trouble to know about. That said, what further needs stating is that Cromwell's life, in this telling, is not the only lens through which the period is viewed. The events of the 1530s remain the focus even when Cromwell is not at the head.

Breaking from Rome

England's split with Rome was one of the more celebrated schisms of the century: Henry demanded of the pope a divorce (technically an annulment, but commonly called a divorce) from his wife, Catherine of Aragon. The pope, for reasons of state and perhaps of religion, delayed making a decision. Henry became frustrated and cut off English revenues to Rome. He then looked to separating from Catherine using domestic institutions and without the permission of the pope. Step-by-step England became schismatic because Henry needed a local clergy independent of Rome but subservient to the state.

But similar processes were underway in staunchly Catholic Spain and France. The Spanish monarchy, under Ferdinand and Isabella, had obtained effective control over ecclesiastical appointments, since pro-forma approval was granted by the papacy to royal nominees. The monarchy had also lessened the power of the papacy to direct and constrain by controlling the publication and implementation of papal bulls inside Spain and its Italian possessions. This power in later years did much to keep Henry on his throne, since without the cooperation of the Spanish king (also Holy Roman emperor), the pope's excommunication order (until 1538) was provisional only and without material effect. In Sicily, part of those Italian possessions, secular independence was even more advanced. There the king operated as permanent papal legate, preventing the takeover of the local clergy by an emissary from Rome. By contrast, the archbishop of Canterbury, William Warham, was superseded as church primate when Thomas Wolsey, already a cardinal, became papal legate and assumed command of the English church. The adjudication of Henry's divorce case was also placed in the hands of two papal legates, Wolsey and Lorenzo Campeggio. And while this token of English subservience was soon to end, as was the payment to Rome of tithes and taxes, Spain had already disavowed its dependency and had discontinued these obligations. Moreover, with the creation of the court of the Spanish Inquisition late in the fifteenth century, all of whose judges were crown appointees, Spain brought the church's judicial powers under secular control.

France was the scene of the last great tug-of-war of the so called *regnum* and *sacerdotium*, the medieval contest between the temporal and spiritual powers. King Philip IV did battle with Pope Boniface VIII; and the king's victory on that occasion (1296–1302) was the tipping point in the centuries-long controversy between church and state. On the heels of that struggle, and through the third quarter of the fourteenth century, the papacy was removed to Avignon, France to exist in what the rest of Europe came to refer to as the Babylonian Captivity. France, clearly, was used to bare-knuckles dealings with the Holy See, including multiple invasions of its Italian homeland in the current period. And like Spain, France too enjoyed the right of censoring papal decrees and the right of filling ecclesiastical offices with candidates chosen by the king. Such patronage made the Gallican church more dependent on the crown than on the papacy and bought the loyalty of noble families whose second sons and spinster daughters found careers as abbots and abbesses.

State-Building

Spain came together as a country after centuries of struggle with the Muslim conquerors of the Middle Ages. By the close of the fifteenth century, all that remained of the Reconquista (the eight-century campaign by Christian Europeans against the Moorish occupation of Spain and Portugal) was capture of the kingdom of Granada in the far south. That fell in 1492. Before then, in 1479, the main work of state-building was accomplished when Isabella of Castile (central Spain) and Ferdinand of Aragon (eastern Spain) joined their kingdoms together. The unification of the peninsula was completed in 1512 with the absorption of Navarre in the north. (Portugal, the exception, emerged as an independent state between the twelfth and the fourteenth centuries when Castilian attempts to regain it finally ended. It was conquered though by Philip II in 1580 and remained part of Spain until 1640.) The other challenge to 'one king, one law, one faith', as Isabella named the unification, were the nobles, whose power expanded in proportion to their usefulness in expelling the Muslims. When not in use, they molested and pillaged the cities, which formed a league of mutual protection styled the Holy Brotherhood. Ferdinand and Isabella brought the Brotherhood and its militias under the control of the crown. They also brought under crown control, or simply ignored, the Cortes of Castile and Aragon, the two most important of Spain's many representative assemblies. The Spanish monarchy thus achieved a degree of absolutism not attempted by Henry and not wanted by Cromwell.

Medieval France was a collection of powerful duchies surrounding an insignificant kingdom confined to Paris and the Ile de France (then a slice of land running south from Paris to Orléans). Until the reign of Philip Augustus (1180–1223), the king's vassals were more important than the king himself. One such vassal was Henry II of England (1154–89), who possessed most of northwestern France by inheritance, and most of southwestern France by marriage to Eleanor of Aquitaine. Henry was far more the ruler of France than was Philip its king. But Henry's son, John, could not hold onto these possessions, losing Normandy, Maine, Anjou, and Touraine to Philip (1204). The breakout from the Paris enclave and the slow march toward statehood began with these acquisitions. Southern France was obtained during the next quarter-century in consequence of a successful church crusade against the heretical Albigensians, whose stronghold was Toulouse. Expansion after that relaxed for a time, as the saintly rule of Louis IX (1226–70) focused on the good governing of what was had already as opposed to the forceful taking of more. In the next centuries, though, the effort revived with the Hundred Years' War (1337–1453), which, in its first stage, was an attempt by English kings to reclaim their lost inheritance;

and which, in its second stage, was an attempt by French kings to extend their hold on the country. In the end, England was expelled from its continental possessions, except for the Calais Pale. The consolidation of France was finally completed under Louis XI (1461–83) who seized the duchy of Burgundy upon the death of Charles the Bold (1477); and under Louis' successor, Charles VIII (1483–98), who acquired the duchy of Brittany through marriage to Anne de Bretagne (1491). Gascony was wrested from English control at the end of the Hundred Years' War, but its incorporation into France waited upon the ascension to the throne of Henry of Navarre (1589), who through marriage and inheritance came to possess the province's divided lands.

Like Spain, the French monarchy emerged from its medieval weakness the recognised master of a unified state. And though it was co-ruler with an Estates General representing all classes of society, this French assembly, in the period between 1450 and 1550, met rarely, was advisory mainly, and had little control over spending. An emergency tax called the *taille*, meant to defend against the English invader, was kept in place and made permanent (1439), thus freeing the king from supervision by the estates. Central power was also established through the use of royal officials recruited from the bourgeoisie, instead of from the nobility. The troublesome magnates who had ruled the roost during most of the Carolingian dynasty (750–987) and during half of the Capetian (987–1328) were largely killed off during the Hundred Years' War (seven thousand of them lost). The Wars of the Roses (1455–85) worked the same magic for England and the Tudor monarchy.

Although a sense of statehood took root in fifteenth-century France, its hold on the public imagination was not enough to dislodge the dynastic politics practiced by the French kings and accepted by their subjects. With a contiguous country at last in place, the sensible policy, one might suppose, was to expand eastward toward the Rhine. But four successive monarchs thought it better to enforce their family's claims to trans-alpine Italian lands. France fought to acquire Naples and Milan as an inheritance of its kings rather than Lorraine, Franche-Comté, and Savoy as an enlargement of itself. England was no different. Henry VIII preferred attacking France, because his ancestors had once ruled there, to annexing Scotland on his northern border. In fact, Cromwell noted the folly of this strategy long before he was a king's minister obliged to execute the king's policies. Cromwell though did manage, once he became a minister, to take first steps toward the creation of the United Kingdom: by eliminating the customary immunities from royal justice enjoyed by some territories; by reorganizing the border councils to increase their dependence on the crown; by extending English administration and parliamentary representation to Wales; and by undermining Dublin's feudal magnates and replacing them in government with English lord deputies supported by an English garrison.

Religion, Reform, Rebellion

As powerful as were the monarchies of Spain, France, and England at the start of the sixteenth century, they were to become more powerful still– certainly in conception and often in fact – as a result of the religious controversies that entangled them all. But the march toward absolutism seemed rather like disintegration to contemporaries whose countries were split by rebellions and civil wars and whose royal houses were hard-put to sustain themselves. Spain suffered the least disruption and was the most ruthless in suppressing dissent. France came close to dismemberment but emerged from the struggle more united than ever. England, the first to grapple with the religion problem, contained the furies of sectarian strife and ended the century a bona fide equal of its continental rivals.

The chief vulnerability of the Tudor monarchy under Henry VIII was the absence of a legitimate male heir. Henry was not seriously challenged by his nobles, but domestic peace could not be assured without a successor in place to continue the line. Unfortunately, Catherine, his wife of twenty years, was past child-bearing age as of 1529. A new wife was therefore needed, the hunt for whom put Henry at loggerheads with the papacy. When the pope delayed granting an annulment, Henry pivoted and attacked his own clergy. English anticlericalism had causes apart from the king's dynastic problems: e.g., the financial burdens imposed by the church; the perceived injustice of canon law adjudicated by opaque ecclesiastical courts; the neglect of ministerial duties by high clergy, coupled with the lax sexual morals of low clergy. Henry tapped into the public's discontent so as to weaken and take over the English church, which, in short order, surrendered its independent legislative powers (enshrined in Magna Carta), acknowledged the king to be its supreme head on earth, provided Henry with his divorce, and stood by helplessly as its monastic colleagues suffered the dissolution of their houses and the confiscation of their wealth. The strategist of this campaign, which turned the church into a department of the state, was Thomas Cromwell (though a few scholars give principal credit to Henry). Doctrinally the church moved toward Protestantism without ever becoming fully Protestant. Henry applied the brakes, and Cromwell so arranged the passengers as to keep as few as possible from being hurled out of the carriage. There were rebellions, and there were persecutions; but England never descended into the civil war that for decades roiled neighboring France. Civil war came in the next century, when the obdurateness of Stuart kings and the radicalism of Puritan dissenters caused England to explode; but for the duration of the sixteenth century, England was kept at peace by the firm hands of Henry and Cromwell, and later by the compromises of Elizabeth I.

Not so on the continent, where the Protestant creed brought bloody religious strife and fresh political thinking. Lutheranism had its first and most lasting impact in Germany, the territory of its birth. Germany was not previously mentioned among the states of the period because its unification was delayed until the nineteenth century – a delay caused partly by Lutheranism. Despite the fact that Luther respected the distinction between church and state and offered a brand of religious reform which emphasised the inner life as a sanctuary from the stresses of the world, he was, willy-nilly, drawn into the political contests of the day. The papacy responded to his demands for reform with threats of excommunication and arrest. Luther, in defense, sought out the protection of German princes, some of whom were happy to extend him their patronage. They came forward because Luther's attack on church corruption provided the perfect excuse for streamlining their governments, the administration of which had been made inefficient and expensive by centuries of ecclesiastical interference. From the start, therefore, a religious reformation with tendencies toward mysticism was co-opted by politics. State endorsement of the Christian faith was of course as old as Emperor Constantine (306–37), but what was newly happening was the multiplication of religions combined with the multiplication of states. Religious non-conformity, always a problem, could not so easily be stamped out if heresy enjoyed the protection of state power. And if state power was not united and overwhelming, but disjoined and contested, then warfare within a state was likely to occur, since resistance to a heretic prince was generally allowed. Disestablishment was off the table because of the presumption that people professing different faiths could not all be loyal to the same state. And toleration of dissent was as yet an unnoticed option, because of the conviction, nearly universal, that religious truth was singular, evident, and of first importance, and that malignity and self-interest, therefore, were all that prevented dissenters from seeing the light.

So alarmed was Luther by the Peasants' Revolt (1524–5), which looked to his anti-authoritarianism as a justification of its own, that he became authoritarian himself in his eagerness to condone the measures taken by princes to suppress the uprising. Moreover, having thrown off the structure and discipline of the Catholic church, he was constrained to invest the secular power with responsibility for preserving the uniformity of the faith. Princes became in effect unmitred bishops, charged with combating heresy and persecuting heretics. Dependence on the princes thus caused Luther to advocate submission to their rule. On the most pressing issue of the age – passive obedience vs. active resistance – Luther stood for order over liberty and for submission to power. But obedience had its limits, since the liege lord of the German princes was the Catholic emperor Charles, whom Protestant subjects could in conscience resist if he forced Catholic worship on them; otherwise the quietism of Luther, joined with the dismantling of the ecclesiastical estate wrought by him, opened the way to an unprecedented enlargement of the secular power. While Henry VIII was no Lutheran, it is easy to see why he found this new creed attractive and why Cromwell, devoted to the crown's supremacy, pushed Henry to adopt it.

The most important of Luther's disciples was John Calvin (1509–64), whose eventual influence exceeded that of the master. Calvin was in temperament more autocratic than Luther, although Calvinism in the hands of second-generation followers came to be associated with resistance and even with democracy. When Calvin was in charge and unencumbered, as with the founding of the government of Geneva, church and state were nearly one, and church was nearly all (or aspired to be). But when Calvinism tried taking root in inhospitable soil, such as France and Scotland, each ruled by Catholic monarchs, passive obedience to sanctified state power was replaced by resistance, rebellion, and tyrannicide. The Huguenots in France and John Knox in Scotland were persecuted nonconformists with little chance of prevailing through persuasion. Hence resistance was condoned in the writings of each: resistance by lesser magistrates, in the case of the former, so as to contain the violence; in the case of the latter, resistance by the public at large, because lesser magistrates were mostly opposed. In France the violence was not contained, however, as eight civil wars were fought over a span of three decades (1562–93). During the wars, dissenting populations were slaughtered en masse (with the St Bartholomew's Day Massacre as the defining event), while kings and party leaders were frequently targeted for assassination. The widespread violence brought a group of thinkers, called the Politiques, to appreciate anew the value of unchallenged monarchical power. They articulated theories of absolute sovereignty and the divine right of kings. But as a practical matter, they also encouraged toleration in circumstances where the price of religious uniformity, ordinarily a good thing, was too high to pay. The price in France was plainly too high, and so coexistence was the sensible alternative, even though coexistence might diminish the sovereignty of the crown. The wars ended when Protestant Henry of Navarre, a Bourbon claimant to the vacant Valois throne, agreed to convert to Catholicism ('Paris is worth a mass,' he said famously – or apocryphally). His Edict of Nantes (1598), which declared Catholicism the official state religion, also extended religious toleration to Huguenots and the right to rule over and garrison their own separate towns. (This state-within-a-state arrangement proved incompatible with the centralizing ambitions of the French monarchy of the seventeenth century, which besieged and conquered these fortified Huguenot cities, suppressed the practice of Protestantism, and finally revoked the Edict of Nantes [1685].)

Calvinism had a different finish in Scotland: after a three-year rebellion, it took over the realm and then helped to chase away a queen. Scotland's king, James V, died young in 1542, leaving behind a French wife and a new-born daughter. The wife, Mary of Guise, ruled (as principal councilor then as regent), while the daughter, Mary Stuart, grew up in France. The Scottish lords disliked submitting to a French female, but they supported her when challenged early by John Knox, wanting to convert Scotland to Calvinism. They abandoned her, however, when Knox returned from twelve years of forced and voluntary exile and organised rioting Protestant sectaries into armed insurrectionists. Meanwhile, Mary Stuart married the French dauphin, Francis (1558), who a year later succeeded to the throne and a year after that succumbed to disease. Six months earlier Mary of Guise had died as well. So when Catholic Mary, queen of Scots, reunited with her countrymen (1561), she was husbandless and motherless, and her native land had just been captured for Calvinism by John Knox. The lords received her coolly; Knox inveighed against her violently; and after six years of sensational romance and lethal court intrigue, Mary was arrested, imprisoned, and forced to abdicate. She escaped the next year and attempted to regain her lost throne. But defeated in battle, she and her supporters sought refuge in England (1568). There she lived under house arrest, and worse, for nineteen years before being executed for treason by Queen Elizabeth, tired of Mary's alleged plotting (1587).

Protestantism never advanced into Spain. The Catholic Reformation stopped it, as did the Spanish Inquisition. An ethnic factor also came into play, for non-conformity in Spain had a Semitic face –Jews and Muslims forcibly converted to Christianity but never assimilated or trusted. The Muslims, called the Moriscos, represented the greater danger because of the power of the Turkish empire in the Mediterranean. Fear of enemies within induced Spaniards to oppress the Moriscos, and quarreling administrators prevented a peaceful settlement of the dispute. In desperation, the Moriscos rebelled, appealing to the sultan for support. But the sultan preferred attacking Cyprus instead, and he left the Moriscos to fend for themselves. They held out for two years (1568–70) in southern Spain before being defeated and dispersed across Castile.

The Netherlands was a different matter. Calvinism seeped in from France, Germany, and England, and the local nobility, at odds with their Spanish overlord, were unable or unwilling to control it. Riots broke out in major cities, during which church-burnings and image-smashing had free rein (1566). In due course the iconoclastic frenzy was suppressed by military intervention and Inquisitional terror; but these reprisals only caused elements of the nobility to organise a proper resistance centered around a group of privateers called the Sea Beggars. Out of money and out of will, Spain agreed to withdraw its forces on condition that the provinces of the Netherlands remain all Catholic. They refused, and in southern cities Calvinist dictatorships were established. The highhandedness of these extremist governments offended the Walloon nobles who reaffirmed their Catholic orthodoxy and renewed their allegiance to Spain. In doing so, they differentiated themselves from the nobles of the northern provinces who came together under the Union of Utrecht (1579), soon to be called the United Provinces. England sent assistance but continued to negotiate with Spain (1585). The assistance angered Philip II, who conceived the plan of attacking England, while the negotiations left the Dutch suspicious and feeling betrayed. Elizabeth had alienated both sides, but she saved herself when the English navy and bad weather defeated the Spanish Armada (1588). Some years later, with the religious wars having ended in France and the country united behind its new 'Catholic' monarch, Henry IV (Henry of Navarre), Spain tried one last time to determine the French succession. This Franco-Spanish war (1595–8) achieved little other than to provide the United Provinces the breathing space needed to solidify their break from Spain and commence the building of independent Holland (completed in 1648).

Statecraft and Diplomacy

For centuries European potentates had been treated to unsolicited instruction by self-appointed advisers offering their high-toned counsel in books called generically 'mirrors of princes.' That practice quickened in the Renaissance in response to the rise of the new monarchies exercising the invigorated powers of their centralised governments. One author who contributed to the genre was Desiderius Erasmus, the most famous intellectual of his time. Erasmus put great store by the role of the prince's adviser and tried himself to become an adviser to Charles, when he was still a boy, and to Henry, when he was newly a king. Neither monarch took him on, so Erasmus wrote to them, and to others, from afar. In his *Education of a Christian Prince*, he laid out humanism's recipe for successful statecraft.

To begin with, writes Erasmus, a prince must be able to count on the loyal support of his subjects. In the case of a hereditary prince, which is the norm, this support is gladly given, unless a prince offends against customary practices and Christian virtue. Thus a traditionalist prince, who is pious, kind, merciful, and humble, is secure within his realm. Only benevolence can win the public's backing, and only voluntary consent is true submission. At the same time a prince must guard against the hatred and contempt of his subjects, which he can best do by: controlling his appetites and passions; economizing on his expenses; discharging his duties with care; and supervising his subordinates closely. A prince should not try concealing his true nature–as exposure is assured–but should be exactly what he appears to be. And what a prince should be, in sum, is skillful, honest, diligent, and upright. These qualities a prince can develop through sound education, in the first instance, and maintain through receipt of wise counsel thereafter.

The commonweal is the prince's foremost concern. In this regard the prince is like a physician applying curatives to a patient. As the responsible physician studies the patient's illness and listens to the patient's complaints, so the responsible prince stays at home and learns about his people and his country. The prince who travels frequently and far squanders his resources and neglects his duty. The prince should govern through laws that are few in number, clear in phrasing, and impartial toward all. He should correct laws corrupted over time and impose only those taxes that are low, temporary, and considerate of the poor. Most of all, the prince should confine himself to the good governance of his realm and not strive for its expansion through marriage alliances or through war. Foreign-born princesses confuse allegiances and fail to deliver the security and comity expected of them; more often they are sources of recrimination, bitterness, and conflict. War is a scourge; it should never be undertaken for light or personal reasons, such as the honor of the prince or the assertion of dynastic claims. These motives concern not the people, whose welfare the prince is obligated to serve. Likewise, diplomacy is a mistake; for what should function as a pledge of peace and an alternative to war is used instead to deceive and ensnare. It is a scandal that Christian princes should even have need of treaties; so how much greater is the scandal that these treaties are little observed and are a pretext for war. Christianity is a pacifistic religion. In order to be true to that faith, the prince should disengage from the competition of states; and if circumstances forbid this posture of isolation and neutrality, the prince should abdicate his throne rather than commit the crimes needed to defend it.

A friend and colleague of Erasmus was Thomas More, author of *Utopia*. More shared the humanist view that peace among states is an incomparable good and that rulers do best who attend to their domestic affairs, forgoing plans for glory in war. In Book I of *Utopia*, his Raphael Hythloday, the fictional traveler to fictional lands, especially the 'nowhere' land of Utopia, satirises the knavery of courtiers and the follies of court life. He imagines a conversation at the court of the French king in which jealous courtiers pitch competing schemes for the conquest of Italy; also a conversation at a second, unspecified court where the subject is the raising of revenues. All proposals involve double-dealing and condone princely greed; all are clever, jaded, and prideful in their liberation from moral constraints; and all are shown up as stupid and wicked when compared with the good sense and simple decency of Utopia's neighbors. The issue is whether any profit is to be had from Hythloday's taking a place at court and contributing his radical counsel to a king. But his counsel, on its own, seems hardly radical – do not invade Italy and do not rob your subjects – however removed it might be from the commonplace practices of the day.

Commonplace indeed. French kings did invade Italy, repeatedly; in pursuit of which they traded provinces, married off princesses, paid tribute, hired mercenaries, bribed adversaries, and betrayed allies. And if the other court alluded to is England's under Henry VII, that king did debase currency, impose fines, sell pardons, and corrupt judges (all charges laid by Hythloday). European monarchs behaved generally the same and were playing catch-up with Italian princes, whose reputation for nefariousness was unsurpassed. Politics in the sixteenth century was violent, and war was regarded as the sport of kings. To the extent that anyone gave thought to the purpose of warfare – beyond face-saving, glory, avarice, and employment – it was for the defense and stability of the realm to be achieved through balance-of-power strategies. England tended to think this way because its off-continent location provided protection and made alliances and war, to some degree, a matter of choice. By siding with the weaker power in a given conflict, England could prevent the emergence of a hegemon able to cross the Channel and occupy the country's interior. During Henry VIII's reign, England sided first with Spain against France, because France was richer and more populous (and was England's historic foe); but when Spain and the Empire united and were together triumphant in Italy, England allied with France. Professionalised diplomacy had by then come into use. England supported resident embassies at the courts of all of the major powers. Most other countries did likewise, learning from the Italians who were the first to develop a diplomatic service. Ambassadors smiled and promised friendship;

they collected information, some public, some private and gathered by spies; they intrigued and conspired; they floated proposals and spread rumours; and they negotiated treaties. Primarily they lied about the true intentions of their masters – and were lied to in turn.

The practice of statecraft and diplomacy refused to be guided by theories of the same. The practice was parochial and this-worldly – the scramble for position and power by ambitious courtiers and territorial states. The theory was universalistic and transcendent – the memory of the Roman Empire and the dream of a Christian republic. Thomas Cromwell took his cues from the rough world he inhabited. His statecraft was as realpolitik as any of the age; but it advanced a purpose larger than his own self-interest or the money-mania of the monarch he served. For Cromwell persuaded Henry to utilise parliament, not only as an occasional instrument for the collection of taxes, but as a partner in power necessary to perpetuate the initiatives of the crown. The English Reformation, which could have rested on royal decrees, rested instead on parliamentary enactments. Parliament was almost continuously in existence during Cromwell's near-decade in office – three separate parliaments convened for eight of ten years; moreover, these parliaments, with one peculiar exception, passed more legislation than any other cluster of parliaments before the nineteenth century. At the time, and in the rush of events, no one could tell for certain whether Cromwell was concealing a despotic absolutism under the cover of a mixed regime; or whether Henry was being schooled by Cromwell in the limits of his own power. Henry expected parliament to bow before his supremacy and comply with his demands; and, for the most part, parliament did as expected. But Henry (perhaps cannily) explained to foreign princes that his policies were not his alone to change, since they existed as statutes passed by parliament; and in the afterglow of Cromwell's demise, Henry declared that 'we at no time stand so highly in our estate royal as in the time of parliament, wherein we as head and you as members are conjoined and knit together into one body politic'. He also had to live with disappointment or delay, as sometimes this compliant parliament did ignore his wishes. The least that can be said is that the habits of a 'king-in-parliament' constitutionalism began their formation in this period.

Imperium in imperio was the medieval concept of multiple sovereigns (e.g., monarch, pope, emperor) exercising simultaneous authority over the same people and lands. Cromwell thought this a dangerous absurdity, and he made establishing the independence and integrity of the temporal, territorial state his paramount purpose instead.

2

The Pre-Ministerial Years

Adventurer, Merchant, Lawyer, Parliamentarian

Thomas Cromwell (1485?–1540), first secretary of Henry VIII and eventual peer of the realm, began life in middling circumstances. His family, several generations preceding, had enjoyed considerable prosperity and position when living in Nottinghamshire. The grandfather, John, moved the family south to Putney, Surrey in order to take possession of a fulling mill leased to him by the archbishop; there the family started a wool-processing business. Cromwell's father, Walter, was the second son of John. An enterprising jack-of-all-trades, Walter owned land in the Wimbledon area, raised sheep, fulled cloth, worked metal, brewed ale, and kept a tavern. An occasional 'pillar of the community' (juryman, constable), Walter more commonly was an outcast in trouble with the authorities. Countless times was he fined for overgrazing his sheep on the Putney commons, for ignoring local regulations pertaining to the sale of beer, and for public drunkenness and brawling. On one occasion he was convicted of defrauding the lord and tenants of the Wimbledon manor and ordered to surrender all of his copyhold property.

Walter had two children besides Thomas, daughters Catherine and Elizabeth. Catherine married a prosperous Welshman named Morgan Williams; Elizabeth married a less prosperous (but more auspiciously titled) sheep-farmer named William Wellyfed. (The Williams' son, Richard, when an adult, changed his surname to Cromwell, after his then-famous uncle; he borrowed fame a second time, posthumously, as the great-grandfather of Oliver Cromwell, Lord Protector.) Little is known of the wife and mother, beyond her having connections to a Glossop family in Derbyshire.

Something of Walter's turbulent nature seemingly passed on to Thomas, who quarreled often and violently with his father and who was jailed as a teen (Cromwell confessed in later life to having been a 'ruffian' in his youth). Perhaps it was a family quarrel which caused Thomas, at age fifteen, to leave England in search of opportunity and adventure abroad. Wherever he traveled in those early years of escape, he ended up in southern Italy as a soldier of fortune in the French army fighting at Garigliano (December 1503). The French lost the battle, and Spain the victor established itself as master of Naples. Meanwhile Cromwell made his way to Florence and the Frescobaldi banking house. Florence then was a republic, and Machiavelli was one of its chief officers, serving as Secretary to the Second Chancery and Secretary to the Ten of War (comparable to secretaries of State and Defense). There is no evidence confirming or disconfirming that the two men ever met, but Cromwell's Frescobaldi association – if in fact it existed – makes an acquaintanceship not impossible.

This and other caveats are necessary since so little is known for certain about the pre-public life of Thomas Cromwell. The sources are few, their reliability sometimes in doubt: a letter by the Imperial ambassador Eustace Chapuys; a story told by the expatriate cousin of the king, Cardinal Reginald Pole; occasional comments by contemporary native historian Edward Hall; a novella by contemporary Italian writer Matteo Bandello; a chapter in the latter-day *Acts and Monuments* by martyrologist John Foxe; and genealogical data in the Wimbledon Manor Rolls.

From this smattering of information, scholars surmise that Cromwell, while in Florence, educated himself in finance and mercantile trade, attained proficiency in the Italian language, developed an appreciation for the cultural advances of the High Renaissance (enough for him to support in later life humanist authors of the 'new learning' persuasion), and either converted to, or resisted converting to, the dark side of Italian politics (a la the Borgias), becoming (or not becoming) what then was called an 'Italianate Englishman' – all of this conjecture, to be sure. It is further thought – but with the sources still sketchy and conflicting – that Cromwell, his business apprenticeship complete, attached himself as clerk to a Venetian trader, traveled beyond Florence to other Italian cities, landed in Pisa, and there encountered a party of English merchants who convinced him to come with them to the Netherlands. Once in Antwerp, the money capital of Europe, Cromwell set up shop as a middleman in the wool trade and acquired basic legal experience through an office held in the Fellowship of Merchant Adventurers, an English outfit charged by the king with opening continental markets to the export of finished English cloth.

Probably between 1512 and 1514, Cromwell returned to England (though still traveling back and forth to Antwerp), because no later than 1514, and probably earlier, he married Elizabeth Wycks, widow of a yeoman of the guard, daughter of a well-to-do shearman, and niece of a former gentleman-usher of Henry VII. Cromwell was marrying up in station, and the advantageous match provided him a place in his father-in-law's sheep-shearing business. Eventually Cromwell took over the enterprise, adding to it money-lending, estate management, notarial services, and a legal practice. The circumstances of

Cromwell's formal legal training are unknown, but before the decade was out he had established himself as a reputed London solicitor, and in 1524 he was admitted to Gray's Inn.

The marriage to Elizabeth produced three children, a son and two daughters. Gregory, the first born, was put under the care of tutor John Chekyng at Pembroke Hall, Cambridge. Gregory's cousin, Christopher Wellyfed, was educated with him at Pembroke. Christopher was by far the better student; indeed, Gregory's progress was so slow that his father, displeased and wanting to blame the tutor, was frequently late in paying Chekyng his fees. By all accounts Gregory was a disappointment. Nevertheless, Thomas Cromwell, years later, did manage to marry Gregory to the sister of Queen Jane Seymour; and later still dull Gregory did manage to retain the baronial title of his disgraced father. Gregory survived his father; but his sisters, Anne and Grace, did not. They died, likely, of the sweating sickness, as likely did their mother; all passed away between 1527 and 1529.

There were other trips to Italy during this time, at least two – one in 1514 and another in 1517 or 1518. The latter is comical in the retelling and shows a light-hearted and inventive side of the character of Cromwell. He and two others representing the Guild of our Lady of St Boltolph's Church in Boston, Lincolnshire, traveled to Rome to secure renewal of pardons from Lenten observances for members of the guild. Rather than submit their petition to the curia and wait for the slow wheels of the Vatican bureaucracy to grind out a reply, the three men went directly to the pope, whom they found at his hunting pavilion outside the city. First they serenaded his Holiness, Leo X, with a 'three-man song'; then they presented him a gift of sweetmeats and jellies which they described as native English fare reserved for royalty. A delighted and satisfied Leo granted them their request then and there. On the journey home – likewise on the journey down – Cromwell occupied himself with memorizing the Latin version of the New Testament, recently translated from Greek by Erasmus. Foxe is the source of this story which he related to demonstrate the proto-Protestant piety of Thomas Cromwell. Whether or not Cromwell's piety was sincere and Protestant, the power of his memory was clearly prodigious (a fact attested to by others), and his command of Latin better than average.

When Cromwell first came to the notice of Cardinal Wolsey is uncertain: 1514 was once thought the date of their initial encounter; 1516 is the date now sometimes preferred; but definitely by 1520 Cromwell was known to the Lord Chancellor, for in that year Wolsey commissioned Cromwell to draft an appeal to the papal curia against a decision in the Prerogative Court of Canterbury in a suit involving a vicar and a prioress. And three years later Cromwell sent a petition to Chancery Court over which Wolsey presided. In between these engagements Cromwell may have done occasional contract work for the cardinal, but the record is blank. It is known, however, that as of 1522 Cromwell was listed as a servant of the marquess of Dorset and that the marquess was an associate of Wolsey (who before reaching greatness once taught the marquess's brothers at Magdalene College), capable, perhaps, of opening doors to more regular employment. But not until the next year, and following a dramatic performance in parliament, did Cromwell enter the service of the cardinal.

Parliament had not been summoned since 1515. Wolsey was wary of parliaments and kept their convenings to a minimum. But in 1523 England was at war with France, and the king had not the revenue to maintain his armies in the field; hence parliament was called to raise £800,000 in new taxes. Parliament balked at the request and sent to Wolsey a counter-proposal for half the amount. Wolsey though was insistent, and he appeared before parliament to demand an answer and compel compliance. Under direction from Thomas More, then Speaker of the House of Commons, parliamentarians greeted Wolsey with 'a marvelous obstinate silence' (in the words of More's biographer and son-in-law, William Roper). Yet in the end parliament yielded, voting to pay close to the full sum in a subsidy spread over four years. Cromwell was a member of this parliament (a sign of how far he had come in the world), and in his first surviving letter, he described his disappointment with parliament's protracted and futile proceedings:

> I among others have endured a parliament which continued by the space of seventeen whole weeks where we communed of war, peace, strife, contention, [etc.] ... and also how a commonwealth might be edified and also continued within this our realm. Howbeit, in conclusion we have done as our predecessors have been wont to do, that is to say, as well as we might and left where we began.

Despite the mocking review, Cromwell was not so discouraged as to abstain from personal involvement. At some point in the debates, he delivered (or at least composed) a fourteen-page maiden speech attacking the government's war policy and the tax increases needed to support it. The speech began, however, with Cromwell shrewdly taking the government's side and stating the case for the conquest of France, adding large dollops of sycophantic flattery and self-deprecation for rhetorical leaven. He observed, for instance, that England had just title to France (in consequence of victories and treaties dating back centuries) and had never received all the tribute that was owed; that his Majesty's honor was at stake,as the king had agreed to lead the attack in person; and that France had been deliberately provocative, refusing return of the dowry of Henry's sister, briefly the queen of Louis XII.

Then came the turn, that 'another kind' of war, 'more available for the speedy achieving of ... desired purposes', should be waged, not against France, but against Scotland – a 'sharper, more violent, and also more terrible' war that conveyed into that realm 'so great and mighty a puissance as shall be able by god's aid, clearly to vanquish [it] utterly and to subdue [it]'. With a rival war plan now placed on the table, many reasons were next adduced weighing against the French campaign, including the king's safety; the cost of the expedition, aggravated by the delaying tactics of the French and by the expense of garrisoning small towns ('ungracious dogholes') en route to Paris; the loss of in-country holdings which had facilitated past invasions; and the unity and provisioning of France, greater than ever before.

The wiser course, therefore, was first to conquer and annex Scotland, 'joined unto us by nature all in one land', and to leave the conquest of France, 'severed from us by the ocean sea', to another time – a policy pithily encapsulated in the common saying that he who 'intends France to win, with Scotland let him begin' (*Prince*, 3: provinces speaking the same language are possessed with ease, whereas provinces speaking disparate languages are possessed with great fortune and industry).

Even scholars critical of Cromwell give his speech high marks for the depth of its analysis, the thoroughness of its presentation, the perspicacity of its policy recommendations, and the cleverness of its ironic humor – a rhetorical *tour de force*. Wolsey also was impressed (if not persuaded – a large invading army was sent forth to France … only to be stymied by bad weather and accomplish nothing), for he invited Cromwell sometime after to join his staff. As of 1524 Cromwell was being addressed as 'councilor to my Lord Legate'.

In the Household of the Cardinal

Wolsey was not much of a reformer (in this age of reformation), but he did embrace the humanist goal of reinvigorating clerical education. To that end he set his sights on founding two colleges, one at Oxford (Cardinal's College) and one at Ipswich (St Mary's). In order to finance these establishments, he resorted to the not unfamiliar practice of closing minor monasteries and redirecting their endowments. Wolsey chose Cromwell to implement the closure and to oversee the construction. The work began in January 1525, after Cromwell had spent a year proving his competence doing the ordinary secretarial labor of transcribing documents and conveying deeds.

Cromwell's early reputation for efficient knavery stemmed from this service performed for Wolsey. Twenty-nine houses were encompassed by the dissolution. Part of the justification was that they lacked sufficient numbers to chant the Holy Offices, an argument persuasive to Pope Clement VII, who issued after-the-fact approval; and part of the justification was evidence gathered (or manufactured) of gross misconduct among remaining members, a charge taken to be slanderous at the time of Wolsey's ouster and included in the indictment against Wolsey. Cromwell's assignment (which he shared with John Allen, soon-to-be bishop of Dublin and Lord Chancellor of Ireland) was to inventory the properties of the monasteries, estimate their value, arrange for the transfer of moveable goods and for the sale or lease of lands, draw up necessary deeds, settle accounts with tenants, and find new residences for the displaced monks and nuns. And because the number of targeted houses was not decided or advertised in advance, intimidation and extortion were involved. Houses able and willing to pay a satisfactory bribe (used by Wolsey to furnish his colleges or pocketed by his agents) were sometimes spared; and benefices that fell vacant were put up for auction. The rough handling of these ill-fated houses greatly aggravated the public hatred already directed against Wolsey. Increasingly Cromwell shared in that hatred, for an attempt was made upon his life (1527), and friends began writing him admonitory letters.

The positive side of monastic closings was the founding of new colleges. Wolsey made Cromwell receiver-general of Cardinal's College. In this capacity Cromwell kept the accounts, drafted documents, supervised construction, and reported on progress. He had good news to convey in an April 1528 letter:

> The buildings of your noble college most prosperously and magnificently does arise in such wise that to every man's judgement the like thereof was never seen nor imagined, having consideration to the largeness, beauty, sumptuous[ness], curious[ness] [of the] most substantial building of the same. Your chapel within the said college [is] most devoutly and virtuously ordered, and the ministries within the same [are] not only diligent in the service of god, but also [in] the service daily done within the same, so devout, solemn, and full of harmony that in my opinion it has few peers.

But all the news was not so good. A breach in the Thames levees caused flooding of the marshes of Lyesnes. The destruction was extensive – 'the most piteous and grievous sights that ever I saw' – and the cost of repair was high – £300, of which £220 was assessed against Wolsey's Ipswich college (possibly because it owned land in the area). Cromwell wrote to request the speedy payment of the funds; and, as if to mollify his master's expected irritation, he declared that but for his timely intervention the damage there would have been much worse:

> Insomuch that if my being there had not been to have encouraged the workmen and laborers, I assure you all the labor and money that has been there spent heretofore had been clearly lost and cast away. And the workmen and laborers would have departed and left all at chance, which should have been the greatest evil ever happened to the country there.

The letter was addressed to Stephen Gardiner, a fellow secretary and rival for Wolsey's attention. Because Cromwell was often away from Wolsey, visiting monasteries and overseeing construction projects, his position in the household needed careful protecting. Thus he appended to his own letter a letter from the master of the works confirming all that he had described ('and to the intent that you may be the more assured of the truth in the promises'). Perhaps Cromwell could not trust Gardiner (an enemy in the years ahead) to communicate to the cardinal, with adequate conviction, the indispensability of Cromwell's talents and services.

If there was competition in the cardinal's household, there also was rapid advancement. The correspondence during these five or so years shows the growing extent of Cromwell's influence, even that Cromwell was becoming the gatekeeper to Wolsey's largesse. He was referred to as the 'right worshipful Mr Cromwell', the 'well-beloved Mr Cromwell', and the 'servant to my lord cardinal's grace'. The Guild of St Boltoph continued to make use of his services, sending highly prized wild fowl through him to Wolsey. George Throckmorton, an important player in the Reformation Parliament, employed Cromwell to settle a dispute and paid handsomely for the assistance. Another suitor, one Richard Bellyssis, beseeched Cromwell to prevail upon Wolsey in the matter of a mintmaster's post, which Bellyssis wanted conferred on the son of its former occupant; as inducement, a horse was promised to Cromwell. The letter of April 1528, cited above, concluded with a recommendation that a petitioner, for whom Cromwell vouched, be granted a vacant Welsh benefice in the disposing of Wolsey. Other letters brought to the cardinal's notice involve the plight of sundry individuals suffering loss and in need of aid (e.g., London merchants taken at sea and held prisoners by the French). Cromwell could be generous and thoughtful as well as grasping and cruel – though an alternate interpretation is that he was merely establishing a patronage network. In the event, such a network did take root, with solicitations received even from members of the nobility, who in gratitude bestowed gifts appropriate to their status. Acting as intermediary, Cromwell became wealthy in his own right, enough so that his friend, Stephen Vaughan, sent him a great chain meant to secure his London residence from trespass by burglars.

That Cromwell was by this time a man of means is further born out by his last will and testament, drafted in July 1529. The will disposed of liquid assets of some £1,600, plus property in land and tenements of unspecified value. Household furniture, kitchen wares, plates, goblets, and assorted articles of clothing were also part of the bequest. Son Gregory was Cromwell's principal beneficiary, with nephews and in-laws replacing him in the event of predeceasement. One sister and her husband were bequeathed the proceeds from a farm (the other sister was dead, as were the wife and two daughters), and a niece was granted a dowry. Friends and servants were remembered too. There were interesting charitable contributions, including dowries for poor maidens, alms for prisoners, and funds for highway construction. Some of these bequests had as their stated purpose the hastening of Cromwell's soul to heaven, along with the souls of Cromwell's parents and of fellow Christians. Indeed, the will's opening bequest – a prayer, in fact – was to almighty God, pleading that the deity accept the soul of Thomas Cromwell; and in a subsequent provision Cromwell bid his executors to hire a reputable priest to sing for his salvation and to be paid for this seven-year service £46 and change – a considerable sum. Similar services were requested of the five London friaries (though their payment was small by comparison). All in all, a very Catholic man did Cromwell appear to be – not a hint in this document of the Protestantism of which he later stood accused.

On the other hand, last wills and testaments were practically the last place where sensible people would express their misgivings about the church. One who did, dying two years later, had his body exhumed and desecrated by the local diocesan chancellor. The chancellor was subsequently reprimanded and fined, but not for religious fanaticism or cruel and unusual punishment; rather because he had encroached upon the king's prerogative of burning heretics, whether living or dead.

The will was written at a precarious moment for Cromwell, and the caution it exhibited – if that was what his orthodoxy amounted to – would not have been enough to save him from harm, nor would the fortune it recorded have been his to dispense to heirs, if harm had indeed come. But in order to explain the gathering dangers of the summer of 1529, it will be necessary to leave Cromwell for a time and consider more generally the history of the period.

3

Henrician England

Military and Diplomatic Background

Henry VIII ascended the throne in 1509. As the second son of Henry VII, he succeeded his father because his elder brother, Arthur, had died seven years earlier. Arthur was briefly married to Catherine of Aragon, daughter of Ferdinand and Isabella of Spain. Henry also married Catherine (1509), who was almost six years his senior. Henry at the time was an adolescent, not quite eighteen.

In the early years Henry governed the realm with the help of forty or fifty councilors, many of them carry-overs from his father's reign. But frankly young Henry did less governing than partying, spending the surplus in the treasury on palaces, pageants, and progresses of the court. And, for as long as the money held out, he spent on military adventures too.

England was allied to Spain because England was opposed to France, portions of which England had conquered and lost during the Hundred Years' War. When Spain under Ferdinand decided to march against France, England under Henry (son-in-law to Ferdinand) decided to join the fight as an auxiliary. An army of 30,000 led by Henry landed in Calais (1513). The English forces defeated the French at the Battle of the Spurs (the enemy cavalry having 'spurred' their horses into terrified retreat) and besieged and captured the towns of Thérouanne and Tournai (two of the 'dogholes' referred to by Cromwell). Meanwhile a second English army, organised by Catherine and commanded by the earl of Surrey, defeated an invading Scottish army at Flodden Field and killed the Scottish king, James IV (husband of Henry's sister Margaret Tudor).

Henry was prepared to renew hostilities the following year, but his ally made peace with France (in fact, had even done so in advance of the fighting). Not to be left in the lurch, Henry married his other sister, Mary Tudor, to the aging French king, Louis XII.

Actually Henry had two allies making separate peace, though they were about to merge and become one. They were Spain and Germany, the latter called the Holy Roman Empire. Ferdinand died in 1516, leaving the Spanish throne to his grandson Charles. Maximilian, the emperor and a Habsburg prince, died in 1519, leaving the Empire and his Habsburg possessions to his grandson, this same Charles, who as emperor was titled Charles V. France was engulfed by a colossus that also was a foe, because the Habsburgs had dynastic ambitions, but also because France and the Empire contested over Italy.

The fighting in Italy began much earlier in 1494. Charles VIII, king of France, invaded, hoping to make good his ancestral claim to Naples and from there to launch an attack upon Constantinople. His successor, Louis XII, renewed the invasion in 1499 (the first force having retreated in 1495 when a five-party pact formed against it); and his successor, Francis I, renewed it again in 1515 (the second force having retired in 1513 after suffering defeat and in anticipation of an Anglo-Spanish attack). Francis was initially successful and captured Milan following the Battle of Marignano. But over time the might of Spain prevailed, and at Pavia, 1525, Francis himself was captured (though subsequently released). Two years later Imperial forces sacked the city of Rome (causing the pope to imprison himself in the Castle Saint Angelo); and two years after that France suffered its final defeat (in this phase of hostilities) at Landriano.

England never fought in Italy. Its function was to harry France from the north. That England did in 1513 and again in 1522–3. But more often England tried practicing a balance-of-power strategy, pitting one country against the other, while promoting itself as the arbiter of continental peace. The person responsible for this policy, and England's chief diplomat throughout these years (and a little beyond), was Thomas Wolsey (made archbishop of York in 1514, cardinal and Lord Chancellor in 1515, and papal legate in 1518). Wolsey's policy followed that of the papacy, namely to weaken France without over-strengthening Spain. Accordingly, Wolsey was less of a pro-Imperialist (i.e., pro-Holy Roman Emperor, Charles V) than some of his kinsmen and was willing to make overtures to France, England's longtime adversary. There was the marriage of Henry's sister to King Louis, already mentioned; and there was the betrothal of Henry's daughter, Mary, to the French dauphin. The latter occurred as part of an international peace accord, brokered by Wolsey in 1518, called the treaty of London, whereby Europe's belligerent powers agreed to a system of collective security (aggression by one resisted collectively by the combined might of all others) and to a crusade against the Turks, who under their new sultan, Suleiman the Magnificent, were laying siege to the city of Belgrade. A follow-up meeting of English and French heads of state extended the good will and ratified the betrothal. This ceremonial event, occurring in June 1520, was styled the Field of Cloth of Gold. It involved thousands of noblemen, prelates, and gentlemen of both countries, who met on a field in France outside Calais, lived for two weeks under tents, banqueted in a temporary palace constructed for the occasion, and entertained themselves with music, dance, and athletic competitions, including a wrestling match between the kings. Wolsey again was the instigator and organiser of the affair.

Of course Wolsey could just as easily tack in the other direction and align England with the Empire. Wolsey harbored the ambition of becoming pope himself (Leo X would die in late 1521), and Charles had more influence with the College of Cardinals than did Francis; likewise, Wolsey's master, Henry, harbored the ambition of becoming king of France, and Charles alone could deliver him that prize. Hence in the early 1520s England moved back again into the Imperial camp, a shift in allegiance symbolised by the new betrothal of Mary (then five) to Charles (then twenty-one). Under the terms of the agreement, England was obligated to supply troops and funds to the emperor, something which England once did fully (in the campaign complained of by Cromwell), but which it was unable to do adequately ever again (popular resistance to taxes). Charles then fought without useful English assistance, and when at Pavia he was victorious, he denied England its share of the spoils. (He had already denied Wolsey the papacy, throwing Imperial support first behind Adrian VI [1522–3], a former tutor of Charles, and then behind Clement VII [1523–34], of the Medici family.) England withdrew from its formal alliance with the emperor and established an informal alliance with France (Treaty of the More, 1525), staying mostly on the sidelines while making promises of aid depending on the fortunes of war. But fortune proved unfriendly to France as its armies were defeated and its presence in Italy removed for several years.

Social and Economic Background

Population was a concern throughout the Tudor period. At the time of Elizabeth's death in 1603, England's population had just returned to the level it had reached on the eve of the Black Death, two and a half centuries earlier. From a high of between four and five million, England fell to a low of two million around the time of the Tudor ascension. War, crop failures, and outbreaks of plague kept death rates up and birth rates down. Midway through Henry VIII's reign, the number was at two and a half million; but from that point forward, with one setback, population grew steadily, topping four million at the turn of the century. The loss of people affected England's military capacities (France had ten times the number), while the addition of people affected staple prices. Inflation was a fact of sixteenth-century life, in England and on the continent.

Nine out of ten people lived on farms where either they tilled the soil or tended domestic animals. With more people to feed, and with a growing portion of arable land converted to pasturage – this in order that the wool and cloth from sheep might be traded for luxury goods purchased by the rich – living standards of the wage-earning poor declined. Such at least was the analysis of pamphleteers decrying the practice of enclosure, though the primary cause of poverty was an expanding population competing for work, food, and land.

The government responded with a host of economic and social reforms. Enclosure was penalised; trade and manufacturing were regulated; wages and prices were controlled; profiteering was proscribed. Land use, grain supplies, urban renewal, and disease suppression all came under the purview of the government. The poor were supervised in order to discourage their gambling, their idleness, and their drink; and even to discourage their social pretension and waste of funds (e.g., sumptuary laws detailing the quality of clothing permitted to the poor); and they were supervised in order to encourage the honing of their martial skills (e.g., archery practice). Poor relief took the forms of alms for the disabled and public works for the able-bodied. Vagabonds were treated as criminals and rebels.

At the other end of the social spectrum, and constituting the citizen body of the realm, were the lords, lay and clerical, the knights, the esquires, the gentry, and the freeholders. The lay lords, or peers, numbered around fifty or sixty, the spirituals about the same, until the destruction of the monasteries caused the loss of the abbots. The peers were the creations of the monarchy and thereafter the accidents of hereditary succession. Stinginess on the part of the monarchy and infertility on the part of the lords kept their number fairly constant. The function of the lords was to extend the monarchy's rule into the provinces of the realm and to support the monarchy with arms and cash in times of need. The knights made up the army's officer corps, at least in by-gone days; in the sixteenth century they served the monarchy at court and in parliament, as representatives of England's thirty-nine counties or shires.

Freehold land worth £40 was the qualifier for knighthood; dubbing by the crown (usually) was the instrument. Dubbed knights numbered between 300 and 600. Knighthood was a non-hereditary title; it ended with the death of the knight, called 'sir.' But the lesser title of esquire was hereditary, a distinction given to younger sons of barons, to first sons of knights, to persons so elevated by the crown, to justices of the peace, and to gentry with requisite land and office. Some 5,000 families counted as gentry; they knew themselves as such by the right they enjoyed to use of a coat of arms, by the formal address of 'gentleman' and 'lady,' and by the courtesies paid to them by their neighbors. Wealthy landowners were gentry, along with clergy, professionals, university graduates, military officers, and government ministers. Below the gentry were freeholders with the right to vote for members of parliament.

The path to advancement in Tudor society, for those at the bottom or in the middle ranks, was business success made respectable by landowning, education used as an entry to the professions or to government service, ordination coupled with the personal skills to rise in the clergy, and marriage to persons of higher status. Cromwell rose by three of these means.

Doctrinal and Dynastic Background

Throughout this period momentous transformations were taking place in the churches, monasteries, and universities of Europe. In 1517 Martin Luther set in motion the Protestant Reformation with the posting of his Ninety-Five Theses on a Wittenburg church door. Luther's objections to corrupt church practices (pluralism, simony, indulgences, etc.) soon expanded into an all-out attack on church structure and church doctrine. He challenged the primacy of the pope in Rome, claiming the lack of scriptural warrant for such a thing. Indeed, the entire ecclesiastical hierarchy, including the clerical order itself, was of suspect legitimacy, since the early church was a community of equals without governance from above.

He further argued that the mediating task of the church, which supposedly made its existence indispensable – i.e., celebrating the mass, administering the sacraments – rested upon the false belief that human beings, by dint of their own virtuous behavior – called 'works' – could accomplish thereby, or significantly contribute to, the salvation of their souls. True belief held conversely that salvation depended solely on faith in God's word – revealed in Scripture, read and interpreted by individuals. Justification by faith alone is what this doctrine was (and is) called.

Lutheranism spread quickly because the church was corrupt and ripe for reform, because the ground had been prepared by humanist authors registering many of the same complaints (Erasmus especially), and because at its point of origin – Germany – no central authority was in place to stop it. Germany was a collection of independent duchies and principalities held loosely together by the emperor, typically a German prince elected by seven of his peers. But the Imperial office was vacant with the death of Maximilian (1519), and its next occupant, Charles, had to make concessions and pay bribes in order to obtain it over his rivals (other German princes, Francis, and even Henry). And though Charles was a determined opponent of heresy (outlawing Lutheranism with the Edict of Worms), his attention was diverted by wars with France and by the need to defend the eastern Empire from attack by the Turks.

In England, Lutheranism spread more slowly, establishing a foothold at Cambridge among radical students and divines who met clandestinely at the White Horse Tavern. Once this new creed reached the public through the import and distribution of bootlegged books, Thomas More, then councilor to the king, led the fight against it, with polemical tracts of ever-increasing vitriol. Even King Henry joined the struggle, authoring his *Defense of the Seven Sacraments* against an attacking work by Luther – for which effort a grateful Pope Leo bestowed upon Henry the title 'Defender of the Faith' (1521).

But Henry would not continue defending the faith – or ingratiating himself with the pope – very much longer. By 1527 Henry was having doubts about his marriage to Catherine, who now, over forty and past child-bearing age, had given birth to but one surviving child, a daughter named Mary (b. 1516). Five others she had miscarried, delivered stillborn, or watched die in infancy. Henry was worried about the succession, since no woman had inherited the throne and succeeded in keeping it (Matilda in 1135 lost it to her cousin Stephen Boulogne). Accordingly, he recognised his illegitimate son, Henry Fitzroy (son of Elizabeth Blount) and elevated him to the peerage as duke of Richmond in preparation for designating him his heir, should that be necessary. Henry also professed concern over the religious correctness of his marriage, since the union of in-laws was thought to be prohibited by Scripture: 'If a man takes his brother's wife', declares Leviticus 20:21, 'it is impurity; he has uncovered his brother's nakedness, they shall be childless'. The five dead children conceived by Catherine might understandably be taken as evidence of God's disfavour (though given the opposite commandment in Deuteronomy 25:5, maybe not), and Henry sometimes understood it so. Others did as well, including a French bishop who questioned the legitimacy of Mary and her value as marital property. Long before that, Henry's father had his misgivings about his second son's marriage to Catherine, and so he secured a papal dispensation (1503) before changing his mind and calling off the engagement. (The decision to marry Catherine, who had remained in England after Arthur's death, was made by Henry following his father's death.)

One other factor came into play. Henry had taken as his mistress Mary Boleyn; but having tired of her after a time, he sought a replacement in her sister Anne. Anne Boleyn had spent her formative years at the French court, sent there as maid to Mary Tudor (1514) and permitted to stay on after Mary's return home (or, as in some accounts, left in France after accompanying her father on one of his diplomatic assignments). Experienced in the ways of courtly romance and politics, Anne knew better than to satisfy the desires of her suitor Henry. She demanded marriage, and reluctantly Henry agreed to her demand (though one scholar reverses their positions), beginning in 1527 the king's 'great matter', the six-year effort to secure an annulment of the marriage to Queen Catherine and a new marriage to Lady Anne.

Annulments were not uncommon (Henry's sister Margaret had gotten one recently), and Henry expected Pope Clement to grant his request. But Henry's timing was bad – indeed it could hardly have been worse – for in 1527 Pope Clement sat in Castle Saint Angelo, a virtual prisoner of Emperor Charles whose forces were pillaging the city of Rome. The abasement of Clement was acutely important, since Charles, the nephew of Catherine, would not tolerate the family disgrace of having his aunt divorced and cast aside; and Clement dared not anger Charles.

Henry handed the matter over to Wolsey, who went into it supposing that a French princess would be Henry's next bride. Rarely at court with the king, Wolsey was slow to appreciate the depth of Henry's affection for Anne. When made aware of the situation (he had been in France attempting to put together a grand continental peace, one which would circuitously accomplish Henry's 'great matter' by making Wolsey acting pope during Clement's captivity), he turned about and through emissaries petitioned Clement to create a commission which would hear and decide Henry's divorce case in England. Wolsey, as papal legate, would preside over the commission along with Cardinal Lorenzo Campeggio, another legate and absentee bishop of Salisbury. The authority to be invested in this commission was a matter of intense and protracted negotiation, but the issue to be resolved was clear, limited, and agreed upon by all – namely, the technical validity of the 1503 dispensation granted by Pope Julius II.

Campeggio was ill, and so his departure for England was put off and his traveling through Europe slowed. He arrived in October 1528 with instructions from Clement to delay convening the court for as long as possible. Campeggio's first move, therefore, was to approach Catherine with the suggestion that she withdraw from the marriage and enter a religious order – effecting thereby a 'spiritual death' which would leave Henry a widower, free to marry again. Catherine was unmoved by the entreaty or by threats delivered by lords. On the contrary, she took the offensive and in November produced a copy of a second Julian dispensation (the original residing in Spain) which corrected many of the deficiencies upon which Henry's divorce suit rested. More delay resulted as Henry insisted that the emperor release the original, something which the emperor was not prepared to do. Clement's illness in February 1529, and false rumours of his death, caused still further delays, as possible successors (including Wolsey) jockeyed for position. At the curia support for the 'great matter' steadily eroded (under pressure from Catherine and the emperor), and in May a reviving Clement declared, 'I have quite made up my mind to become an Imperialist and live and die as such.'

In point of fact, papal sympathy for, or opposition to, the divorce effort was very much a function of facts on the ground. The resurgence of French power in the autumn of 1527 allowed Clement in the winter of 1528 to comply with Wolsey's request for a commission to hear the case; but the decline of French power in the autumn of 1528 and its collapse in June 1529 (Landriano) caused Clement to turn back toward the emperor. Campeggio was again told to delay. And even though the legatine court was convened in June, Campeggio's procrastination, assisted by competent defense of the queen by Bishop Fisher, slowed the proceedings just enough that Campeggio could announce a July adjournment of the court in conformity with Roman custom. Soon after, letters arrived from the curia revoking the case to Rome.

Wolsey was held responsible for the fiasco, and his master was not the sort to take disappointment in stride. Still, Henry needed the outside push of an aristocratic cabal in order to decide upon Wolsey's disgrace. Wolsey's enemies in the nobility, who resented the fact that this commoner, a butcher's son, had replaced them at court, pressured the king to deprive Wolsey of the great seal and of his post as Lord Chancellor. Also, importuning by Anne, who had independent reasons for hating the cardinal, brought the king to inflict additional punishments on his former minister. In early October Wolsey was indicted on charges of praemunire, convicted at King's Bench, and ordered to surrender much of his property, including York Place (coveted by Anne), and (somewhat later) to remove himself to the archdiocese of York, which, though its archbishop, he had never before visited. Meanwhile Thomas More was named Lord Chancellor, and a new parliament, the first in six years, was summoned for November.

4

To Parliament and the Court

Old Loyalties and New

Before Wolsey set out for York, he stayed a while at his lightly furnished Esher manor, south of Hampton Court (now the king's property). Cromwell was there too, and on November 1, All Hallows Day, George Cavendish, Wolsey's servant and biographer, noticed Cromwell praying and weeping near a window in the manor's great chamber. Cavendish questioned the minister – whose attention to the matins Cavendish thought unusual – about his disquieting demeanor, and whether it was his master's misfortunes or his own that was causing his distress. Cromwell answered honestly, if ungenerously, that he feared the loss of all that he had labored to acquire simply for doing 'true and diligent service' for his master: 'And this I understand right well, that I am in disdain with most men for my master's sake and surely without just cause. Howbeit, an ill name once gotten will not lightly be put away.' Cromwell had reason to believe that he was hated and that the cardinal's disgrace would encompass him too, for his friends had written to warn him of the danger. But he was determined not to fall without a fight; thus he pledged to 'ride to London and so to the Court, where I will either make or mar ere I come again; I will put myself in the press to see what any man is able to lay to my charge of untruth or misdemeanor' (*Prince*, 25: better to be impetuous than cautious).

To 'make' his fortune, Cromwell would try obtaining a seat in parliament, set to convene in just two days. The way had been somewhat cleared by letters to his assistant, Ralph Sadler, and a return letter from the same stating that two avenues to the desired objective had been explored, with provisional success along each, and that a fallback third awaited investigation. These avenues were: (1) that Sir John Gage, vice-chamberlain of the Household, had approached Thomas Howard, duke of Norfolk, about seeking the king's permission for Cromwell to sit in Commons, with the reply forthcoming that Henry was 'very well contented [he] should be a burgess'; (2) that Sir Thomas Rush, a Cromwell associate in the Ipswich project, had inquired about an Orford seat in Suffolk, but that word regarding a vacancy there had not yet come back; and (3) that Sir William Paulet, a Wolsey steward, would be asked, if the Orford option fell through, to find a seat in the Winchester boroughs, where Wolsey, as former bishop, had continuing influence. Orford did fall through, Sadler soon learned, but Paulet was able to place Cromwell in Taunton, a corporate town in the Winchester diocese.

Sadler's letter was explicit about one point, that the king's blessing was contingent upon loyalty to the royal agenda; and Cromwell was urged to come to London at once to work out with Norfolk the details of his expected service (that 'you shall know the king his pleasure how you shall order yourself in the parliament house'). Even so, there seemed some anxiety on the part of Gage and others that Cromwell might be drawn too much into Norfolk's orbit, for the letter included this cryptic note of caution: 'Assuring you that your friends would have you to tarry with my lord there as little as might be for many considerations, as Mr Gage will show you who much desires to speak with you.' Thus the nature and extent of Cromwell's obligations were perhaps not yet all decided.

In any event, Cromwell's position was an unenviable one. Wolsey was despised by the court for failing to secure the divorce (in addition to other, longstanding offenses); and those who engineered Wolsey's disgrace were now opening a door to Cromwell's deliverance – but with conditions, which if satisfied would likely exacerbate the problem of 'an ill name once gotten … not lightly [being] put away'. For Norfolk and the court planned on Wolsey's total destruction through a bill of attainder (or a disabling bill), and presumably they planned on public tergiversation from a former Wolsey staffer.

In parliament's opening session, Wolsey was denounced by Lord Chancellor More (with King Henry standing at his side), and a month later a forty-four article indictment was brought against Wolsey in the House of Lords. The indictment passed quickly and easily, but when introduced in Commons, it ran aground owing to the deft opposition of Thomas Cromwell (who, in the words of Cavendish, inveighed against the bill 'so discreetly, with such witty persuasions and deep reasons, that the same bill could take there no effect'). Was Cromwell not playing the part scripted for him? Was he reneging on commitments to his new patrons, the king and Norfolk? Since two of the articles specified corruption by Wolsey servants in the suppression of the monasteries, Cromwell may have had no choice but to defeat the indictment or suffer prosecution under it. But there also were rumours that the king opposed the indictment and consequent fears in some quarters that Wolsey might be rehabilitated in the future. What seems then to have occurred is that in the intervening month the king's wishes and Norfolk's diverged and that Cromwell, in defending Wolsey, was doing exactly as he had promised, that is, 'ordering' himself as the king directed; while at the same time, and luckily, saving himself from legal destruction and retrieving his reputation from the muck – for, as Cavendish reported, 'at length for his honest behavior in his master's case, he grew into such estimation in every man's opinion that he was esteemed to be the most faithful servant to his master of all others, wherein he was of all men greatly commended'. The fact that the king began restoring properties to Wolsey and in February pardoned him (owing in part to Cromwell's labors) does suggest that Henry had intentions different from ranking members of his court. And since Norfolk did not retaliate against Cromwell, it is a fair surmise that Norfolk recognised the change (both in Henry's wishes and in Cromwell's status), adjusted to it, and put off to a more propitious moment the objective of eliminating Wolsey.

It may have helped with relations at court that Cromwell persuaded Wolsey to bestow gifts and annuities from his remaining properties upon prominent lords, including Norfolk's nephew, George Boleyn, viscount Rochford. Overtures were also made to Anne Boleyn, at Wolsey's insistence, though to little profit, and numerous courtiers of the Boleyn faction were, like Rochford, granted pensions. Wolsey was at Esher, then at Richmond, then at lesser residences, until in April he set out for York. (Removing him to York in the far north, and thus beyond the ready reach of the king, was Norfolk's new ambition.) Throughout this time and into the summer and fall, Cromwell functioned as Wolsey's representative at court. Correspondence between them shows a pleading, pitiful, and effusively grateful cardinal trying to make amends and assuage hostilities; and a consoling, commanding, and abundantly confident servant recommending patience and the quick surrender of all that was demanded: The king wanted possession of the cardinal's colleges; Wolsey should cede them without objection (even though their endowments were not quite his to give). The king was hesitant to deliver on his promise to repay the cardinal's debts; Wolsey should suffer in silence and hope for a change of mood. Complaints were made regarding the size of the cardinal's household; Wolsey should effect the true Christian spirit he now professed and live simply. When Wolsey voiced suspicion that perhaps his servant was not doing all that he might, or was doing more for himself than for his master, Cromwell answered with pique and resentment, claiming to have spent from his own reserves more than he had earned as an intermediary. The reversal of roles no doubt strained relations, as did the long duration of Wolsey's dependency; and from April on, the two were separated, though Cromwell resisted invitations to visit the cardinal.

On November 4, 1530, Wolsey was arrested for treason. His Venetian physician, Agostino Agostini, had been apprehended conveying letters to the French ambassador in London, letters requesting that Francis intercede with Henry on Wolsey's behalf. This revelation, on top of Wolsey's unauthorised summoning of the York Convocation, were enough to convince Norfolk and the anti-Wolsey faction that the cardinal was preparing for a comeback and that his exile to York would not last much longer. The prospect of Wolsey's return was a chilling one to contemplate; and so Agostini was induced to add to the evidence the damning particular that the cardinal had been in correspondence with the pope and the emperor, treasonously conspiring to have the king excommunicated and the kingdom interdicted. Fearing proclamation of the same at the coming Convocation, Henry agreed to have the cardinal arrested. No record exists of Cromwell's mounting a defense at this time, but then parliament was not in session and Cromwell may not have had access to the king.

The arresting officers were Henry Percy, earl of Northumberland, whose betrothal to Anne Boleyn Wolsey had scotched years before; and Walter Walsh, member of the king's Privy Chamber, whose authority alone would Wolsey recognise. Sir William Kingston, constable of the Tower and captain of the king's guard, was the officer sent to escort Wolsey back to London for trial. It was to Kingston that Wolsey uttered these two famous statements, recorded by Cavendish: 'If I had served god as diligently as I have done the king, he would not have given me over in my gray hairs'; and, 'I warn you to be well advised and assured what matter you put in [the king's] head, for you shall never pull it out again.' The party never reached London; for Wolsey was ill before departing and ill on the journey. They stopped at Leicester abbey, where Wolsey, a few days later, died in his bed.

Scholars infer much from Cromwell's final year as a Wolsey servant, but from the same evidence exactly opposite conclusions are drawn. Some see infidelity, deceit, contempt, and self-seeking; others see loyalty, diligence, wise counsel, and honest dealing: Cromwell went running to Norfolk, Wolsey's arch-enemy, the critics charge; but Wolsey himself tried appeasing Anne Boleyn, and it was only sensible to make peace with the regnant faction, the defenders answer. Cromwell stood by, the critics complain, as the cardinal's beloved colleges were appropriated or dismantled; but who was Cromwell, the defenders counter, to resist the graspings of the king. Cromwell's letters drip with supercilious put-downs and impatient brush-offs, observe the critics; but Wolsey was loath to accept his degraded status, answer the defenders, and he had to be spoken to bluntly without euphemism and palliatives – plus the patronizing tone detected by opponents is more correctly read as heartfelt sincerity, the supporters insist. Cromwell used the cardinal's wealth to enlarge his own importance, the critics maintain; but an important friend was better able to promote the cardinal's cause, the defenders reason, and in any event Cromwell was justified in looking to a post-Wolsey future.

Whichever account is more accurate – that of conniving back-stabber or steadfast friend – there can be no denying that Cromwell took an enormous gamble in 'making or marring' his future by going to parliament. For once in parliament he would surely be called upon to defend Wolsey or denounce him, and thus risk convicting himself of either complicity or betrayal. And while

Cromwell very likely had the king's approval, the king was a notoriously mercurial character; and had Henry turned fully against Wolsey, the wolves in the court would have descended upon Cromwell. Nor can it be denied that the strategy adopted he executed with utmost skill. Cromwell showed himself (for a second time) at home in the parliament, able through oratory and politicking to achieve his personal objectives. The fact that he survived the year, managed three demanding and contentious clients – Wolsey, Henry, and Anne – without alienating any of them, and emerged a trusted adviser to the monarch and the Boleyns, is proof of exceptional audacity and shrewdness, perhaps worthy of the ascription Machiavellian.

King's Servant

Cromwell was not exclusively Wolsey's agent during the last year of Wolsey's life. Sometime in the winter or early spring of 1530, Cromwell entered the king's service, wearing the king's livery and enjoying the king's protection. But he had no office as such and so was employed on an *ad hoc* basis only, applying his legal knowledge and his experience with the monasteries to the business of facilitating the many property transfers that the cardinal's fall had occasioned. When that fall was complete, with Wolsey's death, royal favour came rapidly to Cromwell. He went from factotum to Privy Council member in the space of little over a month.

Three stories told how this transformation was accomplished. The earliest recorded was by the Imperial ambassador, Chapuys, who explained in a 1535 letter to Charles that Cromwell sought a private audience with the king in order to clear himself of charges made by Sir John Wallop. In the course of the interview, Cromwell sketched out a plan whereby the king would reform the church and by confiscating its wealth become the richest monarch in Europe. Ever the spendthrift, Henry was intrigued, if not yet convinced, and promoted Cromwell to secret adviser and then to Privy councilor.

Reginald Pole provided a different account of the same meeting. Writing in 1539 in his *Apologia ad Carolum Quintum*, Pole described a cautious, scheming, sycophantic Cromwell who wheedled his way into the king's confidence by declaring that the monarchy was above the law and that politics was as an activity excused from the strictures of ordinary morality; also by decrying the presence of two masters in the realm, the king and the church; by deploring the lack of progress on the divorce and impugning the intelligence and devotion of the royal advisers; and by showing a way out of the thicket that had ensnared the king's 'great matter' for half of a year. That way was to imitate the Lutherans and declare independence from the papacy, to use parliament and the English church to decide (favourably) on the nullity suit, and, by dispossessing the ecclesiastical establishment, to fill the king's treasury with riches heretofore unimagined. Again the reward was a seat on the Council.

The third account was rendered by John Foxe in his *Acts and Monuments*. Foxe credited Sir John Russell with introducing Cromwell to Henry, who later summoned Cromwell to a private meeting in the Westminster gardens. There Cromwell apprised the king of the oath sworn by English bishops to the Roman pontiff pledging a degree of allegiance incompatible with loyal service to the king. This was the oath which the king used to good effect a few years later in wringing concessions crippling to the clergy.

It cannot be known if any of these discordant reminiscences of what must have been hearsay reports is reliable as to detail, or if all three are reliable as to their agreed upon message, that Cromwell launched his career as a royal secretary and Privy councilor with a visionary plan communicated at a single meeting. Henry did not act on the advice in the near-term, that much is certain; and he had already embarked upon an anti-ecclesiastical policy of his own, however tepidly. In fact, it would be a year before Cromwell reached the upper-tier of advisers and two years before he was in control of Henry's policy. It is also doubtful that Cromwell at this time would have recommended adopting the Lutheran strategy of separating from Rome, since in a letter to Wolsey written mid year, Cromwell expressed regret about what Luther had wrought: 'The fame is that Luther has departed this life. I would he had never been born.' Cavendish was silent about a dramatic December encounter; he rather reported on the prosaic, near-daily meetings with the king regarding the disposal of Wolsey's lands and temporalities, during which sessions the king arrived at an increasingly favourable estimation of Cromwell. Cavendish wrote that 'by his witty demeanor [Cromwell] grew in the king's favour'; and that

> the fame of his honesty and wisdom sounded so in the king's ears that by reason of his access to the king he perceived to be in him no less wisdom than fame had made of him report ... And the conference that he had with the king therein enforced the king to repute him a very wise man and a meet instrument to serve his grace, as it after came to pass.

The 'meet instrument' that 'after came to pass' most likely was Cromwell's seat on the Council, a position that could well have been granted without the promise of riches and the intimation of supremacy; and the 'conference' with the king could well have referred to not a single conversation but to all of them combined. That said, nothing in this slow transitioning of Cromwell from Wolsey's service to Henry's precludes an abrupt, unpremeditated promotion to the Council based on the impression created and the information imparted during one taut meeting with the king. And three very diverse people attested to that meeting (in which case *Prince*, 26 applies: when trying to be taken on as adviser to a prince, propose a bold plan of action and offer assurances of easy success).

Once on the Council, Cromwell was given routine administrative duties to perform: receiving appeals, collecting revenues, deeding properties, supervising construction, dispensing pardons and reprieves. This sort of work Cromwell continued to do for quite a long while; but since he was also a parliamentarian, he used that venue to promote the king's policies and enhance his own reputation. By the summer of 1531 he was accounted a principal drafter of legislation; by autumn the Venetian ambassador ranked him seventh among the advisers of the king. Cromwell was in the inner circle now, ahead of Gardiner, the king's secretary.

The first year as councilor also saw Cromwell engaged in a campaign to return William Tyndale to England. Tyndale had left England seven years earlier to study with Luther at Wittenburg. A year later, in 1525, Tyndale achieved fame with the publication of his English translation of the New Testament, an abrasively Protestant rendition in its prologues and anti-Catholic editorializing. Stephen Vaughan, acting on his own initiative but with encouragement from Cromwell, ran the campaign from the continent, where he attempted to contact Tyndale and persuade him to venture repatriation. Tyndale had come to the king's notice in a 1528 work titled *Obedience of a Christian Man*. The book argued the case for royal supremacy and was well liked by Henry, who thought that Tyndale, perhaps the foremost prose stylist of the day, could be enlisted as a propagandist on behalf of royal causes. Cromwell supported the scheme and perhaps proposed it. But Tyndale would not abjure his heresy, as was required, and in later writings, included in dispatches from Vaughan, he showed himself no friend of the king's divorce. Henry called off the negotiations, describing Tyndale's opinions as 'seditious,' 'slanderous,' and 'fantastical'; and Cromwell, in a four-page letter to Vaughan, heaped like abuse upon the heretic author and communicated the king's command that Vaughan 'desist and leave any further to persuade or attempt the said Tyndale to come into this realm.' It was not safe to get too far out ahead of Henry, or to continue on a course which Henry had abandoned (*Dis*, III.35: when once employed as counselor to a prince, speak modestly and without passion so as to avoid responsibility for recommended policies in the event of their failure – advice not always followed by Cromwell).

Faction: Political, Religious, Personal

On Council and at court, Cromwell encountered a governing elite divided into two factions, with elements of a third and a fourth about to congeal. Sitting at the top were the Boleyn-Howards, the party which had just orchestrated the fall of Cardinal Wolsey and had succeeded to his status as power behind the throne. Its leader was Thomas Howard, third duke of Norfolk and premier peer of the realm (excepting Richmond, Henry's ten-year-old illegitimate son). A marital connection tied the Howards to the Boleyns: Elizabeth Howard, Thomas' sister, was the wife of Thomas Boleyn, a mere commoner at the time of their marriage (1499). During the previous reign, the Howard family suffered attainder and the loss of their titles and estates, since the grandfather and first duke had unluckily fought with Richard III at Bosworth (1485). Slowly did the family work its way back into favour with the Tudors, first regaining the earl of Surrey title before the dukedom was restored in recognition of the family's services at Flodden Field (1513). The Howards were therefore in straitened circumstances when Elizabeth married Thomas and could ill afford to be genealogically choosey; plus Boleyn was a courtier with talent and prospects.

The diplomatic and administrative skills of Thomas Boleyn accounted in part for his advancement (with numerous properties and offices out of the royal patronage coming his way); and attachment to the Howards advanced the family's fortunes still further. Viscount Rochford was the first title bestowed on

Thomas (1525). It passed to his son George when the earldoms of Wiltshire and Ormonde were added in 1529.

But what principally promoted the Boleyns were the feminine charms of daughters Mary and Anne, whom the king desired and was resolved to have. Henry's affair with Mary began around 1521 and lasted several years to 1525 or 1526, during which time Mary was also the wife of William Carey, a gentleman of the king's Privy Chamber. (Some recent scholarship is of the belief that Mary was the younger daughter, born in 1509. If true, her affair with the king would have begun when she was only a child. Anne's birth is then placed in 1507. Earlier scholarship puts it in 1501, and puts Anne junior to Mary. George is thought to have been born in 1503.) By the time Henry had tired of Mary, Anne was back from France, at court, and with suitors of her own barking their affection, including the poet Thomas Wyatt. It is not known when Henry first noticed her, or whether her father deliberately placed her in Henry's path (Thomas Boleyn is generally accused of pimping his daughters to the king). At some point though, Henry joined the pack of admirers and chased all other contenders away ('*Noli me tangere*, for Caesar's I am,' wrote Wyatt in his sonnet on the wooing of Anne – 'Whoso Lists to Hunt'). The courtship at first was flirtatious and harmless. But by 1527 the 'great matter' had begun in earnest (with attraction to Anne a leading cause), and by 1528 Henry had installed Anne and her retinue in apartments at Greenwich palace, much to the consternation of the queen. Henry's surviving love letters to Anne were probably written in the 1527–8 period. They showed a young woman determined to be kept abreast of divorce-related developments and advising on some of the actions taken.

When Wolsey finally realised that Anne was something more than a throw-away mistress, he began extending favours to the Boleyn family in hopes of buying their friendship. Relations were cordial but suspicious, and before long the parties were entangled in patronage disputes, with Anne either getting her way or profiting from the king's bad conscience when she was thwarted. Wolsey's dedication to the divorce Anne never trusted, and its failure in 1529 she construed as sabotage. She and her friends, such as her cousin Francis Bryan, often insinuated to the king that Wolsey was working against the king's interests. When the end finally came for the cardinal, it was Anne who delivered the final push. That, at least, was the opinion of the Imperial ambassador. Anne had other friends at court, favourites who took their partisan cues from the appetites of the king. Since Henry wanted Anne, they embraced her too, some perhaps too literally, since later, and under much altered circumstances, their past attentions lent credence to the charge of treasonous adultery with the queen. Sir Henry Norris, Groom of the Stool, and Sirs Francis Weston and William Brererton, both gentlemen of the Privy Chamber, fall into this category.

The Boleyn–Howards were united in opposition to Wolsey and in support of marriage of Henry to Anne. But they differed doctrinally, as the Howards were orthodox Catholic (though fashionably anticlerical), while the Boleyns were crypto-Protestant. Hever castle, the Boleyn home, was a receiving point for contraband books, and Anne was herself a committed evangelical, as outspoken as the times and her special relation to the king would allow. The king knew of Tyndale's *Obedience of a Christian Man* because Anne gave the book to him. She also promoted the careers of several leading lights of the Reformation, including Thomas Cranmer and Hugh Latimer.

Two other fissures weakened the Boleyn–Howard alliance: Thomas Howard did not like his niece (who was opinionated and imperious), and he resented the fact she eclipsed him at court and effectively functioned as party head. And Charles Brandon, a significant, if non-eponymous, faction member, was rivaling Norfolk for top spot on the social register.

Charles Brandon was the duke of Suffolk. By Tudor rules of precedence, the Suffolk dukedom ranked second in the peerage (as of 1529, and again not counting Richmond), even though Brandon, its occupant, was parvenu nobility. From the lesser branches of a prosperous merchant family, he was sent to court as a teen where he and a small band of roustabout courtiers became fast friends with the young prince and later king. In 1512 Brandon was knighted. Subsequent military experience readied him for command, and in 1513 Henry made him high marshal of the army invading France. Brandon distinguished himself at the siege of Thérouanne and at the surrender of Tournai. In gratitude for the victories won, and in preparation for marriage to the emperor's daughter, Archduchess Margaret, Henry elevated Brandon to the Suffolk dukedom, bypassing all barons, viscounts, earls, and marquesses in the realm (only the dukes of Buckingham [executed in 1521] and Norfolk outranked him). The following year, 1515, Brandon married, not Margaret, but Henry's younger sister Mary Tudor, the just-widowed dowager queen of France. The union was unauthorised – indeed it was in defiance of the king's instructions; but once Henry got over his rage, he showered estates and offices upon his new brother-in-law, enough that overnight he became one of the richest and most powerful men in England.

As Henry's oldest friend (and favourite jousting partner), Brandon supported the nullity suit as a matter of course, though his support was uninspired and unenergetic; and his wife was against it. He hated Wolsey for undercutting the prestige of the old aristocracy, and he resented Norfolk for being more old-aristocracy than himself. His religious convictions were Catholic, not Protestant, but mainly he was uninterested in sectarian disputes. His peers judged him dull and lazy.

Cromwell became an agent of this group's ambitions, helping at court and in parliament to keep alive the 'great matter' when even the king was losing heart. But Cromwell also organised a following of his own out of remnants of the Wolsey faction. Three important members of the Privy Chamber, Sir Thomas Heneage, Wolsey's representative at Windsor castle; Sir Richard Page, Wolsey's former chamberlain; and Sir John Russell, Wolsey's emissary to Francis I and a casualty of the cardinal's patronage wars with Anne, came to regard Cromwell as their leader; and numerous other servants from the Wolsey household received office and direction from the new minister. These, and many additional recruits, developed over time into Cromwell's private bureaucracy, a government within the government.

Because the 'great matter' provided cover to religious radicals – in the sense that Lutherans could be more public in their views the more Henry despaired of obtaining his divorce from the pope – Lutherans came to form a distinct faction of their own. Anne was their sponsor, but so too was Cromwell, who some scholars believe was doctrinally sympathetic, but who may merely have appreciated and wished to exploit the coincidence of political goals, namely independence from Rome and supremacy of state over church. His Lutheran colleagues included Thomas Wyatt, court poet and diplomat, Anthony Denny, Privy Chamber gentleman, and William Butts, physician to the king. Committed evangelicals, known as the 'brethren', were ensconced in the London inns of court and merchant community; they, along with religious exiles, looked to Cromwell for protection and promotion of the cause.

Notwithstanding their differences, these various families, personalities, and creedal persuasions constituted the king's party and were alike committed to accomplishing the king's divorce. They stood opposed to a conservative party that severally supported Queen Catherine and Princess Mary, traditional Catholic dogma, the supremacy of the pope, and ecclesiastical reforms consistent with the continuing liberty of the church. Their intellectual leader was Thomas More, though as Henry's new Lord Chancellor, More was obliged to be circumspect and publicly neutral. He focused more on the judicial responsibilities of his office, including the revival of heresy trials which his predecessor had long neglected.

On the Council More could count as his allies George Talbot, earl of Shrewsbury, and Henry Courtenay, marquess of Exeter. But by the time of Cromwell's arrival there, the divorce campaign was state policy, and no one on Council dared to oppose it openly. Some actively, if reluctantly, advanced it. Wolsey's destruction, on the other hand, was one objective which this group unabashedly pursued.

At court Sir Nicholas Carew, Privy Chamber gentleman, was a secret oppositionist, by virtue of his loyalty to Queen Catherine (otherwise he was a trusted friend of the king, and another of his jousting buddies). John Fisher, the bishop of Rochester, spoke for conservative ecclesiastics in the House of Lords and Convocation; while Lord Thomas Darcy did the same for the temporal lords. In the House of Commons, similarly minded MPs, calling themselves the Queens Head group (after the name of the tavern they frequented), gathered around Sir George Throckmorton of Warwickshire, their most voluble member. Outside of parliament several of the stricter religious orders were equally vocal, and sometimes truculent, especially the Observant Franciscans of Greenwich and the Bridgettine monks of Syon. But the true center of the Aragon opposition – the Aragonese – was not even an Englishman. He was the emperor's ambassador, Eustace Chapuys, whose conspiratorial labors went well beyond what either Charles or Catherine would countenance.

Besides court and Council, Cromwell's other theater of operation was the parliament, in which he, the king's minister, sat as representative for Taunton. Called in November 1529, the same body reassembled for six additional sessions, ending its work in April 1536. This six-and-a-half-year long parliament passed a legislative package which ratified the king's divorce, changed the succession, severed England from Rome, established the monarchy's supremacy, and reformed the English church. It thus became known as the Reformation Parliament. By the time of its third session, in 1532, Thomas Cromwell was its unofficial head.

5

The Reformation Parliament

Session One – November–December 1529

With Wolsey gone and the 'great matter' brought momentarily to a halt, Henry changed course, directing his ire against the local church for its alleged abuse of power, rather than against the Holy See for its intransigence regarding the divorce. To this end he summoned parliament, charging it with (in the words of Edward Hall) the 'reformation of certain exactions done by the clergy to the lay people'. Anticlerical sentiment ran high in London, and a recent broadsheet by propagandist Simon Fish helped to crystallise the discontent. Copies of Fish's *Supplication for the Beggars* actually littered the streets to Blackfriars monastery, where the opening ceremony of the 1529 parliament was held. (Henry's own copy was given to him by Anne – or by two merchants, as in another account.) Fish charged the English clergy (whom he repeatedly called 'wolves' and 'bloodsuckers') with felonious possession of half of the king's realm and with possession of a tenth of all private earnings and moveable goods. This latter sum, he contended, was collected through burdensome fees (for burial of the dead, probate of wills, distribution of sacraments, court proceedings, etc.) and costly obligations (for pilgrimages, tithes, etc.). So oppressive had been these clerical exactions that the king's subjects had not sufficient remaining wealth to care for the poor or to pay their taxes fully and quickly to the crown. The church establishment, practically an independent state, had conspired with foreign powers to overthrow English kings; and by their occupancy of Council positions and parliament seats, they had prevented passage of, or had simply ignored, English laws not to their liking (e.g., mortmain). Anyone who complained of these outrageous usurpations was charged with heresy in an ecclesiastical court and forced to recant his statements or suffer capitally for his beliefs. The church was the lone arbiter of true and false belief since access to Scripture was denied to laymen. But if Scripture were translated and its reading permitted to all, the people, Fish supposed, soon would discover that the Bible subordinates spiritual power to temporal power ('Give unto Caesar the things that are Caesar's') and is silent about the existence of that ghostly place called purgatory. Purgatory was a church invention, he claimed, used to extract riches from the laity, who were told that punishment awaited them in the afterlife unless indulgences in the present life were procured by cash payments. Finally, unmarried clericals, by their sexual predations, threatened the sanctity of marriage, the stability of the family, and the populating of the realm. The church was a blight upon the land, he concluded, and a rigorous chastising, if not complete excising, was what it deserved.

Inside of parliament the mood was no more temperate or forgiving. The House in particular was incensed by the church's putative oppression of the lay public, as well as emboldened by the king's seeming blessing on a general airing of grievances – for 'God had illumined the eyes of the king' to the 'subtle doings' of the vile bishops, and in consequence 'men began charitably to desire a reformation' (Hall). Six great causes of complaint were identified, several of them anticipated by the Fish screed: (1 and 2) that the fees charged for the probate of wills and the burial of the dead were excessive and extortionate, working to the detriment of the rich and the poor respectively; (3 and 4) that clericals, engaged in agricultural and mercantile enterprises, resorted to unfair business practices, called regrating and engrossing; (5) that high clergy were pluralists and non-residents, depriving parishioners of 'true instruction in God's word'; and (6) that learned university scholars had no place to preach because the unlearned few were greedily occupying multiple benefices.

A committee was formed to review these and other complaints and to return with suitable legislative proposals. Almost certainly Cromwell was a committee member, since corrections to petition drafts are in Cromwell's hand. The debate was heated and descended into name-calling. Bishop Fisher, in defense of church prerogatives, accused the Commons of displaying a 'Bohemian' lack of faith (i.e., were Lutheran heretics). The Commons in reply likened ecclesiastical practices to robbery; and one of its number, a 'gentleman from Gray's Inn' (perhaps Cromwell, one of the six Gray's Inn solicitors), challenged the bishops' appeal to custom with this disarming query: 'The usage has ever been of thieves to rob on Shooter's Hill, ergo it is lawful?' The logjam broke when the temporal lords sided with Commons. Two bills were drafted, one restricting probate fees, the other restricting mortuary fees (the former bill injured the upper clergy, the latter injured the lower clergy; neither injured the temporal lords). Estates below a certain value were immune from testamentary charges, and fixed rates were set for estates above that value. Likewise with mortuary fees: the poor were exempt, and limits were placed on amounts charged and on the places where fees could be imposed – a deceased wayfarer, for example, was to be liable for the fee at the place of his longest habitation, not at the place of his death.

The same dynamic was in play when the issue turned to clerical commerce, pluralism, and non-residency. A bill proscribing the ownership by clerics of farm land and their buying and selling of goods at fair, plus the holding by clerics of multiple benefices and their absenteeism from the same was vigorously resisted by the lords spiritual (so much so that the king had to convene a special reconciliation conference at Star Chamber). But again the lords temporal sided with Commons, and the bill passed, once concessions were made. These concessions favoured incumbent high clergy, in that grandfathering was applied to some plural benefices presently held. Lesser clergy perhaps benefited too by having non-residency allowed to them if university studies were what kept them away from their ministries. Nobles and bishops could partially exempt their chaplains, and the king could partially exempt those clerics serving him in Council, at court, or abroad. While the bill was not gutted by its many provisos, it also did not settle the pluralism/non-residency debate, which occupied parliaments for generations to come.

Henry may have regarded this anticlerical legislation as a second front in the campaign for a divorce, or he may have reasoned that a parliament invited to vent itself against the clergy would be better disposed to relieve the king of his debts. Henry financed his reign by revenues collected from his own lands, by feudal obligations still in force, by seizures of vacant and attainted estates, by custom fees, by fines, by pensions and tribute paid to him by foreign powers, by taxes voted in parliament, and by loans – some forced, some voluntary – granted by his subjects on promise of repayment. Wolsey resorted to forced loans to finance the French wars of the 1520s. Many persons counted on collecting the debt due and listed it in their wills as part of their bequests. But now Henry pressed to have these loans forgiven, and since 'the most part of the Commons were the king's servants' (Hall), and since the lords viewed royal debt-default as a surety against future borrowing, the request was granted and effusively justified in the bill's preamble. Public opposition was acute, however, and so Henry tried to quiet the murmuring by a general pardon for past offenses against praemunire and provisors statutes.

The 1529 session of parliament passed twenty-six laws in all, most of them addressing economic issues and the administration of justice, a few of them private bills resolving quarrels and disposing of property. There also was the matter of Wolsey. It was previously said that the forty-four-article indictment against the cardinal was approved by Lords but rejected by Commons owing to the stout defense mounted by Cromwell. The source is Cavendish, writing after the fact. In contrast, Hall, a parliamentarian himself, told the story somewhat differently. Here the Lord's indictment was more on the order of a petition to the king, reported also to the lower house but requiring no action there and calling forth no defense speech by Cromwell, who is not mentioned. One could suppose, on grounds of proximity to the event, that the Hall account is more reliable; but in doing so one inevitably changes the perception of the Lords from a body hell-bent on destroying the cardinal to a body content with damaging his reputation. For a petition to an inconstant king, as opposed to a bill of attainder or disablement passed by parliament, would afford no guarantee against the cardinal's returning to power. Furthermore, Hall stated that Wolsey confessed to the charges and signed over his property to the king; but since these were actions taken by the cardinal following his praemunire indictment a month earlier, there may be reason to suspect confusion in the Hall narrative, which may extend to the omission of pertinent details. On the other hand, there are chronological confusions in Cavendish too.

The 1530 Prorogation of Parliament

Although the divorce was not front-and-center during parliament's 1529 session, divorce-related maneuvers were underway in the months prior to the session and throughout much of the following year. On the recommendation of two trusted advisers, Stephen Gardiner and Edward Foxe, Henry accepted the suggestion of an unknown Cambridge don and cleric, named Thomas Cranmer, to solicit learned opinion at home and abroad supportive of the nullity suit. The case had been revoked to Rome; should the hearings ever begin, the testimony of scholars and divines from Europe's most reputable universities could tip the decision in Henry's favour. At a minimum the canvassing project would allow others to weigh in and suggest to the Christian world that the decision ought not to be the pope's alone. Royal emissaries were sent to Cambridge and Oxford where they succeeded in eliciting positive determinations, though not without some difficulty (fighting at Cambridge and the stoning of agents at Oxford). Others were sent to France and northern Italy where an oppositionist campaign, mounted by the emperor and the pope, blocked progress. Each party spent lavishly trying to bribe its way to success. In some cases, Henry's cause prevailed, in others Catherine's.

Meanwhile Henry's agents in Rome were instructed to delay the trial, all the while complaining of the tardiness of the Rota's proceedings. Henry had been ordered to appear in Rome or appoint a proctor to serve as his stand-in. He did neither. (Catherine, on the other hand, did send a proctor.) The opinions from Europe were slow to arrive, and Henry feared a negative judgement from the court. Indeed, he had cause to be worried, since the pope had declared in favour of Charles and had crowned him emperor in March 1530. (The election of the emperor by German princes was the first step; papal anointing was the second, although this was a contested requirement in secular circles; first Leo, then Clement, withheld confirmation for eleven years.) An embassy led by Wiltshire represented England at the coronation ceremony held in Bologna. Wiltshire's mission, besides paying respects, was to persuade Charles and Clement to accede to the divorce. As an inducement, Charles was promised the return of a portion of Catherine's dowry. The mission failed – it had no chance – and so Wiltshire traveled to Paris to confer with Francis and to hasten along the university's report. The slow pace of reply caused Henry to postpone the convening of parliament (set for April, then for June, then for October), though the official reason was plague in the city. Parliament did not meet again until January 1531.

In a similar attempt at applying pressure on Rome, Henry summoned the English nobility, episcopate, and abbacies to a June meeting at court where the gathered lords (and a few commoners) were asked to sign and affix their seals to a petition to Clement beseeching his Holiness to rule in Henry's favour lest civil strife reappear in the land. The letter contained no challenge to the pope's authority, though it did include the admonitory mention of other avenues available should the king be disappointed in his appeal. Henry had enough trouble just convincing his own subjects (let alone the pope), many of whom at first resisted the king's entreaty, one of whom pleaded with Henry to return to Catherine, and most of whom rejected the notion that England could settle the matter without recourse to Rome. Moreover, notable opponents of the divorce, such as Fisher and More, were not invited to attend. Clement dismissed the request with an answering letter written in September.

The fact that Henry had been cited to appear in Rome was taken by him as an affront to his royal dignity. His irritation festered, until eventually he attempted something new. In the late summer and autumn, letters went forth to emissaries in Rome instructing them to request of the pope the return of the case to England where a panel of three bishops, or the Canterbury Convocation, or Henry himself would render judgement – whichever arrangement Clement preferred. The quick failure of that ploy brought additional letters advising the emissaries to inform the pope seriatim: (1) that England enjoyed customary immunities from papal interference, which the king was now inclined to invoke; (2) that church law ordained that ecclesiastical disputes be heard locally and not transferred to Rome; and (3) that the English kingship was an independent polity subordinate to no other temporal or spiritual power. Evidence to support any or all of these claims was skimpy (and Clement demanded to see it). Accordingly, the same emissaries were ordered to ransack the Vatican register and libraries across the continent. Their search was less than satisfactory – indeed it tended to prove the contrary. But that did not stop Henry and his courtiers from haranguing the papal nuncio as to how English supremacy was tantamount to imperial power. Since national sovereignty was not yet an established idea, the only way to extricate oneself from the web of feudal dependencies was to occupy a place at the top of the hierarchy. That is what Henry attempted to do, but at this juncture inchoately and timorously. He acted on none of these claims but fell back on the safer policy of foot-dragging at the Rota.

A fifth and final tactic did Henry employ in these months of indecision. He brought praemunire charges at King's Bench against fifteen ecclesiastics; of these John Fisher was the most prominent, while most of the rest were public supporters of Catherine. Their crime was that they had held on to their benefices, against pressure from Wolsey, by submitting to Wolsey's extortionate demands. (One might rather conclude that they were victims, not accomplices.) The purpose plainly was intimidation, adjustments in the balance of power, and perhaps trolling for cash. Nothing though came of these charges, as a few weeks later (October) the indictments were suspended. Cromwell wrote to Wolsey at the time, apprising him that 'the prelates shall not appear in *praemunire*. There is another way devised'. The other way referred either to a garbled suggestion by Clement that Henry resolve his 'great matter' (temporarily) by taking a second wife (i.e., bigamy) – a suggestion which Henry wished not to scuttle by moving against the local clergy; or, as is more generally thought, the other way referred to a bolder plan, still in gestation, to extend the praemunire charge against the entire clerical order, claiming that their cooperation with Wolsey's legatine authority implicated them in Wolsey's crimes. Later the charge would be significantly enlarged to include the mere presence on English soil of ecclesiastical courts, these judged to be a violation of the king's sovereignty.

This enlargement came just in advance of the reconvening of parliament in January 1531 (though there is confusion about when the charge was expanded and when Convocation first heard about it). The sudden change (assuming a January date) could then have reflected the influence of Cromwell, which influence he could then have earned from a signal performance at a meeting with the king in December (see 'King's Servant' above). Some scholars look at the new purpose given to the anti-clerical campaign as evidence of Cromwell's discovery and emergence. Others though suppose that the hesitancy of the past twelve months was deliberate, meant to hide from view a decision, taken already by Henry and belonging to him alone, to affirm his caesaropapism whatever the outcome of the divorce suit. The question is this: would Henry have returned to the Catholic fold, acknowledging the pope's suzerainty, if Clement had granted Henry his divorce from Catherine? Since both yes and no answers are supported by the record, perhaps a compromise interpretation is best: that Henry would have formally submitted to the pope (in order to maintain peace in his realm and to ensure international recognition of his heir), while expecting the drift of events and his own aggressive behavior to render nugatory the effect of that submission. As for Cromwell, it seems clear that he was not responsible for any of the early attempts to shape the proceedings in Rome (i.e., [1] the collection of favourable scholarly opinions; [2] the testament of support from the English nobility; [3] the stalling tactics adopted by English emissaries at the papal court; [4] the declarations of independence on the part of the king; and [5] the praemunire charges against fifteen prelates) since he was too new to the king's service to be noticed and heard.

Session Two – January–March 1531

The legal independence of the English church from secular interference dated back to Magna Carta (1215), the first and last articles of which guaranteed that the church should be forever free and her rights held inviolate. The king at the time, John (1199–1216), was constrained by the barons of the realm to make these and other concessions, because oppressive taxes, enacted in the wake of losses on the battlefield, had weakened his hand. A counter-offensive began a century later when laws were passed in the reigns of Edward I (1272–1307), Edward III (1327–77), and Richard II (1377–99) curtailing papal power in England. By these laws it was forbidden that church taxes of any description be sent out of the kingdom to Rome; forbidden that non-English clergy be named to English benefices by the pope; and forbidden that cases at law be transferred to the papal court without the pleaders first answering for their contempt of the king's prerogatives. Some of these laws were called statutes of provisors, some were called statutes of praemunire. They were never very effective, and in the fifteenth century they had fallen into abeyance and were little enforced. By Henry's day their neglect was complete, for taxes called annates and first fruits were paid to Rome upon the assumption of vacant benefices; English bishoprics, with *ex officio* seats in the House of Lords, were held by foreign ecclesiastics (Salisbury and Worcester by Italians, Llandaff by a Spaniard); and the king's divorce case was appealed to Rome for final disposition.

By custom the convening of parliament was accompanied by the convening of the Canterbury Convocation, somewhere in London (e.g., St Paul's Cathedral) or in quarters proximate to parliament (e.g., the Chapter House at Westminster Abbey). Convocation was prepared to enact its own reform agenda in response to the beating it received from the 1529 parliament, but a new brief filed at King's Bench charging clergy with praemunire offenses against the crown–these the result not of collusion with Wolsey, but of the existence and operation of ecclesiastical courts – sent the bishops, et al. into a panic. They refused admittance to Chapuys and the papal nuncio, for fear that by associating with papists, Convocation would put Henry in a rage. Then came word from the king that a subsidy of £100,000 was demanded of the southern Convocation to defray the cost of the king's 'great matter', and that in return for this sum a royal pardon would be granted. Bishop Fisher had the audacity to inform Henry that such expenses were entirely his own responsibility, incurred in pursuance of a divorce that was entirely unlawful. But the other bishops were not so brave. After abortive dickering over the amount due, they agreed to the king's demand, requesting only that they be permitted to pay the sum in five installments. Henry objected, and Convocation withdrew its offer pending assurances from the crown. The bishops wanted their ancient Magna Carta rights restored; they wanted the meaning of praemunire specified and restricted; and they wanted relief from the anticlerical legislation passed in the previous session of parliament. But Henry had his own terms. While he retreated on the installments issue, he refused to provide Convocation with any of the assurances requested. Instead he made five new demands: (1) that he be recognised as 'sole head and protector of the Anglican church and clergy'; (2) that spiritual jurisdiction called 'cure of souls' be accorded to him; (3) that the rights and privileges practiced by the church be limited to those consistent with the king's regality; (4) that the clergy sue more humbly for the king's pardon; and finally (5) that the laity be included in the clergy's guilt for having utilised the ecclesiastical courts.

The first two of these demands left Convocation gasping for air. Fisher, the mainstay of the resistance, objected that the supremacy now claimed by the king could pass to a successor who was a minor or a woman; and the 'cure of souls' provision suggested that Henry was arrogating to himself the prerogatives of a priest. Negotiations were carried on by advisers of the king, including Cromwell, who appeared in Convocation and had a private conference with Warham, its head. Cromwell may have been the source of the compromise phrasing that confined Henry's supremacy within the (vaguely determined) boundaries of the law of God: *quantum per legem Dei licet* – 'as far as the law of God allows'. It took Henry some time to accept the qualification, but when he did the upper house of Convocation, its silence taken for agreement, consented to the document (and in fact all present members did sign). The lower house though was recalcitrant, and only a majority gave its approval, with some dissenters insisting upon their continuing allegiance to the pope. Further revisions to the prologue redirected the cure of souls back to the clergy and away from the king, who was acknowledged as providing the spirituality traditional temporal assistance. The other demands similarly transmogrified into familiar declarations; and the king's pardon, contained in an act of parliament, effectively reaffirmed the legality of the ecclesiastical courts.

It would seem that Henry had secular supremacy firmly within his grasp and then, inexplicably, let it slip away. Many scholars hold to this view and attribute the misstep to divided opinion among the advisers and within Henry himself. That is certainly possible, assuming that the outcome was a defeat for the king. But Henry now held the title 'sole head and protector' indisputably, while the 'law of God' reservation invited endless dispute and meant nothing definitively absent interpretation. And who most likely would provide definitive interpretation? Some lower clergy tried, but they were quickly brought up on praemunire charges and had to plead for pardon. The bishop of Durham, Cuthbert Tunstall, also tried in a letter to Henry, stating that secular overlordship applied in temporal matters only. Henry pretended to agree, in a long letter of his own, but then he extended the meaning of temporal to everything short of preaching and the administering of sacraments. Accordingly, the king would appoint bishops, control church property, and recognise but a delegated jurisdiction of ecclesiastical courts. In these exchanges the king prevailed, answering clearly, it seems, the question posed above: for Henry would provide the interpretation, unless the church had the wherewithal and conviction to stand up against his pressure. But already clerics had twice backed down under threats of prosecution.

It is not unimportant that Henry, perhaps prodded by Cromwell, involved parliament in these proceedings. Parliament was called upon to ratify the concessions of Convocation by enacting the king's pardon into law. Early in the session a pardon bill was drafted and passed in the House of Lords; but Commons objected on grounds that the pardon did not encompass the laity. Thomas Audley, Speaker of the House, was dispatched by the members to confer with the king and plead for laity's inclusion. Henry treated him roughly and announced that as king he could pardon whom he pleased and do so by royal decree. Apparently Henry was not yet convinced of the indispensability of parliament's approval or of the continued need for the divide-and-conquer strategy which had been used to such good effect in 1529. He may have been standing on his dignity as a medieval monarch and giving vent to exasperation and disbelief over the presumption of mere commoners; or he may have been imagining the cash he might raise if all the realm were held guilty of praemunire and obliged to pay fines in amendment of their offenses. In any event, Audley and Commons were soon relieved of their anxiety, as in March a new pardon for the clergy and a separate pardon for the laity were submitted by the king and passed by parliament. Hall described a thankful Commons, cognizant of its unworthiness in making demands of the king and appreciative of the king's wisdom in withholding his bounty until Commons had shown itself humble and contrite. Again, this obeisance was not quite in keeping with king-in-parliament constitutionalism, but it was fully in line with Machiavelli's advice on how to dispense benefits – i.e., never in response to demands (*Dis*, I. 32, 38, 51).

The main event of the 1531 session took place in Convocation, not in parliament, which was relegated to the sidelines except for the business about pardons. Still parliament was in session, and so it needed to find something to do. It renewed its attack on the clergy, insisting that an English translation of the Bible be permitted by the church; that Council be used in place of bishops to examine suspected heretics and to determine the scope and particulars of religious reformation; and that attempts to roll back the reforms of 1529 (such as that tried by Convocation) be outlawed and subject to penalty. None of these proposals were enacted, however. Poor relief was put on the agenda, but what was passed (licenses to beg for the impotent poor and beatings for the able-bodied) was a far cry from what was proposed (public works and guarantees of a living wage). The king appeared in parliament to demand that poisoning be regarded as a treasonous offense. It seems that someone had undertaken to poison the bishop of Rochester (though the malefactor called it a prank), and the king, fearful for his own life, and fearful of being suspected of involvement in the attempt on Fisher's life, wanted to deter like attacks in the future and to head-off Catholic outrage. The punishment requested and gotten was boiling alive, which was then applied *ex post facto* to the culprit in the case, one Richard Roose. Significantly, parliament was not called on to address the king's divorce from Catherine; the issue came up directly neither in parliament nor in Convocation. But indirectly the 'great matter' stayed alive by the reading of those opinions collected from the universities and intended to influence the Rota. Finally the term ended with a speech by Lord Chancellor More assuring the assembly that matters of conscience and reasons of state inspired the nullity suit, not the 'will or pleasure' of the king. No doubt More, the 'man for all seasons', was acting under orders and trying to put the best face on what he thought was a sordid affair.

Session Three – January–May 1532

If Henry could not yet divorce his wife under law, he could at least divorce her in practice. Catherine was last at court and in the company of her husband in July 1531. Henry abandoned her at Windsor, went off to other quarters with Anne, and sent instructions for Catherine's removal to one palace/fortress after another scattered across the countryside. Until her death in January 1536, Catherine was held under house arrest and allowed only infrequent communication with her daughter, with Chapuys, and with trusted friends. Henry rarely wrote and never saw her again.

All was mostly quiet on the international front. The occasional embassy went forth looking to build support for the king's divorce, but nothing much came of their efforts. Rome was implored to shut down Catherine's appeals trial and threatened with the recall of English envoys if it refused – also without positive result.

Again there were delays in the reconvening of parliament, postponed from October to November, and from November to the next year; and again the excuse was fear of disease. Finally parliament met in mid January 1532, with Convocation starting its term a couple days later. Cromwell had been busy drafting a host of bills touching economic and legal matters, but most of these were never presented. Always strapped for cash, the king rather decided that parliament should address the all-too-common practice of underpaying the monarchy its full feudal dues. Traditionally the crown had collected an estate tax upon the death of the proprietor; but a way around the tax had been found by willing the use of the property to another in advance of the owner's demise. The legal effect was that the owner never died, and the king never got his death tax. Henry proposed a compromise (pay me some, keep the remainder), but his offer was ill received by lords and commoners alike. The bill of uses was tabled, and Henry thereafter was cross with his parliament.

On the divorce Cromwell was preparing legislation designed to achieve the extreme solution – that Convocation, by-passing Rome, deliver a final (no doubt positive) decision, using evidence gathered during the legatine hearings of 1529. But this bill too never came up for debate. For notwithstanding the royal chest-beating of the previous year (I am an emperor!), Henry proved indisposed to unilateral action. He preferred instead to threaten Rome with the loss of English revenues. This was the *Act in Restraint of Annates*. Its preamble traced the origin of annates, or first fruits, to special papal exactions for funding war against the infidel; and it pronounced as unlawful their continuation into these post-crusading times or their use for routine purposes. Henceforth, declared the law's enacting passage, payments to Rome by new occupants of vacant benefices would be forbidden; refusal by the pope to consecrate new bishops would be remedied by English archbishops acting in his place; and papal retaliations, such as excommunication and interdiction, would simply be ignored. Finally, at the discretion of the king, the implementation of the act could be delayed a year. Thus the door was still open for the pope to come around to Henry's way of thinking.

But parliament was disinclined to endorse this expression of nationalism which potentially could put England outside of the

Catholic communion. Cromwell suspected as much, for he wrote to inform Gardiner, away on state business that 'this day was read in the higher house a bill touching the Annates of bishoprics; for what end or effect it will succeed surely I know not'. Henry had to appear in parliament on three occasions to influence the members. Even so, the vote in Lords was close, with all of the bishops voting against; and success in Commons required recourse to the expedient known as 'division', by which MPs supporting king and country moved to one side of the room, and those opposed moved as outcasts to the other.

Anticlericalism was the other main item of business of the 1532 parliament. The complaints of 1529, which resulted in this or that restriction (mortuary, probate, plurality and non-residence, etc.), were recycled by Cromwell, who, with a little scab-scratching in Commons, managed to produce a petition to the king called the *Supplication of Commons against the Ordinaries* (although some scholars put the impetus with Commons). An ordinary was any prelate in possession of jurisdiction not delegated by another. Archbishops and bishops were ordinaries in their archdioceses and dioceses, as were abbots in their abbacies. The *Supplication*, therefore, was a bill of particulars targeted at England's high clergy, accusing them of transgressing the king's prerogatives and of abusing the laity. Twelve charges in total were specified, with most of them focusing on the legislative and judicial powers exercised by the church: for example, passing canons in Convocation without the king's or parliament's consent and in contravention of the country's secular laws; and operating spiritual courts wherein fee schedules were oppressively high and cases protracted because conducted by judges with an interest in delay; and wherein simple souls, subjected to 'subtle interrogatories', faced abjuring their accidental heresies and bearing the faggot, or being handed over to secular authorities and suffering the flames. These, and numerous others, were the grievances of Commons, which Speaker Audley presented to Henry in mid March.

Before the petition was completed and before action could be taken, parliament and the king heard from Archbishop Warham, who at last got his back up, having been supine in the previous session. In late February he formally protested lay interference in clerical affairs, and a few weeks later he repeated his opposition before the House of Lords. To punctuate his perturbation, he hauled in for examination Hugh Latimer, a heterodox preacher popular at court; and he did so a second time when two of his bishops (and agents of the king) set Latimer free. Warham's complaint was that Convocation had been busy, like never before, cleaning its house and enacting reforms; but that this honest labor was now prejudicially represented as a usurpation of the crown's legislative power.

Battle lines were forming when Easter forced a recess of this over-long session of parliament (so long that Audley pleaded for an adjournment, even though in petitioning the king he was by implication requesting parliament's continuation; Henry noted the contradiction and again treated Audley roughly.) During the break two events transpired – one a counter-punch, the other a foolhardy impertinence – which took some of the new bounce out of Warham's aging step. At King's Bench a suit was filed by the king's attorney general charging Warham with praemunire in the unauthorised consecration of a bishop – fourteen years earlier! A ridiculous charge to be sure (Warham said as much), but in the current climate to be expected. Also, on Easter Sunday William Peto, provincial of the Observant Friars, preached against the divorce with the king sitting in attendance. Henry was livid, but the time had not come for the cutting off of heads; instead he engaged the royal chaplain, Richard Curwen, to deliver a rebuttal sermon the following Sunday. Curwen did, and Peto accused him before Convocation of preaching without proper license – from Peto. Convocation took no action, but its mere involvement in the matter caused Henry to cast a scowl in its direction, whereas before his ire was reserved for Commons, hesitant to oblige him on taxes.

Henry now positioned himself as a mediator between his lay and spiritual subjects (whether honestly or not), and in this capacity he passed on the *Supplication* to Convocation for a reply. Stephen Gardiner, the king's secretary and recently elevated bishop of Winchester, was commissioned to answer on behalf of the ordinaries. Gardiner had been abroad during the early debates and was unaware of the changing mood at court, for he set about his work fully confident that Henry, 'sole head and protector' of the church, was friendly toward the clergy and friendly toward Gardiner (assured of the same by Cromwell who related the king's longing for the return of his so called 'right hand'). Thus Gardiner's first reply insouciantly ignored eleven of the Commons' twelve complaints. It addressed the preamble of the *Supplication*, which had characterised lay-clerical relations as inquiet, vexatious, and nearly violent, affecting innocence and disbelief that such harsh words could ever be uttered. The one complaint it did take up, the legislative independence of Convocation, it dismissed peremptorily, though not without many pages of obsequious puffery to prepare the way. Attributing legislative power to Scripture and the holy church, the reply concluded that 'we, your most humble subjects, may not submit the execution of our charges and duty, certainly prescribed by God, to your highness's assent'. Convocation was pleased with Gardiner's effort, voting approval in upper and lower houses; but then it had second thoughts about sending back to the king an answer so incomplete. A fuller reply was thus drafted, touching on all points of the *Supplication*, and was delivered to Henry by late April.

Henry, though, was not pleased at all. Three days later he summoned to court Thomas Audley and a party of MPs. Audley by now had just cause to fear these audiences with the king, but what the Speaker found was a Henry in full opposition to the clergy and ready to embrace parliament and Commons as an ally. For he handed Convocation's *Answer of the Ordinaries* to Audley with this bit of trenchant commentary, recorded by Hall: 'We think their answer will smally please you, for it seems to us very slender. You be a great sort of wise men; I doubt not but you will look circumspectly on the matter, and we will be indifferent between you.' The claim to indifference, at this juncture, could hardly be sustained. The following week an embassy of bishops, all favourites of Henry, were sent to plead Convocation's case and to implore the king to respect the historic liberties of the church. They were rebuffed. The fatal blow was delivered shortly thereafter: Henry's demands that (1) Convocation renounce its legislative power; (2) submit existing canons to review by a board of thirty-two commissioners, half clerical, half lay, and all royal appointees; and (3) keep as law only those canons receiving the king's approval. Lest there be any mistake as to where Henry now stood, Audley was again brought before the king to be apprised of the oath taken by ordinaries to the pope in contravention of the oath they took to the king. This was Cromwell's doing, and legend sometimes traces the idea's first mention to Cromwell's December 1530 meeting with the king. Hall again is the recorder of Henry's threatening words:

Well beloved subjects, we thought that the clergy of our realm had been our subjects wholly, but now we have well perceived that they be but half our subjects, yea, and scarce our subjects; for all the prelates at their consecration make an oath to the pope clean contrary to the oath that they make to us, so that they seem to be his subjects and not ours.

The oaths were read before parliament where they elicited shock and dismay from supporters of the king.

Meanwhile Convocation, aware now of the king's disaffection and sensing grave danger to the integrity of their corporate body, attempted to salvage whatever they could of their traditional prerogatives. They proposed this compromise: that Henry alone, and not Henry and some commission, rule on the legality of canons, and that Convocation's surrender of its legislative powers be good only for the duration of Henry's reign, a monarch of such surpassing virtue. Henry was unmoved and ordered an end to Convocation's session, which at its last meeting, May 15, was visited by members of the nobility, demanding the submission of clergy and adding an addendum to the list of the king's newly asserted powers, that Convocation assemble only upon the king's command.

The ordinaries felt themselves beaten, and they in turn beat down what little spirit surfaced in the lower house. By the time the vote was taken most of the members were not in attendance. Only six bishops voted for the submission and a similar number of abbots, but apparently that was sufficient to constitute a majority. The *Submission of Clergy* was formally subscribed on May 16. It stipulated that never again would Convocation enact laws, that it would convene only upon the king's writ, and that the king and his commission of thirty-two would confirm or discard all existing canons.

Parliament had been prorogued for two days when its titular leader, Thomas More, hearing of the *Submission*, resigned the office of Lord Chancellor and delivered up the great seal. Audley was soon after appointed as More's replacement.

Cromwell had pleased his king, who in April conferred the office of Master of the Jewels upon his minister and in July the office of Clerk of the Hanaper of Chancery. Both were Household posts concerned with financial matters – respectively custody of the bullion reserves in jewels and plate and administration of the Chancery's treasury.

Session Four – February–April 1533

As had happened twice before, the advertised date for parliament's reconvening was not kept; instead of November, parliament came back into session in February. This time plague was not the reason or stated excuse; the actual cause was difficulty in readying legislation.

In the interim, several events of great consequence took place. Archbishop Warham died in August. He was eighty-two. His death had been long expected and in certain quarters long desired. Though by and large accommodating to his king, on the issue of the divorce, Warham would not as archbishop unilaterally sever the union. Moreover, at the time of his death, he was preparing a resistance speech for delivery at Convocation's next meeting. Stephen Gardiner was the most likely candidate to replace Warham; but Gardiner had fallen into disfavour because of his involvement in the *Supplication* affair. Henry looked past other prominent ecclesiastics too –Stokesley of London, Lee of York, Longland of Lincoln – selecting as his nominee a lightly beneficed archdeacon, Thomas Cranmer, currently serving as ambassador to the emperor at Mantua. Besides lack of status, marriage – and to the daughter of a Lutheran divine, no less – was Cranmer's other liability. Cranmer was a priest, and Henry was a stickler on the point of clerical celibacy. Thus not to offend, Cranmer left his wife in Europe, and later, in order to protect his secret, he had her transported to England in a packing crate – such was the rumour at any rate. The choice was surprising, and surprisingly quick, since appointment of a new archbishop would cost Henry the Canterbury revenues which otherwise would come to the crown for as long as the vacancy continued. Cranmer learned of his selection in November; by January he was home in England.

There was cause for hurry. The previous spring France had agreed in principle to assist with the divorce case still pending at Rome. To finalise the deal, a grand summit, on the model of the Field of Cloth of Gold, was planned for October 1532. The English were to support the marriage of Francis' second son, Henry, duke of Orléans, to Catherine de'Medici, Clement's niece, and in exchange the French were to support Henry's marriage to Anne, as well as his divorce from Catherine. In September Anne was elevated to the marquess of Pembroke, in preparation for her presentation to the nobility of France. The conference proceeded as planned: Francis played host to his English guests at Boulogne, and Henry returned the courtesy at Calais. Cromwell was in attendance, his first venture into foreign affairs. Bad weather delayed the embarkation home. And during the delay, or shortly after the arrival at Dover, Anne conceived a child by Henry.

The pregnancy changed everything – or was everything changed by Warham's death, which by removing a barrier to the divorce also removed a barrier to sexual congress? Either way, a child was coming, whose legitimacy and rights of succession required marriage. The time for dithering had passed; and so Henry married Anne on January 25. The union of course was bigamous – and for that reason kept secret from the public – because Henry was still married to Catherine. An archbishop was therefore needed to wave aside papal objections and to divorce the couple himself. Enter Thomas Cranmer – learned, well spoken, and eager to please – the man responsible for the policy of collecting scholarly opinion favouring the annulment. Henry appointed him archbishop on January 10 at a bear-baiting contest. It was not, however, in Henry's power (yet) to create archbishops. Popes did that. So English agents at Rome pressed Clement to issue the provisions for a new archbishop of Canterbury. Amazingly, Clement obliged, and in record time, perhaps because the (conditional) *Restraint of Annates* of the previous year had not been activated, and Henry now paid the taxes using his own money. Cranmer was consecrated archbishop on March 30, well after parliament and Convocation had begun work, but still in time to effect the divorce.

What Cromwell had proposed doing a year before was now official government policy – to use the English church to accomplish Henry's divorce from Catherine. But by what authority would the English church divorce the king, since under existing procedures decisions taken locally were appealable to Rome, and Catherine had so appealed the case? The new plan was to foreclose appeals, or, in instances of appeals already filed, to force their revocation back to England, where a church primate would now be in place willing to follow instructions. The *Act in Restraint of Appeals* was presented to parliament in mid-March. It had passed through eight drafts before reaching its final, and royally sanctioned, state. Even some clerics had been sounded out in advance. The Act began famously with allusion to the imperial theme: 'Whereby [in] diverse, sundry, and old chronicles it is manifestly declared and expressed that this realm of England is an empire.' No chronicles were cited on the occasion, but recycled tales of Emperor Constantine and of King Arthur were much in the air. Geoffrey Monmouth's twelfth-century *History of the Kings of Britain* was particularly useful, since it traced the lineage of Constantine to Brutus, the legendary grandson of the legendary Aeneas, founder of Latium from which sprang Rome. Constantine had been a Roman ruler of Britain before becoming a Roman emperor; and as emperor he presided over a council which established doctrine for the early Catholic church (the Council of Nicaea, 325). Thus through the Constantine connection, Henry's England could claim a Trojan origin older than Christian Rome and, as its former superior, an exemption from the exercise of papal power. The thesis though was not argued (understandably); rather the legislation confidently announced that England's imperial status had been 'accepted in the world'.

Also in the preamble was a description of English society as a polity divided into estates, ruled over by an imperial king, who exercised 'plenary power', and to whom 'natural obedience' was due 'next only to God'. Medieval popes, at the height of their authority, claimed plenary power; so an arrogation of that power resulting in royal absolutism was what the law seemed to envision. But then a place and a purpose was given to the English church – to adjudicate cases arising under divine law – and the endowments from kings and nobles, which had over the centuries made the church great, were portrayed as necessary instruments to the achievement of that mission. Rather than denounce the opulence and grandeur which the church now displayed (as had anticlerical tracts beginning with Fish's), the legislation explained church worldliness as a safeguard provided ecclesiastics from 'corruption and sinister affection'. It was thus allowed that the church enjoyed some constitutional powers, and so absolutism at home seemed not the real objective. Instead, English independence was the objective, and a well-supplied English church was expected to stand beside an imperial king in resisting pressure from the pope, the Holy Roman emperor, or any foreign body with the presumption to tell England what to do. Nor was this independence a new development; it had existed for an indeterminate time and had been supported by a multitude of laws (i.e., Henry's ancestors had been emperors too). Even so, English laws protecting English independence had not been sufficiently well crafted to prevent the continuation of 'appeals sued out of this realm to the see of Rome'. The Act thus declared that all

> causes testamentary, causes of matrimony and divorce, rights
> of tithes, oblations and obventions ... already commenced ... or
> hereafter coming in contention ... within this realm shall be from
> henceforth heard ... and determined within the king's jurisdiction
> and authority and not elsewhere, in such courts spiritual and
> temporal ... as the natures of the causes ... shall require.

Those courts were to be assisted by an appeals process that would remove a case having begun with an archdeacon to the diocesan bishop, and remove one having begun with a diocesan bishop to the provincial archbishop, except that in cases touching the king's business the final court of appeal would be the upper house of the appropriate Convocation. For the moment at least, Henry's 'great matter' still lay with ecclesiastics for disposing. Nor was Rome completely out of the picture, for the *Act in Restraint of Appeals* did not cover all causes – it did not cover heresy, for example.

The king's marriage was under discussion in Convocation before passage of the *Act in Restraint of Appeal,* and so the verdict rendered in Convocation, once Cranmer took charge, was not an instance of a case at law heard on appeal; it was more on the order of an advisory opinion given in anticipation of parliamentary action. As predicted, Convocation decided in Henry's favour, stating that the papal dispensation allowing a brother to marry his sister-in-law had been impermissibly granted (by Julius II in 1503) and that Catherine's first marriage to Arthur had indeed been consummated (a finding denied by Catherine on a point of law at the center of the dispute). The actual divorce was pronounced by an archbishop's court convened at Dunstable in May. Catherine was in residence nearby, but she refused to attend any of the court's sessions or to acknowledge the court's authority to hear the case; she was declared contumacious. After two weeks of testimony, Cranmer ruled the marriage to Catherine invalid, and at Lambeth (the archbishop's London residence) five days later he ruled lawful Henry's marriage to Anne. Anne was crowned queen on June 1, following a celebratory sailing from Greenwich to the Tower and a triumphal procession from the Tower to Westminster. The gathered crowds were more sullen than joyous, however, as Catherine was popular and Anne was not.

After proroguing parliament, a happy Henry again promoted Cromwell, this time to Chancellor of the Exchequer – then a minor post whose occupant kept the Exchequer seal and sat on the Exchequer court. Certainly Cromwell deserved better, but his influence was not yet widely known and may have been intended as a secret.

This provocative action on the part of the English church provoked a nasty reaction in Rome. The pope waved aside all that Cranmer and Convocation had wrought. The divorce judgement he pronounced null and void, and the papal nuncio he recalled. Furthermore, he moved to excommunicate the king of England, though Henry was given the summer months to take back his lawful wife and beg the pope's forgiveness. Tit-for-tat diplomacy was now in full swing and for some time would be the manner in which the two powers related. Annates, which Henry had paid to hurry along Cranmer's confirmation, were henceforth restrained, as was permitted by the 1532 legislation. Agents were dispatched to Protestant courts and capitals, sent there to spread the word of England's break with Rome and to broach the subject of new alliances. An embassy, led by Norfolk and meant to supervise the long-planned meeting of Francis and Clement (Francis was to obtain the marriage of his son to Clement's niece, and Clement – so it was thought – was to grant Henry his divorce) was abruptly recalled, except for a pair of ministers who remained behind to threaten the pope with the prospect of a general council. Their denunciations of Clement caused Francis to despair of English diplomacy. But then Henry had previously despaired of French faithfulness, concluding that Francis was set to betray him to the pope; Henry thus tried doggedly to have the Marseilles conference cancelled (a postponement to October– November was all that Norfolk could manage).

But the amazing thing was that Henry, after announcing his independence from Rome (*Act in Restraint of Appeals*) and after achieving his divorce through the use of domestic institutions – all of this following Cromwell's plan – continued to work his own plan, or that of other advisers, petitioning the papacy for its after-the-fact blessing of the divorce. Clement's reply was, as before, send a proctor to the Rota where the case will be heard; and Henry's reply was, as before, permit entry to my excusatory, who will excuse my absence and ask that the case be revoked to England where it has already been heard. Perhaps one reason for keeping open the papal option – apart from Henry's inveterate indecisiveness – was the disappointing news that pregnant Queen Anne was in September delivered of a daughter. This was Elizabeth, later queen in her own right, but for now just another girl-child who could not easily inherit the throne. Plus she was the younger of two daughters, and so her claim to succeed, should it come to that, could be more in dispute than Mary's. The 'great matter', rather than a thing of the past, was more tightly knotted than ever.

September brought also the arrest of one Elizabeth Barton, the 'Holy Maid of Kent'. Her rise to prominence was indicative of the public opposition which the divorce and coronation had stirred and of the government's need to lay down a marker of what behaviors would no longer be permitted. The Maid had survived an illness in 1525 which left her gifted, she believed, with the power of prophecy. She thereupon entered a convent in the Canterbury archdiocese and fell under the tutelage of local divines. The archbishop took notice of her, as did Bishop Fisher and Thomas More. So too did the king take notice, though only after she began foretelling his doom should he press ahead with the divorce. That was in 1527. Six years later the climate of hesitancy-cum-tolerance had changed. Others besides Barton complained openly of the divorce, and unrest was growing in the land. With the death of Warham the previous summer and his replacement by Cranmer, a Henry partisan, Barton now lacked a patron able to fend off attacks and make excuses for her; while the king, remarried and displeased by its first fruit, lacked the patience to leave this eccentric soothsayer to her seditious musings. He commanded Barton's arrest and interrogation. With prompting (the nature of which is unknown – though back in July Cromwell recommended the torture of two friars associated with Barton), she and numerous followers confessed the fraud that had been perpetrated. The spectacle of examination and recantation was repeated two months later in an elaborate public ceremony, followed by a vitriolic sermon delivered at Paul's Cross. Her destruction came during parliament's next session.

Session Five – January–March 1534

Parliament convened on January 15, but with a diminished number of Aragonese, many of whom had been instructed not to attend. Cromwell was behind this culling of the membership, which resulted in the absence (temporary in some cases) of such stalwarts of the opposition as Fisher, Tunstall, Darcy, and Throckmorton.

Once in session parliament passed a host of bills of a routine economic nature (e.g., an enclosure bill which limited the size of grazing flocks, lauded by Cromwell as 'the most noble, profitable, and most beneficial thing that ever was done to the common wealth … since Brutus' time'); but reformation issues were again its main item of business. The *Submission of the Clergy*, which Convocation had accepted two years prior, now became a statute of parliament. Cromwell had wanted from the beginning to imprint the submission with parliament's sanction, but Henry was content to keep the submission a matter between himself and his clergy. What then was intended by this revisitation of accomplished fact? Commons may have wanted more than what Convocation initially surrendered, for Commons wanted relief from the spirituality's judicial power, whereas the legislative power was all that Convocation relinquished. A party of MPs led by the Speaker beseeched the king to protect the laity from citation to ecclesiastical courts, where the accuser was unknown to the accused, where heresy was charged and burning threatened without just cause, where fees were extracted contrary to equity, and where the clergy sat as judges in cases affecting themselves. But if this was the intent, it was not the result, as the new law was again silent about judicial abuses. Alternately, parliament's revisitation may have been a product of Cromwell's success in selling his king on the idea of constitutional order, in which proper lawmaking requires that king and parliament act in concert; or in selling his king on the pragmatic benefits of spreading responsibility for controversial matters (*Prince*, 19: when beating down the great, deflect anger and hatred by involving a third party). But then a final possibility is that a *Submission* bill was wanted to rectify a defect in the *Act in Restraint of Appeals* – namely that Convocation, a religious body, was the final court of appeals for royal causes. One might imagine that Henry, when reflecting upon Thomas Cranmer as the primate, would have been sanguine and satisfied with Convocation in charge; but when thinking back to Warham or ahead to parties unknown, Henry would have found the arrangement quite disturbing (or Cromwell would have found it so for him, having himself tried to prevent it back in '33). In any event, parliament's 1534 *Submission of Clergy Act* transferred appellate authority from Convocation to a Chancery court. Otherwise the bill repeated the main provision of Convocation's submission, to wit, a commission of thirty-two to review and approve all canons.

Then came another revisitation of past law. The *Act in Restraint of Annates*, conditional upon the pope's behavior and the king's implementation, was now made absolute. Cromwell attempted to have those payments, which the law withheld from the pope, given instead to the king for the defense of the realm, but the past reasoning for cessation, that the bishops were impoverished by the annates obligation, caused the proposal to die in Lords. The bill that did pass, besides ending forever payments to Rome, created a mechanism for the appointment of bishops and archbishops, no longer the province of popes. Upon nomination by the king of a candidate to a vacant benefice, local ecclesiastics were, 'with all speed and celerity, in due form, to elect and choose the said person named'. Failure to do so after twelve days would cause the nominee's election to go forward without ecclesiastical approval; and failure to do so after twenty days would cause the penalties of provisors and praemunire to come down upon the heads of the offending clergy. Not only was the pope's consent irrelevant, so also effectively was the consent of English churchmen. Henry was showing his church what it meant to be 'sole head'.

The campaign to deny the pope his customary powers and to starve the papal see of English revenues was completed with passage of *Dispensations and Peter's Pence Act*. The preamble to the act declared England's independence from outside lawmaking unless acquiesced in by the monarchy and consented to by the people; and, in the context of the power to set aside or amend man-made laws, the preamble imputed lawmaking authority to the combined body of king, noblemen, and commoners:

> It stands therefore with natural equity and good reason that in all and every such laws human, made within this realm ... your Royal Majesty and your lords spiritual and temporal and commons, representing the whole state of your realm in this your most high court of parliament, have full power and authority not only to dispense ... with those and all other human laws of this your realm ... [but] also the said laws and every of them to abrogate, annul, amplify, or diminish as it shall be seen unto your Majesty and the nobles and commons of your realm meet and convenient for the wealth of your realm.

Two years prior Cromwell had attempted the same with the aborted *Submission of Clergy* bill. For not only did the bill describe England as a mixed polity subject to no foreign power; but one draft of the bill included a phrase requiring the king's law to receive the consent of the estates. Cromwell deleted the phrase and then dropped the bill. Presumably the time was not right for an assertion of constitutionalism, which still was disguised somewhat in the *Dispensations Act*, as the focus was on the curtailment of papal power, not on the checking of regal power.

By terms of the act, the archbishop of Canterbury would take the pope's place in issuing dispensations from canon law and in issuing all other licenses and instruments needed for church-approved actions. Furthermore, the householders' tax called Peter's Pence, dating back centuries though amounting in total to very little, was to cease, as were other such little-noticed payments not encompassed by previous legislation. But as with the (conditional) *Act in Restraint of Annates*, parliament provided an escape clause whereby activation would be delayed and the whole measure annulled upon the pleasure of the king – whose pleasure seemed still to include the prospect of reconciliation with the pope. Why postponement or repeal of this minor irritant would cause Clement to reverse his position is hard to fathom. Certainly no reversal was forthcoming, since at about the same time, late March, the Consistory ruled that the marriage between Henry and Catherine was valid under church law and the Holy Scriptures.

It was time now to deal finally with the Maid of Kent, languishing in prison since the previous fall. She could not be prosecuted as a traitor under existing treason statutes (these would change), because her threatening prophecies had been spoken publicly, and even in the king's presence. Accordingly, parliament was called upon to pass a bill of attainder against Barton and several of her confederates, including Bishop Fisher and Thomas More. Fisher confessed to having met with the Maid, but since he had reported the substance of their meeting to the king, no treason was committed – or so he argued (to which Cromwell countered, in a long letter, that Fisher was guilty, because, being in basic agreement with the Maid, he never conducted a proper interrogation, but sought out the Maid simply to hear more of her revelations). Thomas More similarly pleaded innocence, stating that the subject of the king's affairs never came up in his conversations with the Maid, and with two of her associates, and that it was upon his insistence that crown politics were never discussed. The case against More was weaker than the case against Fisher, and Cromwell tried having More's name deleted from the list. Henry though refused, for he was determined to ruin the minister who dared to defy him. A royal commission, which included Cromwell, undertook to interrogate More; but he so effectively parried their attacks, that the House of Lords, hearing the results, indicated its unwillingness to proceed against its former Lord Chancellor. Henry thus relented, and More's name was removed from the bill, though Fisher's was not. Fisher was attainted along with the others; but unlike the others, who in April were executed at Tyburn, Fisher was permitted to purchase a pardon. His life was spared (for the time) at a cost of £300.

But additional trouble awaited Fisher and More. The chief business of the first of the 1534 sessions was passage of the *Act of Succession*. It stipulated that the offspring of Henry and Anne, now the lawful queen – and not the offspring of Henry and Catherine, now the princess dowager of deceased Prince Arthur – would stand in the line of succession, beginning with the first-born son of this marriage (or in the absence of male issue, the first-born son of some subsequent marriage) and then pass to daughters in the order of their birth, with Lady Elizabeth taking precedence. It decreed that 'malicious' opposition to the succession (and to what it implied – the legitimacy of the divorce), whether expressed by deed, by publication, or by writing, was the crime of high treason incurring the punishment of death and loss of property; and that 'malicious' speech, without writing, was the lesser offense of misprision of treason (this a concession wrung from Cromwell) subject to imprisonment at the king's will and to loss of property. Furthermore, refusal to swear an oath of allegiance was also an instance of misprision of treason, with the same punishments to follow.

If not Fisher, then certainly More had it fully within his power to avoid malicious opposition to the new order; and both men were prepared to accept the king's and parliament's right to settle the succession on whom they saw fit. But the text of the oath, not yet codified but soon to exist in a statute of its own, included the phrase, 'You shall swear to bear faith, truth, and obedience alone to the King's Majesty ... and not to any other within this realm nor foreign authority or potentate.' The 'foreign authority' referred of course to the pope in Rome, and the duo rightly reasoned that by uttering these words they would be accepting the supremacy along with the succession. They requested permission to swear a different oath, one that would free their consciences from the sin of denying the pope's suzerainty. Cranmer supported them in this request, but Henry flatly refused ('For in case they be sworn to the succession and not to the preamble, it is to be thought that it might be taken not only as a confirmation of the bishop of Rome his authority, but also as a reprobation of the king's second marriage' – reported Cromwell back to Cranmer). Fisher and More were arrested and imprisoned in the Tower, where they stayed until their executions the summer next.

Again Cromwell was rewarded for services rendered. In April he was elevated to principal secretary, replacing Gardiner who had been too long away on diplomatic duties and too out of favour to retain a post so close to the king – a post which Cromwell would turn into an all-purpose, omni-competent secretariat. A second post soon followed, that of Master of the Rolls. It gave Cromwell an official residence, made him keeper of government documents, and put him in charge of the Chancery clerks; the former post gave him day-to-day control of the administration and put him in charge of the signet clerks. These were both major offices of state.

Those first (serious) overtures to the German Lutherans, back in 1533, began to have effect in the spring and summer of 1534. An alliance was struck with the Protestant city of Lübeck, currently under the sway of sectarian adventurer Jürgen Wullenwever. England was looking for a trading partner outside of Imperial control, and Lübeck was looking for a diplomatic ally to help it determine the succession to the vacant Danish throne, long a prerogative of Hanseatic cities. Lübeck offered to back Henry as a claimant, should a remote kingdom be one of his ambitions. But as Henry never acted on the offer, Lübeck put forward its intended candidate, the Lutheran duke of Holstein, who, to the dismay of Lübeckers, blanched at the prospect of a forced installation and declined to proceed with the plan. Taking umbrage at the obstinacy of the uncooperative duke, the Lübeckers judged him an enemy and invaded his lands. But again they were disappointed, as the duke repulsed their attack and besieged them in return. Meanwhile the Danes decided to choose their own king, electing none other than the duke of Holstein, who accepted the honor and ascended the throne, assuming the title King Christian III. Lübeck ignored the coronation and continued the fighting. Under treaty obligations, England was drawn in, providing financing and some ships. More losses ensued in a perfectly ridiculous war of Lutherans against Lutherans, the very people whom Henry was trying to befriend. Eventually the contest subsided (Wullenwever was executed), and England withdrew from what had become an embarrassing intervention. The cause of this debacle was plainly Henry's 'great matter' and the resulting need for anti-Imperial allies. But it was on Cromwell's advice and by means of Cromwell's agents that Protestant out-reach was tried and thereafter became a regular addition to English foreign policy.

In September, Henry's nemesis, Clement VII, died – this time for real. The man who had obstructed Henry's divorce plans was out of the picture at last. His successor was the Anglophile cardinal, Allesandro Farnese, Pope Paul III (Farnese had thrice supported the divorce in Consistory). Better relations with the papacy were expected (though they never materialised), and in consequence better relations with France were explored. France had of late functioned as England's emissary to Rome, until the explosion at Marseilles a year earlier. But with a new pope came new hope that reconciliation could be achieved, and France was willing to resume its go-between labors. The first step though was uniting the royal households – to which end France proposed that Henry's much betrothed elder daughter, Mary, be betrothed to Charles, the duke of Angouleme (third son of Francis). Of course the damage done to Mary's marital worth would have to be repaired and Mary re-legitimated and restored to the succession (her bastardization was implied though not stated in the *Act of Succession*) – a proposal that did not suit Henry who was set upon a course of brutalizing his daughter and her mother for refusing to acknowledge their demoted status. England therefore made the counter-offer that France use its good offices to secure from Pope Paul a revocation of his predecessor's ruling on the marriage, in exchange for which daughter Elizabeth would be wedded to Angouleme. But a revocation was beyond the influence of France, which likely did not welcome the idea of having its esteemed duke betrothed to a one-year-old of dubious legitimacy – and there the matter rested.

Session Six – November–December 1534

Parliament reconvened as scheduled on November 3. For the most part this second session of the year was a tidying up affair. It codified the king's command over the church by passage of the *Supremacy Act*. The first indication that secular power was supreme came in 1531, with Convocation's recognition that the English king was 'sole head and protector of the English church … as far as the law of God allows'. The second indication came with Convocation's *Submission of Clergy Resolution* in 1532, followed by a parliamentary statute of the same name in winter 1534. The resolution and the statute undercut the independence of the church by removing its legislative power; secular supremacy was the effective result. Now with this third bite at the apple – taken, as said in the preamble, for corroboration and confirmation, for increase in virtue, and for extirpation of heresy and abuses – the king was declared supreme but without mention of that famous saving clause, 'as far as the law of God allows'. The preferred caveat this time was 'on earth' – 'supreme head on earth of the Church of England'. This vague allusion to heavenly supremacy was hardly the equivalent of divine law, with the implication of an ecclesiastical establishment serving as its custodian and interpreter.

The *Oath of Succession* was a corrective measure. The *Succession Act* of the previous session required all subjects to swear their fealty to the king and his heirs, but it did not supply the wording of the oath. That mattered because the extra-statutory oath, which was devised and employed on the moment, brought about the arrest of Fisher and More, who refused to swear. More in fact complained that the oath demanded of him had not the sanction of law. To remedy that oversight, the *Oath of Succession Act* specified the actual language of the oath, which was essentially the oath as administered before.

Another corrective measure was the *Treasons Act*. The *Act of Succession* had made malicious publication (et al.) a treasonous offense punishable by death; but malicious speech, and refusal to take the oath of succession, were left at the lesser crime of misprision of treason, for which the punishment was imprisonment and loss of goods. Under it, Fisher and More were removed to the Tower; but their executions would require that malicious speech be elevated to high treason – which was precisely what the *Treasons Act* did, specifying that talk of the king as a 'heretic, schismatic, tyrant, infidel, or usurper of the crown' was a treasonable offense punishable by death. The immediate targets were Fisher and More. The point was to entrap them through artful interrogation, to threaten them with the gallows for criticisms maliciously spoken (and any pertinent utterance would be so construed), and to wring from them acceptance of the supremacy in exchange for their lives. There were, of course, other targets of the legislation besides Fisher and More and other manifestations of disloyalty besides errant speech; in particular, the withholding of castles, ships, and munitions from the king's use was included in the proscription – a difficult-to-imagine possibility that soon became a reality. The *Treasons* bill was a hard sell in Commons, but still it passed unamended.

The king needed money, and Cromwell had the foresight to say that good governance, and not only the emergency of war, was reason enough to take it. This novel view was articulated in the preamble to the *First Fruits and Tenths Act*, by which annates formerly paid to the pope now were paid to the king. Cromwell tried to accomplish the transfer earlier in the year with the *Act in Absolute Restraint of Annates*, but parliament balked at the proposal. Partly the new argument made the difference, that the king, while incurring 'great, excessive, and inestimable charges' to his own estate, had 'most victoriously by his high wisdom and policy protected, defended, and governed this his realm and maintained his people and subjects of the same in tranquil peace, unity, quietness, and wealth'; and that the sure continuation of these blessings would require 'some honorable provision and remedy'. But mainly the climate had changed, and the king, now recognised as supreme and imperial, was free to do more of what he pleased, while his subjects, liable to charges of treason for almost any cause, were able to do less. The bill provided the crown with a year's revenue of every benefice newly filled and a tenth of the annual revenues of all others. The sum collected was £40,000, ten times the amount ordinarily sent to Rome.

The commoners were not to be exempted from the exactions of a cash-hungry monarch. Their turn came at the end of the session with passage of the *Subsidy Act*, the first general tax-levy in eleven years. The argument about prudent policies issuing in domestic harmony was reprised in the preamble, but with a little more specificity on its second airing. As to the main business – money – the people were to pay a fifteenth and a tenth, and the lords were rated according to the value of their lands. These and other subsidies netted about £80,000.

As usual there was much other business – ecclesiastical, economic, legal, and private – crammed into this six-week session. Parliament adjourned on December 18; it did not meet again for over a year.

The 1535 Prorogation of Parliament

The king's overlordship of the church, enshrined in law, effectively and quickly devolved upon Cromwell, who in January was appointed Vicegerent of Spirituals. Also called vicar general or special commissary, Cromwell was entrusted with the now crucial task of visiting church establishments and assessing their worth. If the church was to be taxed, a detailed cataloguing of church wealth was required. Cromwell named the men to serve as his special commissioners, who in turn named assistants of their own. The most prominent of the group were Richard Layton, Thomas Leigh, John London, and John ap Rice. They descended upon the monasteries and friaries of England armed with a questionnaire, a set of injunctions, and a steely determination to find fault and exaggerate failings. They scolded, they bullied, they tattled (on each other as well as on the inmates); and they proceeded at a blistering pace, finishing their review and filing their report a mere six months after beginning. The report was titled *Valor Ecclesiasticus*; it estimated the value of church property at £800,000.

As mentioned, many besides Fisher and More were to suffer under the *Treasons Act*, and a few in fact suffered before Fisher and More. These were the Carthusians of the London Charterhouse, three of whose monks went to the gallows in April 1535, along with a Bridgettine brother of Syon and a secular priest. Cromwell had issued an arrest warrant for anyone suspected of supporting the pope; and though compliance with the new order was widespread and resistance rare, in a few instances, most involving members of the severer religious houses (e.g., Observant Franciscans), the supremacy was denied or the oath was not taken. Cromwell had trouble with the jury trying the Carthusians, since malicious intent had not been proven to the jurymen's satisfaction; but cajoling by Cromwell, including threats on the jurymen's lives, brought about the required convictions.

The trial of the Carthusians was a warm-up for the main event. In May word arrived that Pope Paul III had elevated Bishop Fisher to the cardinalate (an action somehow meant to please the king but having exactly the opposite effect). Henry was furious, and he railed to his courtiers that while the 'Roman bishop' might give Fisher a cardinal's hat, the English king would ensure that Fisher had no head to put it on. And so began the final act of the Fisher-More tragedy. Interrogations of the famous captives were conducted, with Cromwell twice among the deputation sent to interview More. Little new evidence was gathered, however. Then the solicitor-general, Richard Rich, was sent to get the goods, by trickery if necessary. He relayed to Fisher the king's desire to hear what the bishop of Rochester truly thought about the supremacy; and with that implied guarantee of immunity, Fisher spoke his mind. But his speaking proved fatal, as no immunity was granted, and the prosecution now had the evidence to proceed to trial. On June 17 Fisher was convicted of treason, and on June 22 he was beheaded.

A similar trick was played on More, supplemented by a crucial dollop of fabrication (though the matter is disputed and beyond final resolution). Rich was with More on June 12, sent to his cell, with two others, to confiscate More's belongings. While the attendants were busy gathering up books, Rich posed this hypothetical question to More: If parliament were to make Rich king and make denial of his kingship the crime of treason, would More acknowledge parliament's power to enthrone and punish accordingly? More answered yes, and followed with a hypothetical of his own: If parliament were to decree that God were not God and outlaw all contrary affirmations, would Rich say that parliament acted rightly and that God, therefore, was not God? Rich conceded that the existence of the deity lay beyond parliament's jurisdiction. He then either posed as an intermediate hypothetical the king's headship of the church, to which More, in a lengthy expostulation, let slip his opposition to the supremacy; or, Rich asked nothing further, More answered nothing further, and at trial Rich simply made up the incriminating conclusion, supposedly drawn by More, that if parliament could not make God, God, neither could parliament make the king a pope, or head of his own church. In defense, More observed that he had studiously avoided revealing his mind to the king's councilors, so why would he say all to a character as scurrilous as Rich. Nevertheless, More was found guilty on Rich's testimony. Once the verdict had been pronounced, and as a last-ditch legal maneuver, More challenged the validity of the indictment ('arrest of judgement'), declaring illegal the law under which he was prosecuted, it being the action of a single parliament in contravention of the laws of international Christianity. Now it was clearly stated what had long been clearly understood, that More stood with the universal church under the pope and against the English church under the king. Unimpressed and undeterred, the court condemned More to death, and on July 6 he was beheaded.

The destruction of Fisher and More caused an outcry in Catholic Europe, and the emperor, in particular, was incensed by the brutality. But the emperor at this time had committed himself to a war against Tunis, and he was too occupied with the operations of the fleet to contemplate just reprisals against England. France also was outraged, and also busy with its own affairs, feeling itself liberated by the emperor's absence and judging the moment propitious for renewing its aggression against Milan. But France needed England as an ally, and despite warming relations between the powers, France thought that extortion would be the most efficient means of forcing England's hand. A papal brief sent to the French court asked Catholic princes to cease all dealings with the heretical and (provisionally) excommunicated king of England, and Francis indicated his willingness to sign on unless English aid were forthcoming. To underscore the point that France meant business, English ships docked at Bordeaux were taken into custody. Henry tried to placate Francis with an embassy led by Gardiner. In the meantime Henry himself needed allies among the non-Catholic princes, and so a second attempt was made to establish ties with German Lutherans. The Protestant theologian, Philip Melanchthon, was invited to England (lest he instead go to France – he went to neither). More seriously, and toward the end of the year, Edward Foxe (just named bishop of Hereford) and Nicholas Heath (later named bishop of Rochester), were sent to Wittenberg to confer with Lutheran princes organised under the Schmalkaldic League. Negotiations produced a provisional entente whereby the Germans agreed to resist the papacy generally and its occasional calls for a general council specifically, and agreed to recognise Henry as the League's protector and defender; while the English agreed to assent to the *Augsberg Confession* (catechism of the Lutheran faith) and a confessional creed composed by Melanchthon called the Wittenberg Articles. Further negotiations were planned for the new year, but two years lapsed before they occurred, during which time Henry had many opportunities to hesitate, finagle, and renege.

Session Seven – February–April 1536

Parliament met for its final session on February 4, 1536. As usual its docket was stuffed with proposals for religious and secular reform and with demands for private legislation. Topping the list, however, was a bill for the dissolution of the monasteries. The material health of these establishments had been surveyed in the first half of 1535, and in the second half 'visitors' went forth to take stock of their moral health as well – which, not surprisingly, was determined to be past resuscitation. A new round of anticlerical outrage was ginned up in order to prepare the way for a targeted confiscation of cloistered houses, to be followed by a wholesale take-over in the years ahead. On the block were small monasteries and convents whose annual income fell below £200. Evidently a correlation existed between 'vicious, carnal, and abominable living' and the number of people who lived together – twelve or fewer and the house was a sinkhole of corruption. On one point the bill seemed sincere and considerate, inasmuch as clerics with true vocations were permitted relocation to the larger houses wherein 'religion [was] right well kept and observed' – because they were large; but mainly the bill was interested and cruel, inasmuch as expropriated wealth was transferred to the king and lesser clergy were pensioned off at subsistence rates, with nuns getting the worst of it. The idea was to proceed slowly, picking off the weak and the friendless, and to share the plunder with well-heeled laymen of the nobility and the gentry. Of the 376 houses that fell under this initial ban, 123 saved themselves (for a time) by paying bribes to the crown, to Cromwell, and to sundry intermediaries.

The administration of the *Dissolutions Act* required the creation of a whole new bureaucracy, because Cromwell did not want the money passing through Exchequer, an office more medieval than modern, even with Cromwell at its head. So parliament received, and in due course passed, the *Court of Augmentations of the Revenues of the King's Crown Act*. The act established a court of revenues to record, manage, and dispose of all titles of despoiled lands. Court officials were identified and a chancellor put in charge. The first to hold the chancellorship was Richard Rich. Parliament took another stab at poor relief and at enclosures. This new poor law, while still styled *An Act for the Punishment of Sturdy Vagabonds and Beggars*, conceded that able-bodiedness was not a sufficient condition for employment and that in some instances public works might be needed. A draft of the bill envisioned a national jobs program and the secularization of charity (prohibitions on private alms-giving), these to be paid for by a graduated income tax and a contribution from the crown. But the bill as presented to parliament made job assistance local and voluntary; it retained private alms-giving, though it centralised collection (common boxes) and charged ministers with exhorting their flocks to give generously to the poor. 'Lusty' beggars prone to idleness were to be beaten, mutilated (top of right ear), and incarcerated, in that order – that much had not changed.

The enclosure law tried again to discourage sheep-grazing by penalizing the conversion of tilled soil to pasture and by mandating the upkeep of farm houses. This time though the crown had a stake in the proceedings, inasmuch as all malefactors were

ordered to pay half of their revenues to the king until pasture land
was returned to tillage and new tenements constructed ('suitable
for an honest man to dwell in').

There was trouble in Wales and had been for a long time.
Lawlessness was widespread, and English gentry along the
border were demanding action from the government. For its part
the government was looking to extend the reach of the supremacy
and the number of monasteries subject to dissolution. No longer
adequate was the old system of governance, whereby Wales was
counted a principality under the ostensible rule of the king's first-
born (prince of Wales), but under the practical administration of a
feudal council. In 1534 parliament passed legislation to facilitate
stricter enforcement of law; meanwhile Cromwell replaced as
council president the ineffective John Vesey, bishop of Exeter,
with Rowland Lee, bishop of Coventry and Lichfield. Lee was
a hanging judge. He traveled through the territory in pursuit of
bandits and criminals and of juries who would convict them. He
played Remiro de'Orco to Cromwell's Cesare Borgia (*Prince* 7), an
implacable agent of rough justice serving a master happy to give
him up the moment denunciation became advisable (soon after
Lee suffered disgrace).

When Lee had brought order to the Marches, Cromwell
brought a proposal before parliament to unite Wales to
England, extending the rights and privileges of English subjects
to its western neighbor: common law, division by shires,
administration by justices of the peace, and representation
in parliament. The bill pretended that Wales had all along
been a part of England and that no radical innovation was
contemplated by its statutory incorporation; and it attributed
the opposite view, that Wales was a distinct and foreign land,
to a (minor) difference in language and customs which 'rude
and ignorant people' had played up to foment 'great discord,
variance, debate, division, murmur, and sedition' (*Dis*, I.25:

when reforming an antiquated state, speak as if nothing has changed). The act, *Administration of Law and Justice in Wales in Like Form as in This Realm*, contained a suspensive clause invokable by the king. Passage was easy; implementation was not. Parliament returned to the matter many times.

Calais was another outpost of English rule demanding immediate attention. Its defenses were in shambles, and its administration, under Arthur Plantagenet, Lord Lisle, was incompetent. Cromwell's commissioners reported on the disarray in the autumn of 1535, in time for Cromwell to present to parliament rectifying legislation in the winter of 1536. The *Calais Ordinances*, eighteen pages long, proposed a top-to-bottom revamping of civilian and military rule. The bill passed, but because Lisle was kept on as colonial governor, little good was done. Thence forward, Lisle began working against Cromwell and the Reformation.

On April 14 the Reformation Parliament was adjourned for the last time. A successor parliament (new elections) met in the summer, for just one session.

Cromwell's Program

Cromwell entered the king's service at a time when the attention of the court remained fixed on Rome, notwithstanding Wolsey's failure to wring from Clement an annulment of the royal marriage. The official plan was to pound away at the Rota's closed door, beseeching the pope to reconsider his refusal in light of new punishments which England was prepared to inflict, such as the loss of revenues or the calling of a general council. Cromwell played no role in the formation or implementation of this plan, both because he was new to the Council and because he gave the plan no chance of success. He expressed his misgivings about the *Annates* legislation to Gardiner. The other front on which the king's party fought was at home, against the local clergy, who were presumed to be papists taking orders from Rome. The praemunire campaign, in its first phase, antedated Cromwell's ascendancy; but in its second phase of wholesale attack upon the clerical order, Cromwell's directing hand is clearly in evidence, even if the idea of extorting funds originated with others. Cromwell was involved in the negotiations and may have suggested the compromise that invested the king with his conditional supremacy. Secular supremacy required assertion against the English church no less than against the church in Rome, so it made sense to attack the target which presented itself first. Plus, at some point the English episcopacy had to be put to harness and made to change allegiance, if dissolving the king's marriage was to become its responsibility. Cromwell kept up the pressure in the 1532 session, reviving the Commons' anticlericalism of the 1529 session; and using previous draft legislation still in his possession, he reshaped it into the *Supplication against the Ordinaries*. He stood by Henry's side when the demand was issued that Convocation surrender its lawmaking powers; and he helped to advance that surrender by exposing before parliament the contents of the bishops' oaths and the divided loyalties they implied. Cromwell wanted to involve parliament further, to have the *Submission* be a parliamentary statute and not just a resolution by Convocation. Legislation was drafted to that effect, declaring that ordinances passed by Convocation required ratification by parliament in order to be binding on laity and clergy. The legislation, though, was never introduced and debated. Henry was content – perhaps he much preferred – to have clergy submit to him personally, without any suggestion that parliament somehow shared in the exercise of the surrendered powers.

When More resigned and Warham died, two additional obstacles were removed to a locally produced divorce, as their replacements, Audley and Cranmer, were eager advocates of the king's 'great matter'. The remaining obstacle was the right of appeal to Rome. The *Act in Restraint of Appeals* overcame that. The immediate purpose was to prevent Rome from countermanding a divorce judgement rendered in England. But under Cromwell's skillful management, the much laboured-on *Appeals* bill expanded its jurisdiction to whole categories of cases and linked the divorce initiative to the larger issue of England's independence and the monarchy's supremacy. England was an empire, declared the bill, its polity divided into estates under the rule of a king; its courts, spiritual and temporal, fully competent to adjudicate cases originating at home.

The next step was to deal with the opposition, or to prevent the opposition from ever gaining traction. Hence all elements of society, but the leaders mainly, were compelled to swear their allegiance to the succession and supremacy, or expose themselves as traitors by refusing. Parliament was involved, asked to give its approval to a host of laws, thus making the work of the Reformation its own. And with passage of the *Dispensations Act*, the king gave his approval (whether consciously or not) to the concept of king-in-parliament constitutionalism. All that then remained was to gather up the wealth of the church and apply it to the cause of English greatness.

Cromwell's program moved along another track as well, that of 'commonwealth' legislation focused on social and economic issues. Cromwell attempted to ameliorate hardship and manage the economy with enclosure, poor relief, and price-fixing legislation. And as minister he intervened almost daily in the private affairs of Englishmen, undertaking to resolve disputes and instruct litigants in cases at law.

6

The Fall of Anne Boleyn

Travails of a Queen

As of June 1533 Anne Boleyn was queen of the realm, and as of September she was mother of Elizabeth, whose birth was a deep disappointment papered over by a lavish christening ceremony. In bearing a daughter, Anne had failed in her one, true mission. A second attempt would be needed, and sometime in the autumn she conceived again (though the number and timing of her pregnancies are much in dispute). There also was work to be done to repair her reputation as the concubine who had chased from the throne a legitimate and beloved queen, had hurled England into the maelstrom of sectarian conflict, had complicated the country's relations with France and the Empire, and had wrecked its trade with the Low Countries. Thus she founded a school for needlework and donated the products to the poor.

Apart from successful breeding, Anne's other challenge was to retain the affection of her husband, whose philandering eye, though unremarkable for the period, wandered frequently and had at court many beauties to fall upon. Rumours of a tryst provoked Anne to a jealous rage, causing Henry to remind his new wife and mother-to-be that others – and her betters – had suffered the same before, and that if she persisted in making trouble, he might just return her to the humble circumstances in which he had found her. Chapuys got wind of the discontent in the royal bedroom and pushed Cromwell to confirm that Henry, only months into the marriage for which he had waited years, was tired of Anne and wished to be rid of her. Cromwell would not confirm, but the talk continued. Indeed, Anne's standing at court rose or fell depending on whether a mistress had emerged to compete for the king's affections. The autumn of 1534 was a particularly bad time for Anne. An unnamed inamorata came to court, who so attracted Henry and unnerved the queen that Anne and her sister-in-law, lady Rochford (wife of George Boleyn), hatched a plot to ensnare and discredit the young woman. Lady Rochford, for reasons of her own having to do with an embittered marriage, was the lead conspirator. When Henry learned of her schemes, he had her banished from court, but with spill-over harm done to Anne. Shortly after, another lady was the object of the king's attentions. The scene Henry made at a court ball caused tongues to wag and dispatches to fly from emissaries to their masters back home. Then came a third woman in the sequence, Madge Shelton, Anne's cousin and lady-in-waiting – though a short-lived infatuation it was. In fact, none of these romances occasioned much infidelity – if they occasioned any infidelity at all – but as the mark of the declining influence of the queen, they sullied her reputation and allowed ambassadors to treat her with disdain.

There were shafts of sunlight to brighten the darkness. Pregnancies were a balm to the couple's spirits. After the birth of Elizabeth, Anne was pregnant another three times (unless one was a false pregnancy). The king then would boast of his virility and delight in the expectation of receiving a male heir, while his wife too was vouchsafed her moment of prospective glory. Sadly, each conception ended in a miscarriage, with sullenness and despair descending upon the royal couple. Anne was moody, demanding, and cutting in her speech; but when her temper was under control, she and the king took great pleasure in each other's company, and the court was uplifted by their gaiety. One such time was the spring of 1535: Anne was again pregnant; no mistresses were about to cause Henry to regret his marriage to her; and the terror directed against the pope's adherents had yet to expose its reach and brutality.

Anne's overriding political objective was to ensure the throne for her daughter. The legislative program designed to accomplish the succession proved a complete success, with the 1534 passage of the *Act of Succession*, the *Oath of Succession*, and the *Treasons Act*. These laws did more than designate Elizabeth heir-presumptive; they commanded that individuals swear their allegiance and stifle their objections. But the ferocity of the acts was less a sign of confidence and a surety of the future than an admission that Elizabeth's claim might go unredeemed unless coercive force were applied – which no one could count on following Henry's demise. Thus despite the muscular promotion of the Boleyn cause, the Boleyn women occupied terrain difficult to defend. And leading the assault was a bastardised princess held under house arrest.

Once Elizabeth was born, and once it was clear that Mary would not sign away her patrimony, the two half-sisters – seventeen years apart in age – were brought together in a common and movable household. But it was decidedly Elizabeth's household, not Mary's. For whether they were domiciled at Hatfield Hall, Eltham palace, Richmond, or Greenwich, Mary's situation was tantamount to that of a Cinderella under the supervision of a wicked stepmother (two of them in fact, though their severity was a function of royal command and not of heartless disposition). Henry was angry with Mary, and he wanted her to feel his wrath; he wanted her, and her mother (kept elsewhere), to yield to his will. Anne though was afraid of Mary; and she showed her fear by pestering the king to reduce Mary's support (including food and clothing), to set Mary to labor, to surround her with spies, and to ignore her when visiting. Henry, as usual, was inconstant: feeling paternal, he would forgive and forget, tender some kindness, extend some courtesy, even in the absence of a *quid pro quo*; or, in response to just that absence (and the 'quids' were never forthcoming), he would sink into a choler. Anne was obliged therefore to calibrate her hostility to that of the king's. Not always could Anne simply push for sterner measures; sometimes she too had to offer honey instead of vinegar: for example, the use of her physician when Mary fell ill; or the opportunity to come to court without paying obeisance to the queen. But Mary never reciprocated, never gave in. Anne's reaction, when most exasperated and alarmed, was to demand that Mary and Catherine be sent to the Tower; she even spoke of poisoning the pair and threatened to do the deed when the king was out of the country. Chapuys heard the rumours, those he did not invent himself; and he spread them about in hopes of inciting rebellion in England and invasion from Spain.

Beyond this business of signaling her favour and disfavour, there was one practical measure which Anne could take. It was to arrange for Elizabeth's marriage to a French prince. Anne actually was just trying to keep pace with events, because the French had proposed (1534), and were continuing to press for (1535), a marriage between the dauphin and Mary. If only to prevent such a union, Anne had to put forward her own daughter and demand that the French focus on an Elizabeth–dauphin, or Elizabeth–Angouleme match. Thus when the ambassadors from France requested to visit Mary at Eltham, they were permitted access to Elizabeth only. Their grandiose plan was to unite France and England (against the Empire) by marrying a princess in line to become queen of England to a prince in line to become king of France, and by having their children rule both countries as one. Anne needed Elizabeth to be that princess; but the French wanted Mary. Henry was cool to the whole idea, and eventually the dauphin, Francis, was married to a Spaniard. But in the meantime, during the troubled second half of 1535, there was no concealing the fact that international politics could sideline Anne just as effectively as domestic liaisons.

Those troubles included the outraged reaction to the executions of Fisher and More; the threatened excommunication of the king (for a second time, and for a second time not expedited); the emperor's triumph over the Turks in the Mediterranean; the failure of the summer harvest, brought about, some said, by divine vengeance; the hostility of the London merchants over the loss of their markets; and the overt, and near universal, support given to Mary and Catherine by the women of England. The French ambassador filed a report on conditions in the island state; so bad were they, both material and moral, that the French hardened their negotiating stance across all fronts.

Setting the Stage

News of Catherine's death in early January 1536 came as deliverance to Henry, who dressed head-to-toe in yellow and did a dance with his similarly attired pregnant queen. Anne too thought that she was delivered: her rival, and the object of the public's affection, was gone; her daughter's rival was alone and helpless; and her lawfully divorced husband was now, and even better, retroactively a widower. But the death of Catherine was not the curative it was expected to be. A year earlier Henry had inquired of his advisers about the difficulties of divorcing Anne. He was told that the removal of Anne would by law restore Catherine to her place as queen and Mary to the succession. Loath to contemplate such a prospect, Henry let the matter drop, and Anne escaped divorce proceedings against her. But under these changed circumstances, with his first queen blessedly dead, Henry's attachment to Anne was purely a function of Henry's affection for Anne, and sustaining that affection was always an ordeal.

It was at this juncture that Jane Seymour entered the mix. She was the daughter of Sir John Seymour of Wiltshire, paterfamilias of an ancient Norman clan whose home was Wolf Hall. Henry had stopped at Wolf Hall while on progress (sans Anne) the previous summer. There he met (or re-met) Jane, a woman as unaccomplished and unassuming as his present wife was sparkling and assertive. Plain Jane she was – demur, quiet, and pleasing. Her family was quite the opposite, however – ambitious, conniving, and courtly-wise like the Boleyns. And learning from the Boleyns, they knew better than to allow Henry to satisfy himself too easily. Thus Jane was kept in seclusion, instructed to repel, politely but firmly, all of the king's advances. In January Jane was received at court as a lady-in-waiting to Anne, having once before performed that service for Catherine. The temper of the courtship remained much the same – royal notes and presents returned with a smile – until Henry, coming to terms with his new love's exacting morality, ordered Cromwell to surrender his Greenwich apartments to the Seymours, so that his visits with Jane could be properly chaperoned. This change of living quarters was destined to have fatal consequences a short time later.

January brought yet a third development, more momentous than the other two. The king almost died. On the day of Catherine's internment, and as celebration of the event (January 24), a tournament was staged at Greenwich. Henry, age forty-four, competed in the lists and ran several courses; but in one encounter, he fell from his horse and crashed to the ground. The armoured steed came down upon him, and he lay unconscious for two hours. Onlookers thought he was dead. He was though only stunned, and upon reviving he sent Norfolk to report the mishap to Anne. She was then seven months pregnant, and the fright which the news caused her resulted in (or at least was followed by) a miscarriage five days later. The stillborn baby was a boy. Anne blamed Norfolk; Henry blamed Anne, and he confessed to a Privy Chamber intimate that he viewed his second marriage as invalid because contrived by witchcraft and cursed by God. His terse remark to his bed-ridden wife (related by Chapuys) was non-consoling and seemingly dispositive: 'I see that God will not give me male children. When you are up, I will speak to you.' Anne's position had never been worse: her most recent and perhaps last chance at providing an heir and saving a crown had ended in disaster – on top of which a divorce was now practicable and a replacement was on hand.

The most enterprising of the Seymours was Jane's elder brother Edward (Lord Protector and duke of Somerset during the regency of Edward VI). In March he was admitted to the Privy Chamber. He discovered there and joined up with a secret faction of Aragon adherents, assorted lords and gentry who had been forced underground and into silence all the while Catherine was alive, but who could begin to speak out on behalf of Mary's dynastic claims now that the first-born child stood alone, unencumbered by a barren and discarded mother/wife. The argument they advanced was that the legitimacy of Mary did not hinge on the validity of her parents' marriage, since the marriage was understood to be valid at the time of her birth (called *bona fide parentum* in canon law). Thus Mary could be restored without Henry needing to reverse himself. Included in the party were Edward Neville, Anthony Browne, John Russell, Thomas Elyot, Henry Pole (lord Montague), Geoffrey Pole, and Henry Courtenay (marquess of Exeter and earl of Devon); Nicholas Carew was their leader. Seymour's interest, of course, lay not with Mary as heir-presumptive, but with Jane as future queen; but the path to both objectives lay in sabotaging Anne. Carew's April appointment to the Order of the Garter in place of George Boleyn provided sure evidence that the faction was advancing; but then the king's selection of Boleyn to vote in proxy for an absent lord, as well as the transfer of estates to his father by action of the parliament, were fair signs that favour and influence were in flux.

Cromwell's Coup

Cromwell was active at this time. Diplomacy engaged him, more than did bedroom gossip (though that would come soon enough). As far back as the summer and autumn of 1535 Cromwell began investigating the possibility of a rapprochement with the emperor. (In the estimation of some scholars, Cromwell leaned always toward an Imperial alliance, even though overtures to the Germans marked him in the public's mind as a Protestant sympathiser). England's security was the principal inducement. Discontent over the pace and scope of the Reformation ran deep. Conspirators (including Catherine) were in communication with outside powers. Insurrection was a real possibility; if supported by an invasion, defenses would fail and the monarchy would fall. And the likely invader – the emperor – was never more powerful and never more provoked. In conversations with Chapuys, Cromwell inquired as to terms. The terms were predictable and predictably unacceptable: return to Catherine, to orthodoxy, and to the pope. Nothing came of these discussions; they were premature, plus the object of English diplomacy at the time was a marriage alliance with the French.

The equation changed, however, with Catherine's death. No longer did the emperor have his aunt's honor to defend; no longer was marriage to the 'concubine' an affront to Spanish pride. It became instead a domestic affair important to the emperor only for its effects on the succession. Perhaps then a deal could be brokered. (Wrote Cromwell to Gardiner and Wallop: 'considering upon the death now of the said lady dowager [Catherine] whereby the emperor, having none other cause or quarrel to the king's highness, will of great likelihood by all ways and means seek for the king's highness amity.') Cromwell renewed negotiations with Chapuys in February. What the emperor now wanted was material support in his wars against the Turks, also support against France which had returned to Italy and was fighting to take Milan. He wanted Henry to acknowledge the pope's suzerainty and return to the Catholic communion. Finally he wanted his cousin re-legitimated and at a minimum not precluded from the line of succession. He did not bother himself with Anne, except to offer her a back-channel bribe if she would agree to step down. In fact, he went one step further, as he momentarily reversed his assessment and communicated to the English ambassador at Rome his acceptance of Anne on the throne – the reason being that her continuation as wife and queen would keep Henry out of the marriage market and away from a union with France at the highest level. The court factions were also receptive to the new diplomacy: the Aragonese wanting an Imperial alliance for dynastic, doctrinal, and security reasons; the Boleyns tolerating the same in hopes of distracting from their Francophile past which now threatened to leave them isolated and exposed; and the Seymours expecting divorce to be the consequence, followed by a marriage to Jane. When all of the parties had been consulted and the details ironed out with Chapuys, Cromwell took the proposal to the king.

Henry was at Greenwich, having returned there after the adjournment of parliament on April 14. Chapuys arrived on the 18th, greeted by notes of welcome and an invitation to visit the queen. That he declined to do; but an encounter with Anne as she went into mass was not possible to evade. Informed that Chapuys was standing behind the door through which she entered, Anne turned, bowed, and waited for Chapuys to return the courtesy, which he did (to the consternation of the Aragonese). The dance then continued at dinner, with Chapuys deliberately keeping his distance from Anne, who dined in her private apartments, he in the presence chamber entertained by Rochford; and with Anne making loud protestations against the French, which remarks she had relayed to Chapuys. After dinner came the audience with Henry.

Cromwell and Audley were in attendance, and Seymour arrived a little time later. Chapuys expected a straightforward exchange. He stated the emperor's conditions, adding as a sweetener the emperor's promise to patch up Anglo-papal relations if Henry agreed. Henry's excommunication order and the papal decree stripping Henry of his kingship had been held up by Charles; an agreement now would make these encumbrances go away. But Henry affected surprise, was non-cooperative and temperamental. He summoned Cromwell and Audley to attend upon them and instructed Chapuys to repeat what he had just said. The ambassador obliged, then removed himself to the far end of the room where he engaged Seymour in casual conversation. From this distance Chapuys could not make out the king's remarks, but he could tell that Henry had grown excited and angry with his minister. After some minutes of royal scolding, a flushed Cromwell retired to a window embrasure to take a drink and compose himself, while the king returned to Chapuys. Henry was in a mood, or pretended to be. He demanded that the offer be put in writing; he demanded that the emperor tender an apology for his perfidious practices of ten years; he even rehearsed all of Charles's supposed betrayals; finally, he agreed to review the texts of past treaties but to do nothing more. Chapuys was stunned, as was Cromwell, who confessed his bewilderment to Chapuys as the ambassador was departing Greenwich. Several months of careful negotiations had been blown away in an instant by an inscrutable, intransigent king.

Henry though may have been acting on policy, not pique. Henry was adept at playing the neutral in a balance-of-power strategy. He liked to have options, liked to negotiate opposite alliances simultaneously: with France against the Empire, with the Empire against France, with the Germans against them both. He did not so much like forming alliances, however, and being thereafter obligated. He also liked using his ministers as stalking horses; though in this case it may have been Cromwell who was using Henry, since Cromwell had gotten out ahead of his king and was acting somewhat on his own (this he admitted to Chapuys). In any event, there was advantage in offering but not finalizing an alliance with Charles, since what Henry really wanted was the emperor's acknowledgement that Henry was an emperor too, independent of Charles and independent of the pope. Charles and the pope rather thought of England as a fiefdom and Henry as a vassal. (One reason for the hesitation in depriving Henry of his throne was the belief that as a benefice held in fief by the Holy See, the kingship would revert to Rome, and England would become the pope's to rule.) Thus there could be no going back to the Catholic union, no subordination to the pope as the emperor proposed. Plus the international dynamic in 1536 favoured English neutrality, since the continental powers were again at war and were bidding for English aid.

Cromwell was suddenly in trouble. He had taken the lead in advocating a policy which the king now emphatically rejected, or which the king made all but impossible to achieve (contra *Dis*, III.35). His enemies were circling, principally Anne, who faulted him for vacating his Greenwich apartments in favour of the Seymours. In Anne's mind, Cromwell had become Henry's procurer, having already become Chapuys' confidant and dinner companion. This mysterious relationship (which included the exchange of expensive gifts) once provoked Anne to declare that she wished Cromwell's head off his shoulders. She viewed the minister's tilt toward the emperor as an attack upon herself; and though she chose to play along, she knew that an Anglo–Imperial entente would leave her out in the cold. It may even have been she who persuaded Henry to scuttle the alliance. Moreover, Anne was not alone; she stood at the head of a court party. If she turned against him, the entire Boleyn faction would follow: her father, Wiltshire; her brother, Rochford; the Chamber minions Henry Norris and William Brereton; and Cranmer, the archbishop. From the other side, no solid support could be expected either, for the Aragonese were but comrades of convenience; otherwise they were fixed enemies of the Reformation and of Cromwell its architect. Nor were the Seymours true allies, since the success of their enterprise might lead to the minister's displacement no less than the queen's. Even the lords began to line up in opposition, Norfolk especially; for they anticipated enrichment from the dissolution of the monasteries, and Cromwell was thought to be backsliding in order to appease the emperor.

Over the next six days Cromwell made the fateful decision to destroy Anne Boleyn. He would take the offensive and fight to the death, for in the coup he envisaged, either Anne or he would go to the gallows. Divorce would not be good enough, as divorce would leave Anne her title as marquess of Pembroke and her base in the court; it also would imply the validity of the first marriage to Catherine and the invalidity of the supremacy which ended it. Such a course might satisfy the Aragonese, the Seymours, and the emperor, but it would hardly find favour with the king; nor would it solve Cromwell's dilemma of using allies without serving their purposes in place of his own. He rather would bring charges of capital crimes so heinous as to shock the conscience and cast a pall over all of the queen's supporters, charges that would implicate the Privy Chamber and weaken it as a rival center of power. The queen, now Cromwell's chosen foe, would be undone by her own gross misconduct, leaving the king free to marry again and delighted with the minister who had so freed him. The influence of this new wife (and of her family) would of course be a problem, but ultimately that influence would depend on the birth of a male child, which the king's age and declining health might well prevent, or mere chance as so often before. Lastly, the supremacy would be secure if Mary were forced to accept it (and counted a traitor for refusing); and her acceptance would marginalise the Aragonese in turn. Such was the plan.

On April 24, Cromwell secured from Lord Chancellor Audley (the king was probably not involved) a patent of oyer and terminer. This instrument allowed Cromwell to name a twenty-person commission to investigate unspecified treasons in Middlesex and Kent counties. Such a commission was colourable as a routine enforcement of the *Treasons Act* and not by itself a cause for suspicion or alarm. Commission members included Audley and Cromwell as presiding officers; Norfolk, Suffolk, Wiltshire, and various other lords; a pair of knights; and nine judges. Any four commissioners could take action independent of the larger body. Many of the members may not have known of their appointments or known of the commission's true intent. Certainly the earl of Wiltshire, Thomas Boleyn, was kept in the dark, and possibly most of the others were too – until Cromwell presented evidence to a grand jury targeting the queen (*Dis*, III.6.6: avoid discovery by keeping the number of conspirators to a minimum and by executing the plot at the moment of disclosing it to others). But the evidence had first to be collected, since old stories of pre-nuptial indiscretions would not have sufficed to jolt the king, and since the *Succession Act* (1534) had made gossip about the queen a crime of treason. Cromwell had his spies, but they operated under the catch-22 of disappointing their employer if they reported nothing incriminating about the queen, and exposing themselves to prosecution if they did.

ANNA BOLLINA VXOR HEN

1. Anne Boleyn, Henry VIII's second and most controversial wife. Beginning as allies Cromwell and Anne finished as enemies.

Opposite: 2. Henry VIII and his father Henry VII by Holbein. The elder Henry's usurpation of the throne caused the younger Henry much anxiety about the succession.
Right: 3. Anne of Cleves, Henry VIII's fourth wife. This is the painting by Holbein that persuaded Henry she was a beauty. Henry changed his mind upon seeing Anne at Rochester, and Cromwell, who had brokered the engagement, fell into disfavour with the king.
Above right: 4. Arthur, Henry VII's first son and Henry VIII's elder brother. Arthur's brief marriage to Catherine of Aragon was the cause of Henry's troubles and the occasion for Cromwell's eventual rise to power. From a nineteenth century stained glass window in St Laurence's church, Ludlow.
Top: 5. Anne Boleyn's father, Thomas Boleyn. Thomas' elevation to the peerage was due mainly to the charms of his two daughters, Mary and Anne.

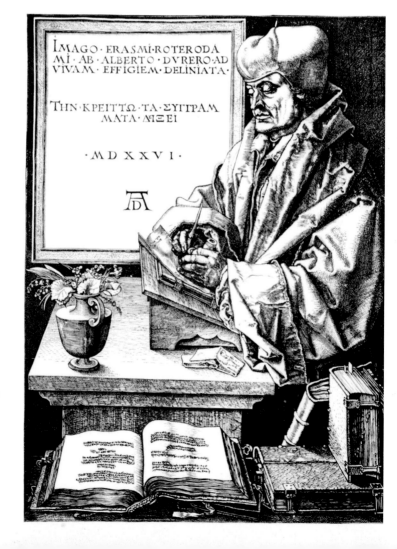

Opposite: 6. Jane Seymour, Henry VIII's third wife who gave Henry what he craved most – a son named Edward. Jane died within days of delivering the child.
Above left: 7. Edward, Henry VIII's son by Jane Seymour. He would later succeed to the throne as Edward VI (r. 1547-53).
Above right: 8. Seal of Elizabeth I. Elizabeth was Henry VIII's daughter by Anne Boleyn. Elizabeth reigned as queen from 1558 to 1603.
Right: 9. Erasmus. This iconic woodcut by Dürer depicts the greatest scholar of the age, Desiderius Erasmus of Rotterdam, at work in his study. The Latin inscription states that the image was sketched from life by Dürer. Cromwell committed to memory Erasmus' Latin translation of the New Testament.

IMAGO · ERASMI · ROTERODA
MI · AB · ALBERTO · DVRERO · AD
VIVAM · EFFIGIEM · DELINIATA ·

ΤΗΝ · ΚΡΕΙΤΤΩ · ΤΑ · ΣΥΓΓΡΑΜ
ΜΑΤΑ · ΔΙΞΕΙ

· M D X X V I ·

KATHERINA VXOR HENRICI · · VIII

Opposite: 10. Catherine of Aragon as a slightly younger woman (c. 1520?). By 1529 Catherine was past child-bearing age and had produced only one living child, a girl named Mary.

Above left: 11. Thomas Wolsey from a drawing by Jacques le Boucq. Not the obese figure of the more familiar likenesses. Cromwell was Wolsey's servant from 1524 to 1530.

Above right: 12. Tomb of Thomas Howard, 3rd Duke of Norfolk and uncle to both Anne Boleyn and Catherine Howard (Henry VIII's fifth wife). Norfolk resented Cromwell, a 'new man,' and worked to bring him down.

Right: 13. Thomas Cranmer from a painting by Gerhard Fliche. As archbishop of Canterbury, Cranmer presided over the court which finalized Henry's divorce from Catherine. Cranmer defended Cromwell at the time of his fall.

Above left: 14. Sir Richard Southwell, by Holbein. Sir Richard Southwell was an East Anglian gentleman who did particularly well out of the English Reformation, owing his advancement to the patronage of both the Duke of Norfolk and Thomas Cromwell. He was present at the conversation in the Tower of London during which, according to the testimony of Richard Rich, Thomas More actually denied Henry's supreme headship. However, questioned in court, Southwell said he had heard nothing.

Above right: 15. Thomas Wyatt, poet and early suitor of Anne Boleyn. Arrested with others at the time of Anne's trial, Wyatt was exonerated and released. *Left*: 16. Sir John Godsalve, Clerk of the Signet by Holbein. Another rare portrait of a supporter of Thomas Cromwell.

Notwithstanding this difficulty, Cromwell's agents were now expected to deliver. But the time was short, and likely they would have failed without extraordinary help from the subject herself. Most historians believe that Anne was innocent of the adultery charges stipulated in the indictment, but they do not represent her as a chaste queen careful about decorum and appearances. She ran her own court, more or less, which she filled with beautiful people playing the game of courtly love; and she placed herself at the center of this swirl of flirtation and romance, admired and doted on by all. Such behavior was common enough for the day; but given the changed circumstance of 1536 (the miscarriage of a son, the loss of the king's affection to another, and international forces arrayed against the current order), Anne would have been wise to concentrate on her needlework and send the musicians away. Some say though that the stress of her marriage and the fading of her looks increased her craving for the attentions of handsome court gallants.

In any event, on April 29 and 30, Anne was overheard conversing with Mark Smeaton and Henry Norris respectively. The latter conversation was the more damaging, though on its own it would not have caused Henry to throw over his favourite courtier. Anne inquired of Norris about the state of his betrothal to Madge Shelton, Anne's cousin and the former mistress of the king. Norris replied that his intent was to 'tarry awhile.' He gave no reason, this widower of five years; so Anne supplied one for him. She conjectured that Norris was procrastinating because he hoped to marry Anne once the king was dead: 'You look for dead man's shoes; for if ought came to the king but good, you would look to have me.' Norris recognised instantly the implication of this remark – a conspiracy against the life of the king by the queen and her lover – and the reckless indifference the queen had shown toward his own safety, since the remark was made in the earshot of attendants who may have been (and were)

Cromwell spies. In protest he declared that 'he would his head were off' rather than contemplate the king's demise. The quarrel ended soon thereafter with one more verbal sally, that by Anne asserting that she could destroy Norris if she so desired, at which point they both understood that to stanch the flow of rumour Norris would have to go to the queen's almoner and attest that Anne was a 'good woman'. He did, only to have a hearsay report confirmed by one of the parties involved.

Anne had been told of Norris' affection a year earlier by Francis Weston, another bewitched courtier. When the married Weston was challenged by Anne to stay away from Madge Shelton, already betrothed to Norris, Weston responded that Norris came to the queen's apartments not to see Madge but to see Anne; and he admitted that his attendance on the queen was inspired by the same infatuation. Thus two esteemed courtiers preferred Anne to the more beautiful Madge, even if only one was brave enough to say so. Such attentions, no doubt, were a tonic to the queen's vanity.

Then came a third admirer to join the competition – Mark Smeaton, the youngest and most handsome of the three, and a talented musician and vocalist. But Smeaton was a low-born commoner, and so when he professed his love, the day before the altercation with Norris, the queen firmly put him down, reminding him that as an 'inferior person' he could not compete for the queen's affections or expect to be spoken to as if he were a nobleman. Smeaton meekly answered that a loving look was all that he desired.

Smeaton's encounter with Anne in the presence chamber at Greenwich was reported to Cromwell, who probably suspected already that the brooding youth had a thing for the queen. Smeaton was the first to be arrested. He was taken to Cromwell's Stepney house on the 30th, interrogated, and possibly tortured. He confessed to three counts of adultery with the queen and may have accused others in the bargain. Later that day, with Smeaton's confession in hand, Cromwell went to several commission members and then to Henry. Cromwell took a chance in accusing Norris, who was Henry's dearest friend, and whose conversation with Anne a disbelieving king might dismiss as inconclusive or interpret benignly. But with proof of one adulterous relationship ready to present, other courtly relationships were construable as adulterous too. Henry was shocked by the revelations (and they must have been convincing since he did not turn on Cromwell for making them). His planned trip to Calais with Anne in the coming days he postponed; though the jousting tournament at Greenwich on the following day he allowed to go forward. He invited Anne to the tournament, even though earlier in the day he had quarreled with her over the rumours, already circulating, of her exchange with Norris. Henry attended the tournament, with Anne at his side, and with Norris and Rochford at the head of competing teams of jousters. After viewing several of the matches and supplying Norris with a fresh mount, Henry abruptly departed the pavilion, leaving Anne behind to watch by herself. He summoned Norris and commanded that he ride with him and a small party of courtiers back to London. Cromwell's stage management must have broken down at this point, because an accused person was not generally admitted access to the king, lest this fount of justice be swayed by fond memories and special pleadings (Anne was properly sequestered). But this time it made no difference that the king overbore custom, for Norris' asseverations of innocence fell on deaf ears. Norris was taken to Whitehall and the following morning escorted to the Tower.

Additional arrests followed in quick succession. Anne was seized and sent to the Tower on May 2, having first been interrogated by Cromwell and select commission members at Greenwich the day before. Also arrested on the 2nd was George Boleyn, Lord Rochford. Rochford was an able and important courtier, fiercely loyal to his sister; if allowed to live, he would plot his revenge and might one day have it (*Prince* 3; *Dis*, III.6.1: injured parties avenge themselves unless the injury to them is absolute – i.e., their own deaths). Rochford's wife Jane, once an ally of Anne, now an unwavering foe, gave testimony of incest committed by the siblings. This was the piece of evidence calculated to shock the conscience, and it probably was included in the package of charges which shocked and repulsed the king. Weston was arrested on May 3. Anne's own distracted ramblings in the first hours of her confinement were what brought Weston under suspicion. Anne disclosed Weston's year-old profession of love and gave full details of the Norris and Smeaton conversations a few days prior. On May 4, William Brereton was arrested. Brereton, like Norris and Weston, was a Privy Chamber groom; but he was older (as old as the king) and not one of Anne's intimates. His mistake was to have gotten crosswise with Cromwell over affairs in Wales. Brereton dispensed royal appointments in North Wales independent of Cromwell; and in defiance of Cromwell he arranged for the apprehension, return, and execution of a Welshman with whom he was quarreling. Cromwell wanted Brereton ruined. Two others were arrested on May 8, Richard Page, also of the Privy Chamber, and the poet Thomas Wyatt, a known Anne-suitor of long ago. They were interrogated but not tried and were subsequently released – their exonerations serving to demonstrate the justice of the proceedings.

Grand juries were convened on May 10, in Middlesex and in Kent, to hear evidence of adultery and treason collected by the commission of oyer and terminer. The charges laid against the queen and her five paramours included twenty counts of adulterous solicitations and sexual relations occurring between the autumn of 1533 and the spring of 1536 (with names, dates, and locations all supplied); also the exchange of gifts as tokens of love; and the charge of conspiracy to kill the king and marry the queen (an elaboration on Anne's remark to Norris). The two grand juries had no difficulty delivering indictments. The evidence was then presented to a petty jury on May 12, which tried Norris, Weston, Brereton, and Smeaton collectively; and to a jury of peers on May 15, which tried Anne and Rochford separately. Anne was additionally charged with poisoning Catherine and conspiring to poison Mary (an inference drawn from Anne's gift of lockets to Norris); and with ridiculing the king's poetry and dress. Rochford in turn faced the further charge of belittling the king's virility by implying that Elizabeth was not Henry's child. All were found guilty by unanimous votes of the several juries. Mercy was extended at the punishment phase, in that all were granted beheading – as convicted traitors they could have suffered that, plus hanging and disembowelment, or, as with Anne, burning at the stake. The men were executed on Tower Hill (outside the Tower compound) on May 17; the queen was executed on Tower Green (inside the compound) on May 19. Anne's execution was delayed a day to allow time for a specialist swordsman to arrive from Calais and to allow time for Cromwell to rid the grounds of foreign spectators, whose reports back home, it was feared, would be harshly critical of the crown.

The Aftermath

Henry did not wait long to remind the world of what, from the royal perspective, necessitated the destruction of Anne Boleyn – namely the desire for yet another queen and yet another try at siring a male heir. On the day following Anne's execution, Henry was formally betrothed to Jane Seymour; and ten days later, on May 30, they were married at Whitehall chapel.

Just prior to these events, Henry set Cranmer the task of devising grounds for an annulment of the Boleyn marriage, which three years earlier Cranmer had pronounced entirely valid. It would not do to invoke the public honesty impediment based on Anne's reputed precontract to Henry Percy, earl of Northumberland; for Percy refused to acknowledge such a contract – both because the rumour of it was untrue and because to change his story now would be to expose himself to the charge of having treasonously deceived the king. Cromwell was accustomed to bending people to his will, but he could see that there was no profit to be had from leaning on Northumberland; so Cranmer had to go elsewhere for his grounds. He determined to rule invalid the papal dispensation allowing Henry to marry within the prohibited degrees of affinity. Clement had granted this dispensation (1528) on the chance that annulling the marriage to Catherine might one day prove expedient, in which case the way would need clearing for a marriage to Anne, otherwise forbidden because of Henry's previous relations with her sister Mary. As before, it was decided that the pope had overstepped his authority and that the dispensation was void. This Cranmer proclaimed on May 17. On May 18, in his capacity as 'English pope', he issued his own dispensation waiving all consanguinity impediments to the king's marriage to Jane.

The reason for divorcing Anne, two days before her execution, was of course not to be rid of a wife, but to be rid of a daughter by that wife. Under the *Succession Act*, Elizabeth stood next in line to the throne, ahead of any female child produced by Jane. Since Henry was seeking a fresh start with a third bride, he judged it advantageous to bastardise all of his past brood; and the parliament which met in June was given the job of adjusting the succession laws to favour Jane's offspring (though at the time of its summoning, in late April, Anne's fate had not been sealed; thus the purpose then was to address an omission in the Reformation statutes which, while making opposition to the supremacy a crime, had failed to make allegiance to the papacy a crime). Cromwell notified Gardiner, away from court, of the change: 'The late princess, Lady Elizabeth, is by parliament pronounced also illegitimate.'

The Aragonese expected great things from Anne's fall. Anne had pushed England toward Lutheranism and alliance with German Protestants; England now would swing back toward Catholicism and alliance with the emperor and the pope. Anne had degraded Catherine and Mary (and was thought to have done worse); Mary now would return to court and to royal favour as heir-presumptive to the throne. Likewise her supporters would come out of the shadows and into bright open spaces of power. But they did not reckon on Cromwell, who moved quickly from investigating the Boleyns to investigating them. Charged by Henry with breaking Mary to the royal harness, but receiving from her the same resistance as before, Cromwell reported back that her continued obstinacy was caused by encouragement from her Aragon friends. Henry agreed and set Cromwell loose on the Aragonese. Some he interrogated, some he banished from court, and some he incarcerated in the Tower. In fact, a full-scale purge was in the works when Mary, wanting to spare her followers the fate that had befallen the defenders of Anne, yielded to Cromwell's demands. She affixed her signature to documents renouncing her legitimacy and her place in the succession (June 15). Henceforth she was the bastard child of a royal concubine, to be done with as the king, her father, saw fit. The Aragonese escaped destruction on the occasion, but only because they abased themselves before the king and his almighty minister. As a mark of his new standing, Cromwell was admitted to the peerage as baron Okeham and invested with the office of Lord Privy Seal, taken from the disgraced Thomas Boleyn. The Seymours too found advancement, Edward to the peerage as viscount Beauchamp and his brother Henry to the Privy Chamber.

7

Rebellion

The Pilgrimage of Grace

The work of dissolving the smaller monastic houses, authorised by parliament, had been put on hold through the spring while Cromwell attended to his palace coup. That now done, Cromwell dispatched his commissioners to close the houses, disperse the inmates, and expropriate the wealth. He also secured through Convocation a formulary of faith more Protestant-sounding than anything previously dared. These Ten Articles, as the formulary was called, combined Protestant teachings on sacraments and justification with Catholic beliefs regarding saints and purgatory – all of it muddled and modified to produce a middle-way, compromise creed. The Articles was then supplemented by injunctions to the clergy, a set of commands from Cromwell as Vicegerent of Spirituals, mandating preaching, education, moral reform, alms-giving, and scholarships for the young. Some care was taken to ensure a friendly reception for this *via media* faith, though in the northern counties rumour determined the public's reaction – a reaction mostly frantic and hostile, and within a few weeks armed and violent.

The uprising started in Lincolnshire in October. The parishioners of St James in Louth, inflamed by their vicar's

Sunday sermon, undertook to keep guard over the church lest the Vicegerent's commissioners, due to arrive, confiscate its valuables in the name of the crown. Some of these parishioners on the following day traveled northwest to Caistor where they roused the inhabitants to a similar resistance. Horncastle to the south of Louth needed no outside agitation; its commons, stirred on by the local clergy, murdered the chancellor of the Lincoln diocese who was there among them conducting the commission inquiry. By week's end (October 7), 10,000 rebels had gathered in Lincoln where their leaders drafted a petition to the king. Among the rebel demands were the restoration of the closed monasteries, the removal of heretical bishops and of base-born members of the Privy Council, and the end of taxes and of enclosures. In short order the number of Lincolnshire rebels rose to between 40,000 and 60,000. Against them the king had only small companies of soldiers, organised into two armies under the commands of the earl of Shrewsbury and the duke of Suffolk. Shrewsbury was profusely thanked by Cromwell for his loyalty to the king and promised 'all such habiliments and munitions'; while the Suffolk contingent was reinforced by arms from the Tower and from workmen from Cromwell's Bermondsey house, both brought to him by Cromwell's nephew, Richard. Even so, the royal armies were under-equipped and vastly outnumbered and had little chance of prevailing in a fight. But the rebels who faced them in and around Lincoln were not actually rebels intent on toppling the regime; they rather were petitioners humbly asking for redress of grievances and wanting nothing so much as pardon for their presumption. Henry did grant them a pardon (except for 140 who were arrested), though their other demands he ignored. Nor did he refrain from expressing his hostility and contempt, calling the Lincolnshire men 'rude commons of one shire, and that one of the most brute and beastly of the whole realm'.

When news reached London of the Lincolnshire uprising, the king fully expected the nobility and gentry of the region to rally to the government's side. Countless letters communicated this expectation, and countless responses gave reasons why the lords and the gentlemen were slow to comply. It seemed that their lives were threatened – or so they claimed – if they refused to join the rebels and if they refused to provide leadership to the rebels' cause. They all professed loyalty even while they made excuses for disloyal behavior, and so the king was at straits to know who were his friends and who were his enemies. Similarly, the rebels were at straits to know whether the grandees pressed into service were aiding them or aiding the king. Was Lord John Hussey, for example, a rebel (he met with the insurgents and promised to do their cause no harm), or was he a king's man (he fled his home in Sleaford in advance of the rebels coming to get him, and he made his way to the royalist camp disguised as a priest)? No one could say for sure, including Hussey himself. Uncertain leadership and concomitant tension between the classes were two reasons why the Lincolnshire rebellion collapsed so suddenly. Another was the essential moderation of the rebels, engaged as they were in a remonstration with the government more than in a rebellion against it and trusting too much in the benevolence and wisdom of the king.

One dramatic instance of seemingly coerced leadership occurred in early October when Robert Aske, a Gray's Inn lawyer, was stopped while traveling through Lincolnshire on his way to London. His captors obliged him, as they had numerous gentlemen in the area, to take an oath in support of the uprising; but soon thereafter he put himself in charge and was readily deferred to as the natural leader of the group. No longer coerced (if ever he was), Aske was indefatigable in organizing a similar resistance in the East Riding district of Yorkshire. He gave the rebellion its name, the 'Pilgrimage of Grace'; he provided the rebels their uniform, or identifying badge, the Five Wounds of Christ; and he composed his own oath for others to take:

> You shall not enter into this our Pilgrimage of Grace for the commonwealth, but only for the love you do bear unto almighty God his faith, and the holy church militant and the maintenance thereof, to the preservation of the king's person and his issue, to the purifying of the nobility, and to expulse all villain blood and evil councilors against the commonwealth from his Grace and his Privy Council of the same.

Aske was the force behind what proved to be the primary insurgency, which began in Yorkshire just as the disturbance in Lincolnshire was drawing to an end. Over the next few days, Beverly, the Wolds, Holderness, and sundry towns at the confluence of rivers emptying into the Humber all rose up, their inhabitants marching on York and taking the city (surrendered by the mayor) within the week. As Yorkshire was home to several medieval castles, these too were attacked. Some held out – Scarborough and Skipton; some capitulated – Pontefract and Hull. Pontefract castle on the Great North Road was by far the most imposing. It was besieged by the rebels and surrendered to them by its constable Lord Thomas Darcy, an elderly courtier-warrior of the Aragonese persuasion. The quick capitulation of mighty Pontefract (October 20) caused deep dismay and suspicion back at Windsor where the king and Cromwell were then residing. Darcy's submission was seemingly another instance of a local dignitary forced to do what in the event he was inclined to do, perhaps even eager to do.

The king's response to the Yorkshire troubles was at once psychological and material. A messenger was dispatched from Nottingham charged with informing the insurrectionists that Lincolnshire was quiet and under royal control. News of

Lincolnshire's surrender was meant to deflate the spirits of Yorkshire rebels. But when the messenger reached Pontefract, Aske would not permit him to address his followers. This occurred on October 21. On the following day, word arrived of a royal army approaching Doncaster and commanded by Shrewsbury. Also a second army was on the march, organised and commanded by Thomas Howard, duke of Norfolk, forced into retirement by Cromwell (the disgraced Anne Boleyn was Norfolk's niece) but now needed by the king. The royal contingent was small, however – 9,000 combined, against 20,000 to 40,000 rebels. These forces faced off at Doncaster with nothing between them but the river Don. With a victory here – a likely prospect – the rebel army could have marched toward London practically unhindered. (Suffolk was in the field with 4,000, Exeter with 2,000, but they and smaller detachments could easily have been picked off in detail; as an indication of the danger facing the king, the battlements of the Tower were reinforced at this time.) But as before in Lincolnshire, the rebels, or their leaders, did not want to defeat the king but to force a change in government policies. Aske hesitated; and using as his excuse the rising waters of the Don, he agreed to stand down and talk, when Norfolk, seeing clearly the desperateness of his situation, offered negotiations.

A meeting between Norfolk and individuals selected for hostage exchange occurred on the 27th, followed by a more public meeting on Doncaster bridge, led not by Aske, but by Pilgrim luminaries capable of earning Norfolk's respect. The Pilgrims' demands tracked closely those of their Lincolnshire compatriots: return to the true faith; restoration of the church's ancient liberties; repeal of obnoxious Reformation statutes; removal of heretic bishops and of base-born advisers to the king. By this last was meant Cromwell, Audley, and Rich, the persons held most responsible for the dissolution. Norfolk benefited from the rebels' extreme antipathy toward Cromwell, since it was widely presumed that Norfolk, remembered as the hero of Flodden Field (second in command to his aging father), would be Cromwell's high-born replacement at the head of the Privy Council. The king was not their enemy, the rebels believed, except insofar as wicked advisers had poisoned his mind. Norfolk played upon this wishful thinking, promising vaguely a northern parliament to redress rebel grievances and a royal pardon for all, while assuring the king in private letters that he, Norfolk, had no intention of keeping his word. Unfortunate it was for the rebels that the man whom they trusted was the second most devious in the realm, surpassed only by Cromwell.

The plan was for Norfolk and two of the Pilgrims (Ralph Ellerker and Robert Bowes) to travel to Windsor for a meeting with Henry, after which these Pilgrim-emissaries would return with the king's reply. That reply, full of venom for the rebels, offered pardon for all but ten unnamed leaders, while objecting to the list of rebel complaints and/or dismissing them as baseless. It was not an answer likely to win hearts and minds among the Pilgrim host. Henry, it seems, was slow to comprehend the danger posed by the rebellion. But another round of discouraging dispatches persuaded him to halt the emissaries' return, to hold them for some three weeks under house arrest, and, during the interim, to send heralds north with promises of rewards for those of the gentry willing to renounce their actions and renew their loyalty to the crown. Norfolk also wrote to Darcy asking that the lord betray Robert Aske; to which invitation Darcy replied: 'I cannot do it in no wise, for I have made a promise to the contrary, and my coat was never hitherto stained with such a blot.' Darcy regarded the offer as so unlike a nobleman that he supposed it to have originated with the base-born advisers around the king, that is, with Cromwell.

The emissaries returned on November 17, and on the 21st they reported to a council of Pilgrims held at York. They had only a verbal message from the king, to the effect that Norfolk would be coming to Doncaster carrying a written reply and the offer of further negotiations with three hundred of the rebels (*Dis*, III.6.20: immobilise a conspiracy by providing a distant opportunity on which it can focus). Upon hearing this from emissaries who vouched for its truthfulness (though while in custody they had effectively gone back to the royal side), the rebel leadership divided between those who wished for peace and wanted to think well of Norfolk and the king, and those who were hot for battle and confident of victory and who thought that negotiations were a ruse designed to give the king time to gather his forces. Speaking for them was Sir Robert Constable, an old warrior with battlefield honors dating back to Henry VII. Constable had in his possession a captured letter from Cromwell to the keeper of Scarborough castle, Ralph Evers, threatening stern retaliation for rebels once the insurgency had come to an end ('if these rebels do continue any longer in their rebellion, doubt you not but you shall see them so subdued as their example shall be fearful to all subjects while the world does endure'). This letter Constable read; but the peace party was too hopeful to be deterred from continuing talks with Norfolk. The meeting would go ahead, once the Pilgrims had managed to sharpen their demands, for Norfolk did tell them of Henry's dissatisfaction with the previous version.

 For three days the Pilgrims met at Pontefract (December 2–4) where they thrashed out the Pontefract Articles, a list of twenty-four grievances touching issues religious, dynastic, political, economic, and personal. The four or five complaints of previous petitions ballooned into twenty-four because Aske had canvassed the towns of the north and because hundreds of representatives had assembled in Pontefract. Regarding religion, the Pilgrims wanted heretical writers proscribed (both German and English) and heretical bishops put to the flames; they wanted the secular supremacy undone, or that part respecting cure of souls; suppressed religious houses they wanted revived and the dissolution ended; corrupt commissioners and other agents of the crown they wanted disciplined or controlled; they wanted traditional church liberties restored, such as sanctuary and benefit of clergy; and they wanted curbs placed on first fruits and tenths – all of these changes to be codified by parliament. Their dynastic demands were for Princess Mary's re-legitimation, lest a vacant throne go to the Scots, and repeal of that provision of the second *Succession Act* (1536) empowering the king, in default of issue, to choose his own successor. Their political demands included the removal and condign punishment of wicked counselors, with Cromwell, Audley, and Rich specifically named; fair elections, untainted by royal interference, for shire-knights and burgesses; a new parliament, as promised by the king, summoned shortly and held in the Pilgrimage-friendly north (York or Nottingham) to legislate on matters raised by the rebellion; repeal of statutes enacted during the uprising; and regular use of common law. Economic complaints focused on taxation, inheritance, and enclosures. The personal liberties demanded were the right to bear modern arms, i.e., the crossbow and the handgun; the right to trial in vicinage, or trial in York for those living above the river Trent; and the right to free speech, meaning an end to treason for words.

The Pontefract Articles, placed under the microscope of scholarly investigation, has lent support to the thesis that the Pilgrimage of Grace was an elite operation more than a populist movement. It is noted, for example, that some of the grievances originated with Robert Aske and with no one else (e.g., concern for the pope's spiritual headship); that some reflected the interests of the propertied few (e.g., objection to statutes of uses); and that some required insider knowledge available mainly to London courtiers and parliamentarians (e.g., Cromwell's guiding role in the Reformation and his responsibility for the dissolution). This revisionist thesis thus holds that the Pilgrimage was a planned affair by adherents of the Aragon cause who, outfoxed by Cromwell, organised an opposition in the northern provinces to counter Cromwell's ascendancy at court. The commoners were in the rearguard, not the vanguard, the argument goes, and all protestations of compulsory oath-taking were self-interested exculpations dreamed up after the rebellion had failed. The fact that much of the extant literary source material comes from memoirs, testaments, and confessions composed by captured Pilgrim leaders pleading extenuating circumstances for their treasonous behavior does buttress the case. And certainly the crown did not accept the claim that the uprising was merely a commoners' crusade, for it punished the leadership more severely than the rank-and-file. On the other hand, the people's eagerness to take as true all dark tales about the doings of government (e.g., a tax on 'upper-class' foods consumed by the poor) means that public opinion was set on rebellion with or without the leadership of elites. Recent histories have returned to this interpretation, placing substantial, if not complete, responsibility on the common folk of the north – who, by the way, did know enough about Cromwell to denounce him and his associates in the lyrics of one of their ballads:

Crim, Crame, and Riche [Cromwell, Cranmer, Rich] / With three Ls, and the Liche [Longland, Leigh, Layton, and the bishop of Lichfield, Rowland Lee] / As some men teach / God them amend / And that ask may / Without delay / Here make a stay / And well to end.

Perhaps then it is best to suppose that the Pilgrimage was a genuinely populist movement, which, once up and running, was co-opted by the gentry, but with the glad consent of the people, habituated to elite rule; that the gentry took charge partly out of fear, partly out of ambition, but mainly out of concern that without their guidance a justifiable resistance would become a revolution destructive of all social order; finally, that at some point (to be spoken of next) the gentry made a separate peace (or thought that they did), opted out, and effectively handed the Pilgrimage back to the people, which they, the gentry, then helped the king to crush.

While the Pilgrim leaders were thus occupied with drafting their bill of complaints, the king was occupied with letter-writing to Norfolk, his negotiator and general. These royal dispatches, vague in their directives and ill-informed of facts on the ground, expressed distrust of Norfolk and contempt for the insurgents. Increasingly violent, they demanded, in exchange for a pardon, total submission of the rebels and the surrender of ten of the ringleaders for special punishment; and they threatened war in the event of refusal. But just as the conference at Doncaster was set to begin, on December 5, Henry, perhaps influenced by Suffolk on station in Lincolnshire, softened his position, offering at last a general pardon (no exceptions), a continuation of the truce, and the promise of a parliament at a place and date to be determined. It was a great good fortune for Henry that the conference was delayed a day while Norfolk waited on Shrewsbury to arrive on the scene and that his modified instructions thus reached Norfolk before commencement of the meeting; since if Norfolk had been obliged to say what Henry truly thought and still intended, the Pilgrims would have refused him, fighting would have ensued, and the king's forces would have suffered defeat unless saved by the weather. But as it happened, Norfolk was permitted to take a conciliatory line, which the Pilgrim peace advocates interpreted as proof of the king's good nature and of his willingness – when free from evil advisers – to placate his subjects and conclude with them an honorable peace. In three days of negotiations, the respective parties came to agreement on most items contained in the Pontefract Articles. The monasteries were a sticking point, however, since the Pilgrims were adamant in demanding their restoration and Norfolk was adamant in keeping their valuables for the king. Here the parties finessed and put off, agreeing to a compromise whereby the monasteries would formally submit to the king's commissioners, the king would waive their submission and restore their independence, and parliament would determine their status once and for all. Other items were not closely considered, like Mary and the succession, but Norfolk could point to the promised parliament as the place for resolving such matters. Indeed, the specter of a parliament served his purposes well, as Aske and the others came to believe that not every detail needed settling before proceeding to the next stage. And all that was in writing was the king's pardon, in transit from London.

Aske took the agreement and the assurance of pardon back to his supporters gathered at Pontefract. Eloquent and charismatic, Aske succeeded in persuading the gentry and some 3,000 commoners that the deal which had been struck was a good one indeed. With their hurrahs ringing in his ears, he returned to Doncaster, only to learn upon arrival that the hurrahs of Pontefract had turned into boos. Rabble-rousers among the commons had sown doubts about the trustworthiness of the gentry conducting the negotiations and about the reliability of the promises made (would there be a parliament soon and in York?). Aske was obliged to return and repeat his performance, which he did to the satisfaction of the assembled. Thereafter, back in Doncaster, he surrendered his title of captain and removed the badge of the Pilgrimage, the Five Wounds of Christ. He was once again a loyal subject of the king. In appearance at least, the Pilgrimage was over, with solid gains made by the rebels.

That solid gains were in fact made could be detected in the reaction of the king. Henry was not pleased. He thought that his honor had been inadequately defended by Norfolk and the others. Honor required that someone pay for the rebellion – but the pardon exonerated all – and that the loot from the monasteries be entirely his to enjoy or dispense. Henry wanted blood. What he got was a peace with traitors who extracted concessions and made him look weak. Cromwell felt obliged to reply to rumours circulating on the continent that Henry accepted ignominious peace terms because the loyalty of his soldiers was in doubt. An unequivocal refutation did Cromwell send to Gardiner and Wallop serving in France:

> there is no thing more false than that the commons assembled for the king's part were so faint and unwilling that they would not have done their duties, if it had come to extremity … and I am assured … that the most part of the king's retinue in manner wept when they were commanded to retire, considering the rebels were not more extremely punished.

It rather was consideration for the safety of his forces, Cromwell explained, as well as clemency toward the rebels – who could be put to good use once 'healed and recovered' from their corruption – that induced the king to stay his hand.

But then there was another way of viewing the outcome, one not in need of the minister's rosy-eyed representation. Many of the rebel demands were never acceded to, such as the surrender of Cromwell to his enemies; and the pardon, as it turned out, was incomplete–more the promise of a pardon than an actual pardon granted and in hand. It required rebellious subjects to petition for personal pardons at the king's courts in London. Few commoners had the time or resources for the trip; hence their future safety would depend on parliament's action or the king's good will. The gentry could make the trip, and did – Aske among them, meeting privately with Henry on January 5 – but their journeys to the capital only highlighted their separation from the commons whom they purported to represent.

This division in class interest, now back on the surface for the commons to see and resent, was the catalyst which set off a third round of rebellion and which provided the king his excuse for reneging on his Doncaster promises. John Hallam, a farmer-firebrand from East Riding, and the person responsible for turning the Pontefract crowd temporarily against the peace accords, was of the opinion that erstwhile rebels needed a card to play, an asset in their hands, during the long winter months of 1536–7 as the north awaited its parliament and the material satisfaction of its demands; for otherwise the king might take back what he had given, and the gentry might support him in his betrayal. In concert with another hothead, Sir Francis Bigod of North Riding, an Oxford-trained Lutheran pressed into service by the rebels and a convert to the cause ever since, he concocted a plan whereby the castles at Hull and Scarborough would be taken by stealth. Hull had been occupied by rebels during the uprising; but under the terms of the Doncaster peace, it and Pontefract were restored to their royal keepers. Hallam was to raise a new rebel army from the towns of East Riding, sneak its soldiers into Hull on market day, and then take the castle by surprise. But his army in the event consisted of himself and twenty others, and the mayor had been alerted to the impending attack. Hallam tried to postpone, regroup, and go again; but he was captured when he went back into Hull attempting to rescue those of his comrades trapped inside.

Scarborough was Bigod's assignment. Bigod though contemplated a rebellion grander than Hallam's, one on the scale of the original Pilgrimage and able to imperil the crown; and he went to Beverley and places north to raise the forces he would need. In the meantime, he gave Scarborough to a subordinate, George Lumley, who amazingly took the town with only 140 men and a letter from Bigod. But Lumley did not move immediately to seize the castle. He was a friend of Ralph Evers, the Scarborough castellan, who was away in London securing his pardon. Lumley warned Ever's father to keep his son clear of Scarborough since the castle was about to fall under siege. Then, like Bigod, Lumley went off to collect additional forces. Since it rarely is a good idea to inform the enemy of what one is planning to do, another fiasco was set to unfold: Evers returned, took command of the castle, repelled the attack (led by Lumley's subordinates), and arrested the attackers.

Hearing of Hallam's fate in Hull, Bigod rushed south with a force of 800 hoping to pressure the city into releasing his colleague. Emissaries were dispatched to open negotiations; most of these were taken prisoner. Letters were sent to Aske, Constable, and other Pilgrim leaders asking for help and advice; in unison they answered that the treaty was good and should be respected. Unable then to raise an army in East Riding, Bigod decided to move west toward rebel-happy Richmond. But before leaving the area, and while in Beverley, the contingent still with him was surprised, scattered, and some of it captured. The remnant headed northwest and then dispersed, and Bigod, alone, went into hiding. A month later he was seized in Cumberland.

News of Bigod's capture came as Norfolk was entering York, sent to administer an oath of allegiance, to gather information about the past rebellion, and to punish all infractions since the pardon; also to shut down the monasteries, gather up their wealth, and reassign their inhabitants without apparent regard for the fact that this suppression was supposed to be a *pro-forma* and momentary thing. Nor did his commission make mention of a parliament, much less of the time and place of its occurrence. (Wrote Cromwell by way of justification: 'their chief article which next their pardon was for a parliament for that they might have their pardon therein confirmed, they remitted the appointment of the same wholly to the king's Majesty without the naming of time, place, or any other thing touching that matter.') His instructions were drafted in advance of any report of the assaults on Hull and Scarborough; they thus reflected how narrowly the king interpreted the agreement and his determination to squeeze from it every possible advantage without plainly violating its terms and provoking further trouble. Henry operated under no such constraints once it was clear that some of the rebels had returned to rebellion.

More returned than just Hallam and Bigod and their hapless followers. In the northwest, tempers flared when in February the earl of Cumberland, Lord Clifford, on word from Norfolk, tried arresting Pilgrim malcontents who had taken sanctuary in the Kirkby Stephen church tower in Westmorland. A skirmish ensued, in which the lord's forces, border bandits led by his son Thomas, were badly beaten and chased half-way back to Carlisle, home of the family castle. With some incitement by agitators, Westmorlandshire was up in arms, and with help from its neighboring counties, it mustered a rebel force of 6,000 men; these then marched on Carlisle.

But as the assembled mass prepared to assault the battlements, it was attacked from outside the city; and before it could reorganise itself, a second company attacked it from inside the city. The rebel army quickly broke rank and was routed, with hundreds killed and hundreds captured. Norfolk was in North Riding at the time. Informed of the Kirkby Stephen incident and expecting the assault on Carlisle, he organised his own army on the spot, composed of northern gentry (as he brought no army with him from the south), and he double-timed them westward to Carlisle's relief. But when he arrived, all that remained was the hanging of prisoners, seventy-four in all, many of them picked at random. To prevent the 'premature' removal of prisoner bodies, iron chains were used in lieu of rope, until the supply of chains was exhausted. (The removal of rope-hanged bodies caused Cromwell to convey to Norfolk the king's impatience with the progress of the investigation: 'And touching the depositions taken of certain women [with respect to] the cutting down and burial of the traitors in Westmorland and Cumberland ... the king's highness thinks verily that if the said depositions had been earnestly taken ... the principal doers and occasioners of the same would have been ere long identified and apprehended.')

Now the retribution began in earnest. Monasteries and abbeys were treated brutally, especially those which had allowed themselves to be restored, but even some which had nothing to do with the Pilgrimage. On the king's order, the Bigod men captured at Beverley were rounded up and tried (their captor had previously released them on bail); and when they were found innocent (forced into service, they said), the king demanded the names of the jurors who set them free. Of course Bigod was killed, along with Hallam, Lumley, and numerous others associated with the 1537 uprisings. These had already been under arrest. For those not yet arrested, the standard procedure was to order their appearance in London. So terrifying was the prospect of coming to court, that one former dissident, only lightly involved in the Pilgrimage and thereafter scrupulously correct, tried mounting a new rebellion rather than answer the king's summons. This was Sir John Bulmer; he and his wife were executed. Many of the lords and gentry were executed too (two hundred or so), irrespective of the pardon granted to them, because violation of the pardon by a few effectively cancelled its protections for all. In law the pardon held, and efforts were made to contrive treason charges based on post-pardon events (which is why the king and Cromwell were so set on convicting the Beverley men, since they were to give evidence of misprision against some of the rebellion's original leaders). The success of these efforts allowed Cromwell to declare (to Wyatt): 'If they had not highly offended since the king's pardon, his majesty had never remembered their precedent offenses nor imputed the same to their charge.' But in practice post-pardon loyalty made no difference for those who had once defied their king (*Prince*, 18: a prudent prince does not keep faith after promises made have served their purpose). Darcy, Aske, Constable, and Hussey all met their ends. They had been loyal, even useful, since the pardon, and for that reason went south to London confident of receiving the king's commendation. Instead they were incarcerated, examined over weeks and months (obliged to give written answers to interrogatories), placed on trial, convicted, and executed. Darcy was the most eloquent and memorable at his examination, charging Cromwell with responsibility for all that had transpired:

> Cromwell, it is you that art the very original and chief causer of this rebellion and mischief, and art likewise causer of the apprehension of us that be noble men and do daily earnestly travail to bring us to our end and to strike off our heads; and I trust that [ere] you die, though you would procure all the noblemen's head within the realm to be stricken off, yet shall there one head remain that shall strike off your head.

In point of fact, Cromwell was a backstage player in the suppression of the insurgency. He was not a soldier, and fighting rebels was soldiers' work. More than that, he was anathema in the north, and his appearance there would have incited the rebels even further. Indeed, so hated was his person and name, that Richard, his nephew, was declared by the rebels *persona non grata* and forbidden admission to meetings in which peace was discussed. Norfolk, not Cromwell, was the lead player in this drama, chosen to be the king's voice and arm. The Pilgrimage, therefore, presented Norfolk his main chance to repair and enhance his standing at court. He led the king's armies; he saved the king's throne by avoiding battle when victory was unsure; he deceived, betrayed, and drew blood on the king's behalf. Norfolk gave Henry a total triumph in the north, while minister Cromwell, as Darcy said well, was the rebellion's chief origin and cause.

And yet nothing improved for Norfolk. In consequence of the insurgency and the discovered need for reformed government in the northern counties, Norfolk urged that nobles like himself be placed on the Council of the North. Cromwell urged that 'new men' like himself, loyal and competent gentry, be placed on the council instead. Cromwell's plan was to extend the reach of the central government into the untamed hinterlands of the realm, and 'new men' beholden to the crown, not feudal magnates with ambitions of their own, were the better instruments for the task. The king took Cromwell's advice and sent Norfolk back to his home in Kenninghall. That Cromwell was able to best Norfolk at the duke's moment of supreme service to the crown meant that Cromwell, Lord Privy Seal, had now reached a stature comparable to Wolsey's. And like Wolsey, Cromwell had gained an enemy intent on his destruction.

Reginald Pole, Cardinal And Provocateur

For those rebels who contemplated an England without Henry, Reginald Pole, the expatriate scholar and cousin of the king, was a person of great interest. As a young man, Pole was sent to Italy by Henry to pursue an education. Later, while in Paris, Pole was requested to collect opinions supportive of the king's divorce. The mission was unwelcome but completed nonetheless, and upon Pole's return in 1530, Henry offered his promising relative (who then was not even a priest) the see of Winchester or the archbishopric of York, both formerly occupied by Wolsey. Pole declined and received permission to return to Italy and continue his studies (1532).

It was a matter of some importance to Henry that Pole approve of the divorce and of the Reformation that accomplished it; but Pole, like More, could not bring himself to say that he did. Had Pole been in England, the *Treasons Act* would have been used to convince him; but since he was in Padua, the most Henry could do was to ask Pole, through others, to explain himself: 'to declare truly and plain without colour or dark of dissimulation, which his Grace most princely abhors. He does not wish for a great volume or book, but the most effectual reason plainly and briefly set forth.' Pole wrote 'a great volume or book', over two years, and then sent it to Henry. It arrived in May 1536, just after the execution of Anne Boleyn.

Titled *Pro Unitatis Ecclesiasticae Defensione* (*In Defense of the One Universal Church*), the book took Henry at his word (his dislike of dissimulation) and declared forthrightly the author's belief that the church was a universal institution with the pope at its head; that England was a dependent body obligated to submit and obey; and that defiance by a part against the whole was a rebellious act warranting invasion and deposition. As if that were not enough, it also compared the king of England to Nero, Satan, and a dirty barrel. Henry was not amused, though he held his temper long enough to invite Pole back to England for clarification and further dialogue; and he enlisted Pole's mother in a letter-writing campaign meant to lure the wayward son home. But even naïve Reginald was not that naïve, since the gallows surely awaited him if he returned. Instead, at the insistence of the pope, he became a cardinal of the church (though still not a priest) and papal legate to England, dispatched to Flanders where he was to muster support for the Pilgrimage of Grace and be on call for crossing the sea and expelling Henry from the throne. In some circles it was bruited that Pole, a Plantagenet, would marry Princess Mary, a Tudor, and together rule as king and queen. In other circles it was remembered that a quarter-century old prophecy had accurately foretold the rise and fall of Wolsey and that this same prophecy had further predicted the coming of a second 'Red Cap' to reconcile a divided land or to destroy it utterly.

Pole's mission, begun in early 1537, was already too late for the Pilgrimage proper, which by then was well into its truce phase. But it was not too late for Bigod, Hallam, and the rebels of Westmorlandshire – if the pope had not delayed until spring releasing the bull of legation upon which Pole's authority rested …if Henry had not pulled diplomatic strings to have Pole chased out of Flanders and into neutral Liege …if the operation had been adequately financed …and if a dozen contingencies had fallen into place. None did, however; and instead of harassing Henry from afar, Pole was himself harassed, as Henry put a bounty on his head and unleashed Cromwell's network of spies to apprehend or assassinate him. Many attempts were made, including the infiltration of Pole's household by a Cromwell agent whom Pole either won over by kindness or scared off by intimations of exposure; either way the assassin left with his task unaccomplished.

For the most part, through the spring and summer of 1537, Pole just sat and waited, hoping that events would break his way and justify his legateship. But the continent's powers, Francis and Charles, remained at war, and irritating Henry, much less threatening his throne, was not an idea that interested them. In August Pole returned to Rome to participate in a general council scheduled for November.

The Exeter Conspiracy

As mentioned, Reginald Pole was a Plantagenet. He was the grandson of George, duke of Clarence, the younger brother of

Edward IV of the house of York. Pole was, therefore, a scion of the White Rose faction (from the Wars of the Roses: White Rose for York, Red Rose for Lancaster), as were his brothers Henry, lord Montague, and Geoffrey. White Rose Plantagenets were never entirely comfortable with the Tudor dynasty, nor were the Tudors entirely comfortable with them, executing those of their clan with the genealogical credentials and personal ambition to covet the crown (*Dis*, III.4: no prince is secure on his throne while those who have been despoiled of it are still alive). In recent years, more cordial relations had been maintained, marked by royal emoluments bestowed (e.g., Reginald's education expenses) and subject services performed.

Two other White Rose noblemen prominent at this time were Henry Courtenay, marquess of Exeter, and a grandson of Edward IV, and Edward Neville, a descendant of John of Gaunt and Edward III. These two, the Pole brothers, and assorted relations and friends met socially, drank liberally, and complained indiscreetly about Reformation England under Henry and Cromwell. Courtenay had done somewhat more in the past, involving himself in a Cornish uprising in 1531, for which imprudence he spent a brief time in the Tower. His wife Gertrude, marchioness of Exeter, had been more imprudent still, visiting the Maid of Kent, communicating with Chapuys, and urging Mary to resist her father's demands that she accept her bastardization and surrender her title (for which interference the marchioness likewise spent a brief time in the Tower). The communications with Chapuys, in 1535, telling of the king's threats upon the lives of Catherine and Mary and urging a response by the emperor, were plainly treasonous acts, comparable to efforts by Darcy and Hussey in 1534 to contact Charles and persuade him to invade. But Cromwell and his investigators never learned of the marchioness' dealings with the Spanish ambassador; and her husband, while certainly friendly to the Aragonese, had remained loyal during the northern rebellion, commanding and recruiting forces for the king. Courtenay, more recently, had let slip remarks mildly critical of the king's advisers: e.g., 'Knaves rule about the king; I trust to give them a buffet one day.' Similarly, Montague had lamented the destruction of the monasteries in a letter to his cardinal brother. But for the most part, the Exeter Conspiracy consisted of harmless grumblings by White Rose and Aragon elements. These persons, in their hearts, may have been enemies of the government; they may have wished for dynastic change in England; under the right circumstances, they may even have worked to bring it about. But they did not join the rebels of the Pilgrimage of Grace; and in the post-Pilgrimage period, they were not actively conspiring against the crown. Their real crime was their connection to Reginald Pole and the continued danger which Henry perceived from that quarter.

In the summer of 1538, Francis and Charles struck a truce which ended their two years of fighting. The pope attended the summit at Nice, as did Cardinal Pole. Peace between the powers meant to Pope Paul that the time was right to pressure England into renouncing the Reformation and reuniting with the universal church. To King Henry, however, peace meant that England was again vulnerable to invasion and that as a precaution the last vestiges of domestic opposition needed to be removed. Accordingly, he instructed Cromwell to eradicate the White Rose faction.

Cromwell hardly needed any prompting. Already he had learned that a merchant named Hugh Holland had been conveying letters from the Poles to the cardinal, warning him of spies and assassins. Geoffrey Pole, recognised as the weak link, was arrested in August and taken to the Tower. Examined repeatedly over the next several months, he tried his best not to implicate his family and friends; but he broke under the strain and twice attempted suicide. The information Geoffrey provided, of the sort noted above (idle statements of discontent, but which Cromwell characterised as 'certain proofs and confessions') allowed the follow-up arrests of Montague, Neville, Exeter and his wife, various friends and supporters, and Margaret, countess Salisbury, mother of the Poles. Servants were questioned and premises ransacked. A search of the countess' Warblington home turned up a piece of cloth embroidered with the Five Wounds of Christ, the emblem of the Pilgrims, and encircled with marigolds and pansies, claimed by Cromwell to represent the union of Mary and Reginald. Since nothing incriminating was gotten from the countess during interrogation, this one piece of material evidence was used to prove her culpability. In cases where letters were found, their contents were twisted to reveal hints of treason; in cases where no letters were found, burning was presumed and guilt imputed. (Chapuys wrote fake letters to Mary so if questioned she would have something safe to show.)

The Exeter conspirators, eleven in all, were charged with plotting to seize the crown and kill the king and his family. One was fined but not tried, Thomas West, lord Delaware. Two were convicted but not executed – Geoffrey Pole and lady Exeter, the former pardoned for having given state's evidence, the latter kept in the Tower until 1540 and then pardoned and set free. Lady Salisbury was also kept prisoner, but rather than pardoned and released, she was executed in 1541 in retaliation for a new uprising in the north. The other principals were all executed in December and January: Exeter, Montague, and Neville, plus Holland and two priests. The last of the conspirators, Nicholas Carew, was arrested only after he had served on the jury which indicted Exeter. Some remark in some belatedly discovered letter pointed to Carew, but the case against him was slim: consorting with villains, failing to give evidence, burning letters. Nevertheless, he was found guilty in February 1539 and executed in March. Later that spring parliament passed an omnibus attainder act condemning the Pilgrimage rebels, the Exeter conspirators, and those known traitors who had escaped the king's justice, Reginald Pole in particular.

The Geraldine Revolt

As the Pilgrimage of Grace was drawing to its conclusion in the winter of 1537, a separate revolt in Ireland, begun three years earlier, was likewise finishing up – or being finished off – with the execution of the Geraldine earl of Kildare, Thomas Fitzgerald, and five of his uncles. These six, imprisoned in the Tower for a year or more, suffered execution at Tyburn in February 1537.

Ireland was a papal fiefdom entrusted to English care in the days of Henry II; and since those days – the late twelfth century – Ireland had been a drain on English resources. Henry VIII wanted Ireland to pay its way, if not enrich the royal treasury, and Cromwell thought he knew how to turn Ireland into a money-making venture and also a willing subscriber to the new supremacy. But as with the reorganization of the Council of the North, he vied with a rival plan put forward by Norfolk. Norfolk proposed a continuation of the live-and-let-live practice of old, a policy of benign neglect whereby the Irish warlords effectively governed themselves, while paying cost-free homage to the crown. No improvements were anticipated, but then neither were there new dangers and new expenses to be incurred. Norfolk was a temporiser. Cromwell was a chance-taker. He advised aggressive action and suppression of the magnates. He prevailed in Council and became the maker and manager of Irish policy until his own fall from favour.

English power in Ireland was exercised through the office of lord deputy. In the days of Wolsey, the office alternated between the Fitzgeralds, earls of Kildare, and the Butlers, (then) earls of Ormonde, with an English agent used instead when neither seemed suitable or when neither would tolerate the other. One such agent, Sir William Skeffington, was put in charge in 1530, and for two years Ireland was generally quiet. But in 1532, the earl of Kildare succeeded in having Skeffington recalled and himself appointed to the post (for the third time). His administration was characterised by harsh repression of the Butlers and of outlying clans and by neglect of the English living inside of the Dublin Pale. He caught the crown's attention when he ordered the transfer of royal cannon from Dublin to the family stronghold at Maynooth, this in response to indications that Cromwell and John Allen, the archbishop of Dublin (and a former colleague in the service of Wolsey), had been conspiring to bring him down. Allen's reports reversed the recall of 1532, with Kildare summoned to London to explain his actions and Skeffington shortly after reinstalled as deputy in his place. Kildare arrived in March 1534 and was sent to the Tower when his son Thomas refused to comply with a royal summons of his own. A false report of Kildare's execution (though the earl did die in custody in September) caused Thomas, nicknamed 'Silken', to renounce his allegiance to the crown and raise a rebellion throughout the land. Among the first casualties was the archbishop, who, attempting an escape by sea, was apprehended and killed when a storm blew his vessel back to shore. With little to stop their progress, the rebels enjoyed a successful fighting season capped off by the siege of Dublin. Skeffington and his English army arrived only in October. They marched on Dublin and dispersed the outgunned rebels, who regrouped at Maynooth castle for the decisive battle. These medieval fortresses, once impregnable, were no match for the new cannon of the day; and so the walls of Maynooth came tumbling down, its defenders scattered, captured, or killed (March 1535). Fitzgerald was away at the time recruiting reinforcements, who, in light of developments, proved hard to find and hard to keep. Many of his allies gave up, submitting separately to the royal authority. Fitzgerald

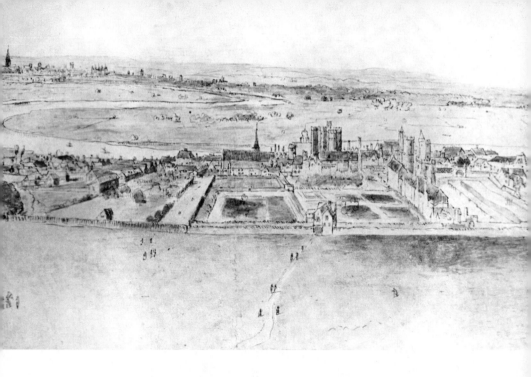

Above: 17. A view of the Tudor palace at Greenwich, massively and expensively rebuilt by Henry VII. Henry VIII was born there, and it remained his favourite residence. Nothing of the Tudor building now survives above ground. It was at Greenwich, in the spring of 1536, that Cromwell hatched the plot to bring down Anne Boleyn.

Below: 18. The Tower of London, *c.* 1550 by Anthony van Wyngaerde. The Tower was a fortress, prison, royal residence, and the home of the royal archives. Cromwell was sent to the Tower in June 1540.

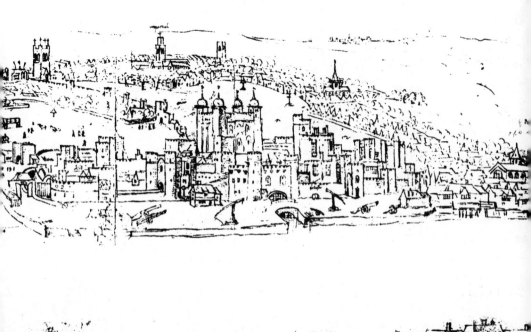

Great Hall,
by Wolsey, 1528

Tennis court
G

Preaching
place

'Holbein' gate

King St Gate

Weomynster Hall (the seat of the law courts)

Stare Chamber

House of Commons
(formerly chapel of St Stephen's)
from 1547 until the fire of 1834

House of Lords

Court of Requests

Henry VII's chapel

Abby

Opposite: 19. Plan of Westminster palace, showing the Great Hall, the Abbey, and the two houses of parliament, all of these situated on the Thames, the main highway connecting London, Westminster, Lambeth, Hampton Court, Southwark, and Greenwich. Cromwell was never Speaker or Lord Chancellor, but he effectively ran the House of Commons from 1532, and the House of Lords from 1536. The drawing is from a later version of the 1578 map known as Ralph Agas' map, although not in fact by him.

Above: 20. A view of Westminster, *c*. 1550, by Anthony van Wyngaerde. Westminster was the seat of the royal courts of justice, the meeting place of the parliament, and the nearest thing to a fixed capital that England possessed. Cromwell's December 1530 meeting with King Henry occurred at Westminster; this was the meeting where Cromwell allegedly revealed his plan of reforming and despoiling the church.

Below: 21. Whitehall palace, *c*. 1550, also by van Wyngaerde. As York Place this had been the traditional Westminster residence of the Archbishops of York, and had been extensively rebuilt by Cardinal Wolsey. It came into the king's hands on the fall of Wolsey in 1529 and was further rebuilt. It was used as a principal royal residence until largely destroyed by fire in the 1690s. The cost of enlarging Whitehall and other palaces caused Cromwell to complain: 'What a great charge it is to the king to complete his buildings in so many places at once... if the king would spare for one year how profitable it would be for him.' Henry secretly married Anne Boleyn in the turret room of Whitehall.

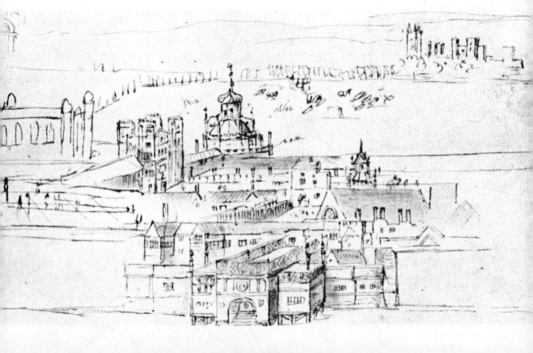

Above: 22. A drawing for the painting of Sir Thomas More and his family by Hans Holbein,
c. 1527. The painting itself was copied by Rowland Lockey in 1593, and the original does not survive.
Holbein painted portraits of many English aristocrats and courtiers, including Thomas Cromwell.
Below: 23. Windsor Castle – a royal palace and fortress, and home of the Knights of the Garter. It was at
Windsor on 11 July 1531 that Henry saw Catherine of Aragon for the last time. It was also at Windsor that
Henry and Cromwell awaited news of the Pilgrimage of Grace.

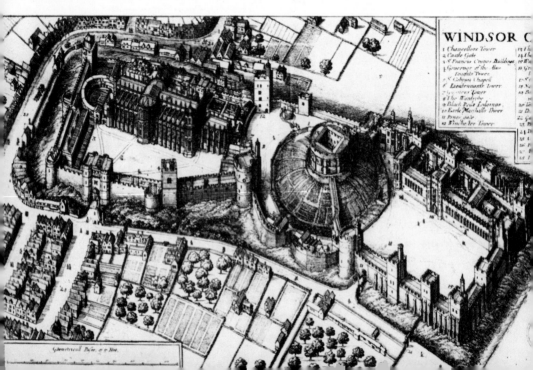

Anglici Matrimonij.

Sententia diffinitiua

Lata per sanctiss.imum. Dñm Nostrum. D. Clem-ñtem. Papã. vij. in sacro Consistorio de
Reuerendiss.moꝛum Dominorum. S. R. E. Cardinalium consilio super validitate Ma
trimonij inter Serenissimos Henricum. VIII. & Catherinam Angliæ Reges contracti.

PRO.

Eadem Serenissima Catherina Angliæ Regina,

CONTRA.

Serenissimum Henricuɱ. VIII. Angliæ Regem.

Clemens Papa. vij.

Hristi nomine inuocato in Trono iustitiæ pro tribunali sedentes, & solum Deum præ oculis habentes, Per hanc
nostram diffinitiuam sententiam quam de Venerabilium Fratrum nostrorum Sanctæ Ro. Ec. Car. Consistorialiter
coram nobis congregatorum Consilio, & assensu serimus in his scriptis, pronunciamus, decernimus, & declaramus,
in causa, & causis ad nos, & Sedem Apostolicam per appellationem, per charissimam in christo filiam Catherinam Angliæ Reginam Illustrem a nostris, & Sedis Apostolicæ Legatis in Regno Angliæ deputatis interposi-
tam legitime deuolutis, & aduocatis, inter prædictam Catherinam Reginam, & Charissimum in christo filium Henricum. VIII.
Angliæ Regem Illustrem, super Validitate, & inualiditate matrimonij inter eosdem Reges contracti, & consumati rebusꝗ alijs in
actis, causæ & causarum huiusmodi latius deductis, & dilecto filio Paulo Capissucho causarum sacri palatij tunc decano & pro
pter ipsius Pauli absentiam Venerabili Fratri nostro Iacobo Simonetæ Episcopo Pisaurien. vnus ex dictis palatij causarum Auditori
bus locumtenenti, audiendis instruendis, & in Consistorio nostro Secreto referendis commissis, & per eos nobis, & eisdem Car
dinalibus Relatis, & mature discussis, coram nobis pendentibus, Matrimonium Inter prædictos Catherinam, & Henricum An
gliæ Reges contractum, & inde secuta quecunꝗ fuisse, & esse validum, & canonicum validaꝗ, & Canonica, suoꝗ debitos de
buisse, & debere sortiri effectus, prolemꝗ exinde susceptam, & suscipiendam fuisse, & fore legitimam, & præfatum Henri
cum Angliæ Regem teneri, & obligatum fuisse, et fore ad cohabitandum cum dicta Catherina Regina eius legitima coniuge, illamꝗ
maritali affectione, & Regio honore tractandum, & eundem Henricum Angliæ Regem ad præmissa omnia, & singula cum
effectu adimplendum condemnandum ommbusꝗ iuris Remedijs cogendam, & compellendum fore, prout condemnamus, cogimus, &
compellimus, Molestationesꝗ, & denegationes Per eundem Henricum Regem eidem Catherinæ Reginæ super inualiditate, ac foe
dere dicti Matrimonij quomodolibet factas, & præstitas fuisse, & esse illicitas, & iniustas, & eidem Henrico Regi super il
lis ac inualiditate matrimonij huiusmodi perpetuum Silentium imponendum fore, & imponimus, eiusdemꝗ Henricum Angliæ Re
gem in expensis in huiusmodi causa pro parte dictæ Catherinæ Reginæ coram nobis, & dictis omnibus legitime factis condem
nandum fore, & condemnamus, quarum expensarum taxationem nobis imposterum reseruamus.

Ita pronunciauimus ·I·

Lata fuit Romæ in Palatio Apostolico publice in Consistorio die. XXIII. Martij. M. D. XXXIIII.

Blosius.

24. A copy of Pope Clement VII's 'definitive sentence' in favour of Catherine of Aragon and against
Henry VIII. Issued on the 23 March 1534, after vain calls to Henry to give up Anne and return to his
first wife. It was ignored in England.

King Henry the eyght.

The Byble in Englyshe, that is to saye the content of all the holy scrypture, bothe of ý olde and newe testament, truly translated after the veryte of the hebrue and Greke textes, by ý dylygent studye of dyuerse excellent learned men, expert in the forsayde tonges.

Prynted by Rychard Grafton & Edward Whitchurch.

Cum priuilegio ad imprimendum solum.
1539.

Last page spread, left: 25. Henry VIII in Council. This appears to be a formal session, with the king seated under his 'cloth of estate'. In practice the council normally met without the king, and attendance was usually about a dozen. Close ties to Henry made Cromwell the unofficial head of Council, even though its co-presidents were the dukes of Norfolk and Suffolk.

Last page spread, right: 26. Title page from the Great Bible, printed by Richard Grafton and Edward Whitchurch, 1539. Enthroned as God's vicar, Henry symbolically hands out the Word of God to the spiritual and temporal hierarchies of his realm, headed by Thomas Cranmer on his right and Thomas Cromwell on his left.

Above: 27. Europe circa 1530s.

SCOTLAND

Northumberland

Cumberland

Durham

Westmorland

Yorkshire

Lancashire

Cheshire

Derbyshire

Nottinghamshire

Lincolnshire

Shropshire

Staffordshire

Leicestershire

2

Norfolk

WALES

Warwickshire

Worcestershire

Northamptonshire

Huntingdon

Cambridgeshire

Suffolk

Herefordshire

Bedfordshire

Gloucestershire

Oxfordshire

Buckinghamshire

Hereford

Essex

Berkshire

1

Wiltshire

Surrey

Kent

Somerset

Hampshire

Sussex

Devonshire

Dorset

Cornwall

1 Middlesex
2 Rutland

28. The map shows England divided into counties. County representation in the House of Commons was by knights of the shire; enfranchised cities and towns were represented by burgesses.

29. The Pilgrimage of Grace 1536–7.

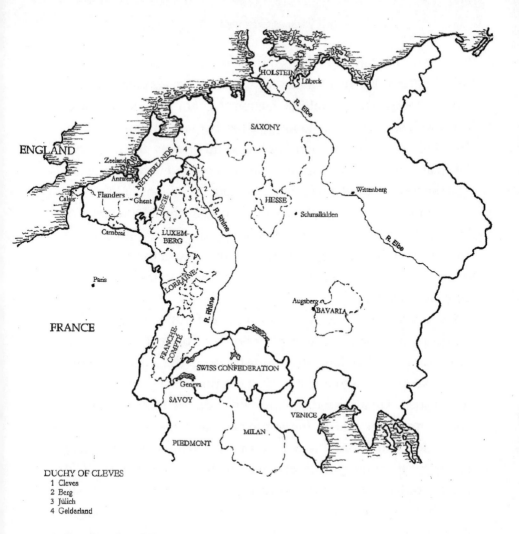

ENGLAND

HOLSTEIN
Lübeck
R. Elbe
SAXONY
Zeeland
Wittenberg
Antwerp
NETHERLANDS
Calais
Flanders
Ghent
HESSE
Schmalkalden
Cambrai
LIÈGE
LUXEM-
BERG
Paris
LORRAINE
R. Rhine
R. Elbe
FRANCE
R. Rhine
Augsberg
BAVARIA
FRANCHE-
COMTÉ
SWISS CONFEDERATION
Geneva
SAVOY
VENICE
PIEDMONT
MILAN

DUCHY OF CLEVES
1 Cleves
2 Berg
3 Jülich
4 Gelderland

30. Germany *circa* 1540.

himself surrendered in August on the promise of personal safety from the deputy. In October he was sent to London and the Tower. Because the Geraldine faction was not yet a spent force, Cromwell was forced to honor pledges, bargain, and prevaricate. Treachery was used to round up the family heads, three of them taken at a dinner to which they had been invited to discuss peace and the future of Ireland (*Prince 8*: imitate the actions of Liverotto da Fermo, who having thrown a banquet for the leading men of Fermo, killed them en masse and seized the town). In February 1536 the Geraldine uncles joined their nephew in the Tower. The following February, when control had been reestablished, they all were executed.

Cromwell was never able to turn Ireland into a money-maker for the crown (suppressing the Geraldine revolt cost £40,000), but he was able to place English administrators in the office of deputy and to keep the magnates at bay, whose power he either broke or diminished. He also managed to persuade the Irish parliament and clergy to accede to the supremacy and the succession, to sever ties with Rome, and to cooperate with the dissolution of the local monasteries. Reformation thus came to Ireland, if only at official levels. But the corruption that before was Irish, now became English, as Cromwell and his agents immersed themselves in bribe-taking and extortion. Ireland was never so rebellious as to provide a base for continental invaders, but neither was it ever truly pacified. In the end Ireland was judged more a mess than a marvel, and it counted against Cromwell at the time of his fall.

8

Henrician Protestantism and the Return to Orthodoxy

The Dissolution of the Monasteries

The closing of the monasteries was done partly in retribution for the role some played in the Pilgrimage of Grace; and those so involved saw their abbots and priors executed in the aftermath. The houses of Kirkstead, Barlings, Bridlington, Jervaulx, and Whalley suffered this fate. They were deemed forfeit because of the crimes of their heads. Houses less complicit were sometimes obtained by threats of attainder; such was true of the Cistercian abbey of Furness in Lancashire. Others surrendered voluntarily, notwithstanding their size, which for the time protected them from legal confiscation, because their members anticipated the coming of a general dissolution and wanted to settle accounts ahead of the rush. Pensions, benefices, and new positions in the secular clergy called 'capacities' were at stake. In some cases Cromwell appointees had been previously installed, and surrender for them was agreeable, if not planned. Three abbeys balked at shutting down, and their leaders were investigated, accused of treason, and sent to the gallows: Thomas Marshall of Colchester, Hugh Cooke of Reading, and Richard Whiting of Glastonbury. Cromwell wrote a memorandum which either commanded or merely presumed Cooke's and Whiting's executions even before their trials: 'The abbot of Reading to be sent down to be tried and executed at Reading with his complices; similarly the abbot of Glaston at Glaston.' Guilt by association was the order of the day: the account books of the Court of Augmentations listed fines imposed upon counties for the offense of tolerating the continued existence of nearby monasteries resisting surrender.

Because the suppression of 1537–8 ran far beyond what the *Dissolutions Act* of 1536 had required or allowed, a new law was passed in 1539 designed to legalise retroactively all prior acquisitions, as well as legalise those acquisitions yet to come. The *Act for the Dissolution of Abbeys* emphasised the voluntary character of the submission and the totality and permanence of the transfer:

> Where diverse and sundry abbots, priors, abbesses, prioresses, and other ecclesiastical governors ... of their own voluntary minds, good wills, and assents, without constraint ... or compulsion of any person or persons ... have severally given ... all their said monasteries, abbeys, priories, nunneries, colleges, hospitals, houses of friars ... to our said Sovereign Lord his heirs and successors forever.

To those monks and nuns driven from their houses under pain of death (9,000 uprooted in all), the insouciant falsehood that they left of their own free wills must have been especially galling.

By March 1540, the dissolution was over. Waltham Abbey in Essex was the last to go. In a span of four years, a millennium of religious history had disappeared. Commissioners carted away every piece of movable property. Lead was removed from church roofs, and church walls were quarried for their stones. Nothing but ruins remained a mere two generations later.

A modest attempt was made to reuse the windfall wealth for the purpose of religious reform. Six new episcopal sees were created out of the eighteen promised, and some suppressed houses were transformed into collegiate churches. But the bulk of the wealth – some £100,000 in annual income, £1,500,000 in sale value; plus countless wagonloads of movable goods – went to the king. Cromwell had redeemed his pledge to make Henry the richest monarch in Europe – or at least richer than at any time in his reign. It was hoped that monastic wealth would provide the crown an endowment sufficient for all of its needs and that taxes would no longer be required of the populace. Under ordinary economies, the crown's finances would have been stable and secure for decades to come. But Henry was careless, lavish, and wide-eyed ambitious. He spent the revenue with abandon, building, for example, his fabulous Nonsuch palace in Surrey, meant to overawe King Francis' Chambord chateau; and landed property he bestowed upon his favourites. Cromwell managed to steer some of the bounty toward coastal defenses; and he managed to include the rural gentry in the distribution of estates. They and their heirs thus came to support the Reformation that had brought them prosperity.

The dissolution was an opportunity for Protestant convictions to gain respectability. Monastic orders were creatures of the papacy, less subject to episcopal control than were parish churches. The suppression of the houses, therefore, further undermined the power of the pope in England. Suppression also invited the destruction of religious shrines, such as that to Thomas Becket at Canterbury, destroyed in 1538. The visitation of shrines was a 'work', in Protestant theology, and forbidden for that reason. No less abhorrent was belief in relics and their miracle-working properties. The famous Rood of Grace and the Blood of Hailes were investigated by Cromwell's commissioners and unmasked as frauds. The first was venerated as a living crucifix; but upon examination it was discovered to be full of 'certain engines and old wire with old rotten sticks in the back of the same, that did cause the eyes of the same to move and stare in the head thereof like unto a lively thing.' The second was a vial of liquid venerated as the blood of Christ. Examination showed the substance to be blood-like, but nothing besides tradition could establish it as the Savior's blood; and when the bishop of Rochester, citing hearsay evidence, denounced the substance as duck blood instead, the relic was discredited. In order for Christianity to become gospel-centered and Protestantised, it was necessary that shrines, relics, saints, and images all be expunged from the faith.

The Bishops' Book

Another action set in motion by the Pilgrimage of Grace, or deferred until the rebellion's end, was elaboration upon the Ten Articles of 1536, the new catechism of the English church issued by Convocation under Cromwell's headship. In February 1537 Henry created a commission to flesh out the full meaning of the Articles and to publish its findings for all to read. The commission was chaired by Cromwell, as the Vicegerent of Spirituals; its members consisted of the bishops of the realm and twenty-five of the lesser clergy. From the start the commission divided along conservative–radical lines. The conservatives, such as Stokesley of London, wanted a more faithful adherence to Catholic doctrine, especially acknowledgement of the sacramental character of confirmation, extreme unction, holy orders, and matrimony. The Articles had recognised only the Protestant-approved three – baptism, communion, and penance (this last a disputed sacrament among Protestants) – and was silent about the remaining Catholic-approved four. The radicals, such as Latimer of Worcester, wanted a vernacular Bible in the hands of the laity, since direct access to the word of God would liberate believers from the expository monopoly held by church doctors. On the matter of sacraments, the radicals let a visitor speak for them, a Scottish theologian named Alexander Alesius, whom Cromwell invited to witness the proceedings. Alesius took the position that Scripture confirmed the divine institution of only two sacraments, baptism and communion, and that all others were human-made, the product of hazy custom and conciliar decrees. The radicals gladly supported his advanced views. But the conservatives were offended; and to keep the peace, Cromwell encouraged Alesius to write down his opinions for circulation, but to refrain from attending future meetings.

Edward Foxe, bishop of Hereford and vice-chair of the commission, was the person most responsible for crafting the compromise statement, for compiling the various parts, and for editing the whole. The book that went forth in July 1537 was titled *The Institution of a Christian Man*; but it was commonly known as the *Bishops' Book* because when completed it had not received the imprimatur of the king. Henry gave the book only a casual review. When finally he did study the work, in December, he discovered that he did not care for it at all; for by his lights, it exuded Protestant heresy. Particularly obnoxious was its affirmation of 'justification by faith alone'. This red flag of Lutheran doctrine suffused the text, causing Henry, as supreme head, to make 246 alterations. In one instance he inserted two small adverbs, 'only' and 'chiefly', which effectively converted 'justification by faith' into 'justification by works'. It did seem to be his conviction that faith was but a profession of belief, not a transformative experience putting the believer in communion with God, and that works mattered greatly, making individuals accountable for their deeds. He insisted upon inclusion of all seven sacraments – having written a defense of the seven against Luther in 1521. The *Bishops' Book* restored the four sacraments missing from the Articles, but it accorded them second-class status to the other three. Henry objected to the distinction, while creating a distinction of his own, one which gave pride of place, ironically, to matrimony. But his corrections were not all reactionary. He let stand the book's Protestant description of the clergy as a body charged with preaching the word more than administering the sacraments or saying the mass; also as a body close to the laity, lacking an indelible mark that sets it apart; and as a body whose members are equal, not separated hierarchically into bishops and priests. Henry even did the bishops one better by removing the modifier 'holy' from holy orders.

It was Cranmer, the archbishop, who had to deal with Henry's editorial improvements. Cranmer instructed, argued, tried involving Cromwell, and put up a brave defense; but in the end he yielded on most points. Cranmer sent the revised version back to the king in the spring (1538). But as it was more than Henry was prepared to review a second time, permission was granted to publish the book unchecked, provided that it was issued under the bishops' names. It thus became the *Bishops' Book*, not the king's (a book called the *King's Book* came out in 1543). The withholding of the royal seal meant that the formulary was still in flux and that doctrinal battles would continue.

The English Bible

Humanist thinkers of the northern Renaissance pegged Europe's rebirth less to the reclamation of ancient art and literature, as the Italians had done, than to the revitalization of an original Christianity contained in the books of Scripture, translated into vernacular languages, and disseminated by the printing press, recently invented. Erasmus took the first half-step with his 1516 Latin translation of the Greek New Testament (bypassing the Latin Vulgate, utilised throughout the Middle Ages). Thomas More applauded his friend's effort. But More was less welcoming of William Tyndale's English translation of the New Testament in 1525; for by then Martin Luther had appeared on the scene, and vernacular translations had become the rallying cry and chief demand of the Protestant heretics (plus Tyndale's version included prologues and marginalia that were aggressively anti-Catholic). Whether to proceed then with the translating project was for Catholic intellectuals a controversial matter, one made all the more problematic by the doctrinal hair-splitting and sectarian quarreling which access to the Bible had produced among German and Dutch Protestants.

The king was cool to the idea in 1530; and his attempts to recruit Tyndale's pen in 1531 blew up when Tyndale disclosed his hostility to the divorce and conditioned his return to England upon the king's sanctioning a vernacular translation of the Bible. But several years later – with the Reformation by then a success – new clerics, new counselors, and a new queen had come to the fore, men and women better disposed toward Protestant belief and practices. The king yielded to their collective importuning, and upon request by Convocation (December 1534), he authorised work on an English translation to go forward. The official plan involved piecemeal translations by ten of the bishops; and while some applied themselves competently and diligently to the task, most did not, and in 1538 the project was abandoned. The fall-back plan relied on a translation by Miles Coverdale, begun in 1534, completed in 1535, and brought to England in 1536. Coverdale was a one-time Augustinian friar and Cromwell friend, who had thrown off his cowl and moved to Antwerp to immerse himself in Lutheran thought. Lacking knowledge of Greek and Hebrew, he provided no original translation but stitched together previous and partial translations by Luther, Zwingli, Tyndale, and others, while imparting to the whole a consistent and mellifluous phrasing of his own. A new title page was added meant to smooth the path to royal approval: its dedication described Henry as the 'chief head of all the congregation of the church'; its frontispiece, a woodcut by the great Hans Holbein, showed Henry in the line of succession of Old Testament prophets and New Testament apostles. Thus flattered, the king bestowed his blessing on the Coverdale translation, ignoring its dependency on Tyndale and objections from the bishops (still slogging away on their official version). It sold out quickly, and two new editions were printed.

Soon though it had a competitor. John Rogers, a chaplain to the Merchants Adventurers in Antwerp and an associate of Tyndale and Coverdale, produced a rival translation in 1537, which likewise earned the king's sanction. Rogers adopted the pseudonym Thomas Matthew; and so his translation was known as the 'Matthew Bible'. It was better liked by Cranmer and the bishops, because its translator knew the ancient languages, and because, with notes appended to the text, it satisfied the bishop's exacting standards of scholarship. Still the Matthew Bible borrowed from Tyndale, from French translators, and from Coverdale.

Then came a third Bible, the 'Great Bible', called that because of the size of its type. In this Bible, Cromwell had a personal stake, having invested hundreds of pounds in the venture. The work was a revision of Matthew, done though by Coverdale and by Coverdale's printers, Richard Grafton and Edward Whitchurch. It also was outsourced to a French printing house because English technology was judged unequal to the task. A special license was needed from Francis I, which Gardiner, the English ambassador, managed to obtain. But the license fell short of affording essential protections from the inquisitor-general, who in December 1538 shut the operation down. Fearing arrest, Grafton and Whitchurch fled to England. Cromwell appealed to Francis to intervene, to permit resumption of the work, or, at a minimum, to allow the printed sheets, the type, and the presses to be sent to England. Two months later permission to ship was granted, and by April 1539 the book was finished.

In anticipation of its publication, and before the excitement occasioned by the inquisitor-general, Cromwell issued a second set of Vicegerent Injunctions. In September 1538 he ordered that a copy of the Great Bible be purchased by every church in the land, to be paid for by parsons and parishioners equally. To help defray the expense, the price charged was set at about a quarter less than what the printers had said would be needed, unless a monopoly on the printing of Bibles were granted to them. A five-year monopoly was thus granted, but to Cromwell, not to the printers, whose profits depended on licensing by the minister. The Injunctions further ordered that the Bible be displayed for convenient reading by the laity; that lay-study be strongly encouraged by clergy; and that obscure scriptural passages be referred to learned men for proper exegesis, lest interpretive attempts by the laity result in disputation and scandal ('refer the explication of obscure places to men of higher judgement in Scripture'). This caution showed that the Reformation was content to move at a measured pace toward its Protestant desideratum – lingering indefinitely in a *via media* faith that involved the laity right up to the point where their participation became embarrassing. Unrelated to Bibles, but no less important, was the injunction to parish churches to keep a register of births, deaths, and marriages. Country people were suspicious of the registers at first, because they seemed like instruments for easy taxation; but their main use, besides providing a census of the population, was to settle cases involving impediments to marriage.

Overtures to Germany

In the spring of 1538, about when the *Bishops' Book* was being published and plans for the Great Bible were being laid, England tried a third time to establish diplomatic ties with the Lutherans of Germany. The last effort resulted in a joint accord signed by ambassadors Foxe and Heath making Henry the protector of the League of Schmalkalden, while committing Henry to acceptance of the *Augsberg Confession* and the Wittenberg Articles. For two years nothing further happened; but now that England was moving rapidly in a Protestant direction, the time seemed right for finalizing the alliance. Certainly Cromwell believed that his king had since come a long way and that with a step or two more he could satisfy the Germans and have them as allies. In May the German embassy arrived. Its head was Franz Burkhardt, vice-chancellor of Saxony; accompanying him were Frederick Myconius, a noted Lutheran theologian, and George Boyneburg, a lawyer. Matrimonial proposals constituted the primary business; but theological conformity was what interested the Germans most. Would the English church show its enlightenment by outlawing clerical celibacy and private masses? Would it endorse the distribution of communion in both species (wine as well as bread) to the laity? Cranmer was ready to agree; but his negotiating team included conservatives like Stokesley and Tunstall who were not. Their interest lay in the status of the sacraments denied by Protestants. Would the Germans, they countered, moderate their radicalism and accept the time-honored teachings of the church in these matters? Positions hardened over the summer months and into the autumn. Neither side was quite ready to make the concessions needed for an alliance; nor did the king much like being told by his inferiors what he must believe. In October the Germans gave up and departed, but with gifts and words of thanks from the king and the promise to try again.

That he did, early in the next year, dispatching Christopher Mont to Germany to renew negotiations with the leaders of the Schmalkaldic League. The result of Mont's talks with John Frederick, elector of Saxony, and Philip I, landgrave of Hesse was a new German embassy sent to London and arriving in April 1539. Again Franz Burkhardt was the head; his associate was Ludwig von Baumbach, a counselor to Philip. Cromwell involved himself closely in these discussions, some of which took place in his home. He arranged for a debate at St James palace with Privy councilors and the Lord Chancellor present and participating. He pressed the case for alliance and explained its advantages to the king. But before action could be taken – and indeed all the while the negotiations were in progress – the international terrain was shifting seismically, ending all hope of England's coming to terms with the Schmalkaldeners (see 'The Cleves Alliance' in chapter 9).

The Heresy Trial of John Lambert

In point of fact, Henrician Protestantism had reached its apex some months prior to the spring of 1539. Its actual zenith was the previous summer; for by then the larger monasteries were falling almost daily; religious shrines were coming down too; the Ten Articles, adumbrated by the *Bishop's Book*, was as yet the authoritative formulary, enforced by a second round of Vicegerent Injunctions; vernacular Bibles were in print, in multiple translations, and up for sale; and the campaign against the White Rose was underway. But almost simultaneous with the destruction of White Rose adherents was the trial and execution of a prominent Protestant sectary. This was John Lambert, born John Nicholson of Norwich.

Lambert began his trouble-making career at Cambridge's White Horse Tavern, the meeting place of England's first Lutherans. With him in the mid-1520s were Hugh Latimer, Robert Barnes, Thomas Bilney, William Tyndale, and others of a radical bent of mind. After his time at Cambridge, Lambert served as chaplain to the Merchant Adventurers in Antwerp, where he dipped deep into the waters of religious extremism, proselytizing on behalf of the Anabaptist creed. Upon his return to England in 1531, he was examined by Lord Chancellor More; but with help from the archbishop, William Warham, Lambert managed to escape. Another archbishop, Thomas Cranmer, came to his defense in 1536 when the duke of Norfolk brought charges of heresy. Again Lambert eluded serious punishment; he was imprisoned briefly, but then set free to continue his unorthodox preaching. By 1538 he was openly professing the Sacramentarian heresy, and even fellow radicals like Barnes thought it prudent to rein in his excesses. In November Lambert was ordered to appear before the archbishop for interrogation. But rather than submit, as he had once before, Lambert foolishly challenged Cranmer's jurisdiction and appealed his case to the king.

Henry was pleased to be called upon in this way. He liked theological debate for its own sake; and for policy's sake, he welcomed the opportunity to pounce on a heretic, since fences needed mending with Europe's Catholic powers. Whitehall was chosen as the place for the trial. Grandstands were constructed in the banquet hall to accommodate the crowds; spiritual and temporal peers were in attendance; and Henry, as Solomonic judge, sat on his throne attired all in white. An opening speech by Richard Sampson, bishop of Chichester, stated the premise and set the tone: the establishment of royal supremacy and concomitant rejection of papal authority was not an invitation for schismatics to run loose in the land. The burden was on Lambert to prove that he was not a schismatic, more particularly to recant his Sacramentarian beliefs and affirm publicly the Lord's presence in the sacrament of the altar. Henry put the question to him, and Lambert confessed that he could not in truth acknowledge the Eucharist to be the body and blood of Christ. The king thought otherwise, and to make his point, he produced Christ's words spoken at the Last Supper and over the raised bread – *Hoc est corpus meum* ('This is my body.'). What could be clearer than that? He then turned the accused over to the bishops for five hours of pile-on interrogation. At the end of their questioning, Henry spoke again, asking (in the words of John Foxe), 'What say you now, after ... all the reasons and instructions of these learned men? Are you not yet satisfied: Will you live or die? ... You have yet free choice.' Lambert replied, 'I commend my soul unto the hands of God, but my body I wholly yield and submit unto your clemency.' Henry assured him that there would be no clemency, for he, the king, would 'not be a patron unto heretics'. He called on Cromwell to read the sentence of guilt. Four days later, on November 20, Lambert was burned at Smithfield. Cromwell praised the king's person and actions in a letter to Wyatt:

> It was a wonder to see how princely, with how excellent gravity and inestimable majesty his highness exercised there the very office of a supreme head of the church of England, how benignly his grace assayed to convert the miserable man, how strong and manifest reasons his highness alleged against him. I wish the princes and potentates of Christendom ... to have seen it.

With Lambert's destruction, Henry was signaling Charles and Francis that while England was independent, it still was Catholic; and he was signaling Cromwell and Cranmer that while reform was wanted, the king alone would determine its limits.

What some of those limits were the king announced in a royal proclamation released on the day of Lambert's trial. Henceforth, the proclamation read, there would be no importation of books printed in English and no domestic printing without a license; also no translations into English without inclusion of the translator's name and no annotated Bibles printed or imported without permission of a named Privy councilor or bishop. Anabaptism and Sacramentarianism were proscribed and their adherents given ten days to exit the country. Public discussion of the sacraments was disallowed, except by university scholars. Neglect of and contempt for the rites and ceremonies of the church were forbidden; and unless specifically abolished, these rites and ceremonies (e.g., processions, purifications, offerings) were to continue in use. Clergy were enjoined to honor their vows of celibacy, and those having married were banned from administering the sacraments and holding offices and benefices. Otherwise clergy were instructed to preach clearly and simply the word of God so as to dampen superstition and strife among the laity. Finally, Thomas Becket, nemesis of King Henry II, was denied his status as martyr and saint, and images of him were ordered removed from all churches and use of his name ordered dropped from all services. Thus did censorship, persecution, and top-down control over doctrine and liturgy become the instruments of Henry's headship.

The 1539 Parliament and the Act of Six Articles

Concurrent with the arrival of the second German embassy in April 1539 was the convening of parliament. Described as the 'most tractable' parliament ever because of the winnowing of personnel worked by Cromwell, it nonetheless delivered a stinging set-back to Cromwell's Reformation project. The return of Stephen Gardiner from a long stint as ambassador to France was part of the reason. Early in the session parliament was informed of the king's desire to have diversity of religious opinion banished from the land; and a committee of lords was thereupon appointed to come up with articles of a uniform creed. The committee's membership divided evenly between reformers and conservatives, and the committee's deliberations, in the few days of meetings allowed to the bishops, were contentious and deadlocked. Norfolk intervened imperiously to declare the effort a failure; and, on Henry's orders, he instructed parliament to compose a new formulary in response to six propositions. The very stating of the questions, touching the issues of transubstantiation, communion in both species, clerical celibacy, vows of chastity and widowhood, private masses, and auricular confession, indicated that a return to orthodoxy was in the offing. Lest there be any doubt as to how the wind was blowing, the king communicated his wishes by visiting Lords and revising the draft legislation. Still, a prorogation was needed before this 'most tractable' parliament fell into line. It declared the bread and wine on the altar to contain the real presence of the Lord and nothing else (consecration having removed all trace of the natural substances); it declared the full Eucharist to be in the bread alone and the taking of wine by lay-persons not needed and not to be insisted upon; it reaffirmed the importance of celibacy and denied priests the right to marry; it made observance of vows of chastity and widowhood obligatory under the law of God; it approved of private masses as contributing to the consolation and benefit of Christian people; finally, it judged auricular confession, or confession to a priest, expedient and necessary and to be continued in use – all Catholic positions hotly resisted by Protestant reformers. But what gave the *Six Articles* its special bite – and its nickname 'the whip of six strings' – were the punishments attached: burning at the stake and forfeiture of goods, without the opportunity of abjuration, for anyone denying transubstantiation, the first article; imprisonment and forfeiture of goods for first-time offenders against the other five articles; for second-time offenders, death.

In the aftermath, two reform bishops, Latimer of Worcester and Nicholas Shaxton of Salisbury, resigned their positions, or were forced to resign. Cranmer survived and in fact was invited by Henry to write down his objections to the new legislation. Cranmer's small treatise, dictated to a secretary, was in transit across the Thames when a bear, swimming in the river, got loose from its handler and climbed aboard the skiff, sending both secretary and treatise into the water. The bear-handler retrieved the treatise; and learning of its heresy (from an orthodox priest in town), he headed for Hampton Court and Bishop Gardiner, who was expected to pay handsomely for such a prize. But Cranmer's secretary reached Hampton Court and Cromwell first, who intercepted the bear-handler before he could get to Gardiner. The treatise was reclaimed, and the archbishop was saved the embarrassment of having to defend himself from accusations by his conservative antagonist.

This 1539 parliament, which, as noted above, dissolved the larger monasteries, created new episcopal sees, and attainted past rebels, was additionally famous for giving royal proclamations the force of law. As judged by the preamble of the *Proclamations Act*, royal proclamations went little heeded in England 'for lack of a direct statute and law to coerce offenders'; and the 'regal dignity and the advancement of the commonwealth and the good quiet of [the] people' suffered in consequence. Nor was the king able to fulfill his executive responsibilities by affixing 'speedy remedies' to the country's problems, since he had to wait on parliament to assemble and to grant him legal authority. It therefore was decided that royal proclamations should be 'obeyed, observed, and kept as though they were made by act of parliament'. Three restrictions did apply (but with heresy proclamations exempted): Council was to be consulted; the lives, liberties, and estates of subjects were to be protected; and existing laws were not to be overridden.

Proclamations were not new with the passage of the act. Henry had used them before as had all of his predecessors. What was new was the legal sanctioning of the practice by act of parliament. In the estimation of some scholars, parliament had effectively surrendered its lawmaking authority to the crown and 'the golden age of Tudor despotism' had begun. Other scholars, however, disagree, supposing that a step had been taken toward bringing the royal prerogative under the panoply of parliamentary power. Much attention is paid to Cromwell's role in the matter and to whether the minister intended the autocratic or the republican result. The fact that he assisted

Henry in packing the parliament (nullifying the results of the 1536 Canterbury elections so as to favour the royal nominees: 'I require you on the king's behalf, that notwithstanding the said election, you proceed to another and elect those other') is proof to some of his despotic proclivities. The fact that he once requested a judicial ruling about the legality of proclamations (one in 1535 regulating the export of coin) is proof to others of his rule-of-law proclivities. Probably he inclined both ways, because probably he recognised the emerging importance of a deliberative assembly and the continuing importance of an energetic executive, each supplying the deficiencies of the other. But there can be no knowing for sure, since at the time there was no clear understanding of the powers of government, much less of their separation and interaction. Still, the 1539 parliament was hardly one to stir the hopes and aspirations of limited-government advocates.

9

Matrimonial Diplomacy

From the summer of 1536 to the summer of 1538, England enjoyed easy relations with its continental neighbours, France and Spain. They were again at war over Italy, and their hostility left England free to strike friendly poses and play the neutral arbiter. Given that these were the years of domestic insurrection (the Pilgrimage of Grace, the Exeter Conspiracy), the sparring abroad relieved England of the danger of a coordinated rebellion-invasion (something Reginald Pole was trying belatedly and fecklessly to arrange). So safe did Henry feel that he issued a manifesto denouncing the pope's planned general council at Mantua and permitted Cromwell and Cranmer to take the English Reformation in a decidedly Protestant direction (Ten Articles).

What set France and Spain to fighting was the death of the heirless duke of Milan (Francesco Sforza, in November 1535) and the determination of Francis to claim the duchy for himself, having attempted the same two decades prior. In preparation for the main assault, French armies spent the spring overrunning towns in Savoy and Piedmont. Charles countered by attacking along France's southern coast and north from the Low Countries. Neither side gained much advantage, as defense stymied offense in both theaters of war. Finally, when resources were exhausted, the king and the emperor decided to call a halt; and under the auspices of Pope Paul, a truce was negotiated at Nice in June 1538.

Wife Shopping

In the midst of these events, King Henry once again entered the marriage market. His union with Jane Seymour, in May 1536, issued in the birth of a baby boy, Edward, in October 1537. At last, after several wives and many lost heads, the king had his male heir (Edward VI, r. 1547–53). But Henry had the queen who performed this signal service for only twelve days more. Jane died on October 24 of complications from the caesarean delivery. Never one to mourn his dead wives, Henry put out feelers for a replacement queen within the week.

Cromwell directed the search outward, concerned that an English bride, in elevating her family, would bring to court a new faction potentially hostile to the minister himself. Henry too seemed tired of the troubles caused by English in-breeding and was eager to exploit the freedom which a legitimate heir provided.

Early overtures regarding prospective mates reflected the confidence of a diplomatically secure monarch capable of stirring jealousies and alarms all across Europe. Henry would consider the hands of the French king's daughter, Margaret, or the duke of Guise's daughter, Mary, preferring whichever of the two the Scottish king, James V, was himself eyeing and planning to wed ('inquire … in what point and terms the said king of Scots stands towards either of them, which his highness is so desirous to know,' wrote Cromwell to England's ambassadors). The marriage would thus serve the purpose of wrecking Franco–Scottish relations; and Henry was sufficiently sure of his bargaining position and personal desirability that he expected the French to renege on promises made to the Scottish king, even though in doing so they would be offending a valued ally of long duration. Mary of Guise, the favourite, was sounded out in December 1537, and in February a picture of her was obtained for royal perusal. But Henry had miscalculated his appeal and mistimed his declaration of interest. For preparations were well advanced by the start of the year for a James–Mary union; and by May the two were wed.

Henry was not discouraged. An Anglo–Imperial alliance would do just as well as an Anglo–French alliance. Plus the lady he had now in mind was perfectly pedigreed to disrupt continental affairs in ways advantageous to England. This was Christina, the daughter of the deposed Danish king, Christian II, the niece of the emperor, and the widow of the duke of Milan. If she were heir to the duchy (its future was then uncertain), Henry would be in possession of a prize fought over incessantly by Francis and Charles and able to determine its allegiance. Hans Holbein was sent to draw sketches of the girl, and private interviews were conducted by gentlemen of the Privy Chamber. Cromwell composed the speech that the emissary delivered: 'It may please you ... to sit so long at some such time ... that a servant of the king's highness being come hither for that purpose may take your physiognomy.' The king liked what he saw and heard. There were, however, difficulties with the alliance, some of them caused by Henry's self-satisfied over-reaching. Henry demanded England's inclusion in any peace negotiations between the powers, and he demanded the emperor's promise to oppose the general council, called by the pope but already past due. At the same time Henry was hoping to accomplish two unions at once, his to the duchess of Milan (Christina), and his daughter Mary's to the infante of Portugal. But Mary was illegitimate – at her father's insistence – and an illegitimate offspring was an indifferent marital prize. Also, the duchess was the grand niece of Catherine; so impediments applied and dispensations would be needed. But who would provide them? Here was a question impossible to resolve, since the Reformation's validity would either be confirmed or repudiated by the choice of agents – the Canterbury archbishop or the Roman pope. (The Imperial camp referenced this very problem whenever it suited their purposes to delay. Cromwell described their concerns thus: 'that for the duchess' part, the matter cannot be concluded without the bishop of Rome's dispensation for nearness of blood', since 'the dispensation to be had in this realm [England] ... should not be sufficient'.) Nor was the duchess, a mere teenager, keen on the idea of taking a husband with a record of brutalizing his wives. She remarked sardonically that if she had two heads, she might then chance it. Henry though was excited by the prospect of the match, and the duchess for him was the frontrunner in the marriage sweepstakes.

More proposals were soon to follow. The French in May came up with a double-marriage scheme of their own – of Mary to Francis' youngest son, Charles, and of Henry to Louise of Guise, younger sister of the 'loved-and-lost' Mary. Again, Henry was excited; and again Holbein went forth to sketch the intended. Cromwell orchestrated the entire campaign, showing exquisite sensitivity to the delicacies of third-party wooing. Then in August a third Guise sister entered the lists, Renée, the most beautiful of them all. More travel for Holbein, who while in France was given the names of three additional maidens to draw for Henry – a sister and two cousins of Francis. That made five on the French side (Mary of Guise was now married, and Margaret, the daughter, was never seriously in the running, for she was 'not the meetest'). Pictures were not obtainable of them all, and in any event Henry wanted to see for himself in a matter that touched him so nearly. Thus he proposed that the bevy of beauties assemble in Calais for his personal inspection. He thought that he was being efficient; the French thought that he was being a cad, and they embarrassed him by contrasting his boorish behavior to the chivalry of the Round Table knights. Eventually though the French agreed to send one lady only, for any more would be to treat the noblewomen of France as hackney horses for sale at auction.

War Fever

Henry's request was not only gauche, but inopportune, as summer 1538 saw the end of hostilities between France and the Empire. The truce of Nice, above mentioned, changed the game board dramatically, with England no longer the courted ally but instead the heretic outcast. England was not party to the negotiations (one of Henry's marriage demands), and English interests were not advanced by the cease-fire, projected to last for ten years. Under its terms, France would return its acquisitions in Savoy and Piedmont, in exchange for which the duchy of Milan would go to Francis' youngest son. Shortly after, Charles and Francis met again at Aigues Mortes to continue the good cheer of Nice and to join together in recriminating Henry.

The pope appreciated this favourable turn of events and moved to have published his much-threatened and much-delayed excommunication order against Henry (December 1538). Indecisiveness was not the cause of delay, rather the want of enforcement power. For it was no use excommunicating Henry and threatening him with the loss of his crown, if France and the Empire were unwilling to do their part to pressure England. Their part entailed the suspension of diplomatic relations, the cutoff of international trade, the postponement of Turkish operations, and, should sterner measures be needed, the incitement of insurrection and the invasion of the island. After Christmas, 1538, Pope Paul made Reginald Pole his emissary to the Imperial and French courts, charged with enlisting Charles and Francis in a crusade against England. (Only days before Reginald's brother, lord Montague, had been executed by Henry.) At the same time Paul raised David Beaton to a cardinal of the church and returned him to Scotland, his native land, to encourage King James to join the crusade. Finally, in January 1539, Charles and Francis signed the treaty of Toledo, committing each ruler to consultation and agreement before marital and political alliances could be formed with England.

Henry's England had never been this imperiled before – not in 1535 when the emperor was outfitting a new fleet; not in 1536 when the Pilgrims were in open rebellion. Catholic Europe, at peace and united, was at last able to chastise the schismatic Henry and turn back the Reformation. And in the early months of the year, Catholic Europe seemed willing as well. France and Spain recalled their ambassadors without clearly indicating that others would take their places. Imperial warships rendezvoused at Antwerp and Boulogne, and transports in great number were brought together at Zeeland; meanwhile English vessels in the region were seized and impounded. Thomas Wriothesley, England's ambassador to the Netherlands, relayed to Cromwell intelligence of impending war: 'The French king, the bishop of Rome, and the king of Scots are in a league to invade England this summer, and ... the emperor will allow certain Spaniards to go to Scotland, as it were, against his will, who shall swear never to return until they have avenged the dowager [Catherine].' More overt measures had been taken by the emperor as well, and more formidable forces had been assembled, which, if directed against Henry (not yet clear), would make England 'but a morsel amongst these choppers'. England in turn commandeered foreign vessels docked at London and at Southampton. But England needed an ally to meet the danger, and, as usual, it looked to Germany for aid.

In negotiations with the Schmalkaldic princes, Christopher Mont proposed a marriage alliance uniting England to the House of Cleves, a duchy along the northern Rhine strategically positioned between the emperor's possessions in the Netherlands and in Germany. Henry would wed the elder daughter of the duke – Anne – and Mary would wed the son – William, soon to be the duke himself. Cleves was not a member of the League of Schmalkalden, for Cleves was not Protestant. But neither was it orthodox Catholic, since like England it had thrown off the suzerainty of the pope. In fact, Duke John's religion was closer to Henry's than that of any other ruler in Europe. At the same time, the duke was 'family' to the arch-Protestant elector of Saxony and Schmalkaldic head, John Frederick, who had married the Cleves daughter Sybille. The elector agreed to promote the English alliance. His support was key, since William, upon inheriting from his father in February 1539, promised not to marry off either of his sisters – Anne or Amelia – without consulting John Frederick first. In order to demonstrate the earnestness of the proposal and the solid hope for success, Mont was instructed to communicate to the Cleves representative that the 'Lord Privy Seal [was] much desirous thereof'.

During these anxious winter months (and presciently for some years before), Cromwell directed a massive build-up of the country's defenses: forty warships constructed and preparations made for conscripting merchant vessels in case of need; castles built at vulnerable points along the southern and eastern coastlines; beacons set up on hilltops; and levies mustered from shires across the realm – all of this effort paid for by the wealth of the dissolved monasteries. In order to impress the enemy with England's readiness for war, Cromwell took the French ambassador, before his return home, on a tour of the royal armoury in the Tower of London and of Cromwell's own armoury, boasting that there were twenty more 'particular armouries' kept by lords and gentlemen far better supplied. The ambassador was duly impressed, admitting to Cromwell that Henry was 'the prince best furnished thereof in Christendom' (*Dis*, II.10: arms, not money, being the sinew of war, show the enemy your armoury not your treasury).

Perhaps it did matter that the realm had moved quickly to repair its tottering defenses and that Castillon, the ambassador, reported back evidence of England's competent vigor. But other factors were also in play, causing the air to seep out of the invasion balloon. Charles was reluctant to turn northward when his main theaters of operation lay in the south and in the east. He was happy to bluff and encourage others to fight for him, but little else would he do. When Reginald Pole came calling, Charles refused to commit: he would not publish the excommunication order or terminate commerce, much less agree to invade. Francis, for his part, was willing to commit, on condition that Charles was in the English campaign to the end; but few were the signs to indicate Imperial constancy. Thus Reginald Pole was advised not to come calling – the excuse being that Henry would catch on to the plot – but to stay at the papal city of Carpentras where he had gone to await further instructions. Instructions never came from Francis summoning Pole to court, and Pole bided his time through the spring and summer of 1539 dodging assassination by Cromwell's men.

The high tide of war panic crested in mid March then began abating by April. A new French ambassador, Marillac, arrived unexpectedly to assume the post vacated by Castillon. He was warmly received at court, and warmly did he assure Henry of Francis' enduring friendship. Marillac did not of course reveal the true nature of his mission, which was to keep Henry in a 'good humour' while Francis waited on the emperor to decide about war. But since Charles was not going to decide for war, Anglo–French relations continued to improve through the weeks ahead. In consequence, the parliament of 1539 adopted policies conciliatory toward the Catholic continent, most especially the *Act of Six Articles*, meant to remove the rationale behind the pope's crusade for orthodoxy and unity.

The Cleves Alliance

The converse of better relations with France was worse relations with Germany. The embassy that arrived in the spring representing the Schmalkaldic League was at first cordially entertained, for Henry was not yet sure that France and the Empire had abandoned their invasion plans. But as Henry grew more confident, his attitude toward the Germans grew more obdurate. They wanted a Protestant England; he wanted a defense alliance against the Empire, rooted most likely in his marriage to a Cleves kinswoman or his daughter's marriage to a Cleves duke. Then a shock from without caused these difficult negotiations to collapse (see 'Overtures to Germany' in chapter 8). The Schmalkaldeners, who had been meeting with the emperor's representative since February at the Frankfort diet, in mid April initialed a treaty, which, for its duration, forbade the emperor from meddling in the religious affairs of the League and which forbade the League from taking on any new members. Henry learned of the treaty in May. He charged betrayal, and was right to do so, for England's discussions with the League had been predicated on the assurance that Henry would become its head. The emissaries were ordered to pack their bags and leave, which reluctantly they did after vain attempts to prove good faith and point out English benefits accruing from the Frankfort accords.

The Cleves alliance was a somewhat different matter, since Cleves was not part of the League. Negotiations for Henry's marriage to Anne continued uninterrupted, with Christopher Mont, Nicholas Wotton, and William Petre serving serially as lead ambassadors. In a March dispatch, Mont reported favourably on

Anne's appearance, saying that everyone thought she excelled the duchess of Milan 'as the golden sun does the silver moon'. Still, a picture was needed to confirm her unparalleled beauty. The local artist, Lucas Cranach, was then ill, but luckily portraits of Anne and Amelia had been painted six months earlier. Their delivery was promised as soon as they could be found in storage at Cologne. But were they faithful representations? Mont spoke only second-hand; and Wotton confessed that he was in no position to vouch for the likenesses, since he had seen 'but a part of [the women's] faces, and that under such a monstrous habit and apparel, was no sight, neither of their faces nor of their persons'. To this objection, his counterpart, the chancellor, replied, 'Would you see them naked?' Probably he would, if he could; but plainly he could not, propriety disallowing what caution demanded; so the women were examined fully appareled. Petre arrived in July to perform the inspection and to hurry along the portraits, as yet not produced. Hope for these wayward pictures ran out in August, and Holbein was sent to do sketches and then paintings, as so often before. Meanwhile Wotton, in August, commented on Anne's character and accomplishments:

> She occupies her time most with the needle ... she can read and write her [native tongue, but] French, Latin, or other languages she has none, nor yet can she sing nor play upon any instrument, for they take it here in Germany for a rebuke and an occasion of lightness that great ladies should be learned or have any knowledge of music. Her wit is good, and she will no doubt learn English soon when she puts her mind to it. I could never hear that she is inclined to the good cheer of this country ... Your Grace's servant Hans Holbein has taken the effigies of my lady Anne and the lady Amelia and has expressed their images very lively.

The desirability of Anne's person was only one facet of the negotiations, which both sides had reason to delay. Duke

William was hesitant to enter into an alliance ostensibly hostile to the emperor; and he felt his pride insulted when imposed upon to accept an illegitimate daughter for a wife. He required considerable and constant persuasion by the elector of Saxony and the English emissaries before warming to the idea. And when he did warm, the elector suddenly cooled – his drop in temperature caused by the passage of the *Act of Six Articles* in early summer, which reinforced the German impression of Henry as intransigently Catholic or perfidiously profane. There also was a legal question regarding Anne's marital eligibility, since a 1527 precontract betrothed her to the son of the duke of Lorraine. In moments of worry and indecision, the terms of the precontract seemed unbreakable to the Germans and the documents pertaining to the case impossible to locate and provide. Henry in turn was facing the prospect of marrying many degrees beneath his station, uniting his Tudor greatness to a minor German duchy by way of a second daughter at that. Moreover, the best explanation for the inclusion of Amelia's portrait along with Anne's – the former offered though not requested – was that the Germans were planning a last-minute substitution of Amelia for Anne, leaving Henry with a third daughter instead of a second. Also, Henry hoped that France and the Empire would return to their normal bellicosity and that a German marriage would not be necessary – the Germans, in general, being such difficult people on points of religion. Finally, in mid summer the emperor re-floated the idea of Henry's marrying the Imperial candidate, the duchess of Milan. Some time was required to examine – and dismiss again – this alternative choice. Thus in July both sides stopped to reconsider.

In August, though, things began to change, and not even the arrival of Wotton's unflattering description was enough to arrest the building momentum. Charles refused to sign the Frankfort treaty negotiated by his representative in April. Since the

Schmalkaldic Germans were now released from their obligations to the emperor, they again became available for alliance with England. Henry valued their friendship on those occasions and to that degree that he feared the enmity of France and the Empire (though these geopolitical considerations are minimised by one scholar). And in late summer, he had cause again to fear. His tilt right with the *Six Articles* had not earned him the good will he expected. Francis was playing him, as he came to realise; and the pope was still pressing for publication of the bull of excommunication and deposition. Meanwhile Charles was prevailing upon Francis to join in the fight against the Turks. Then it was learned that another summit was planned between the French and the Imperial heads of state, at Loches for later in the year. But what Henry found most disconcerting was the report that Francis had offered Charles safe passage across French territory. Given the history between these monarchs – including the imprisonment of Francis by Charles fourteen years earlier – entrusting the Imperial court to the French king's protection was an incredible act of faith, one which the ambassador described as 'either a great remedy to the affairs of Christendom, or, on the contrary, the greatest inconvenience which could happen in our time'. By the same token, the show of confidence which such a journey represented was 'the greatest honor a king of France ever received'. It also was understood that Henry was the loser, or would be if the journey came about, since one of its stated purposes was 'to stop the mouths of those who sought to sow jealousy between the two princes'.

The journey had also a military objective to go along with the diplomatic. In May a rebellion had broken out in Ghent over issues of taxes and religion, and Charles was determined to bring order to Ghent, the city of his birth, in person. Crossing overland through France was the easiest way to reach Ghent in east Flanders. But once in country – and here lay the problem – he might well endanger Cleves, not very far away.

The Cleves duchy was a recent composition consisting of the provinces of Jülich, Berg, Cleves, and Gelderland. Gelderland was added only the previous year, 1538, as a direct bequest to William from the heirless Duke Charles of Egmont. Charles, an inveterate adversary of the emperor, was set on willing his estates to whoever would cause the emperor the greatest aggravation. Originally that was the king of France; but local opinion was opposed, and so Gelderland went instead to William (not yet duke of Cleves). The emperor, however, thought Gelderland rightfully his, and he cautioned William not to accept the inheritance. But William ignored the caution and accepted what was given. Relations deteriorated from then on, with William viewed at court as a disloyal vassal. And now the emperor was coming to suppress rebellion in Ghent and perhaps thereafter to conquer Cleves. William needed an ally, and Henry topped the list of available candidates.

The elector of Saxony's approval was still required but was not easily to be gotten, Henry having so offended with his disdain for 'true religion' and his ill treatment of Saxony's ambassadors. But eventually John Frederick saw the danger to Cleves, and he even feared for the safety of the Schmalkaldic cities. His consent was communicated to Cromwell by way of Burkhardt at the end of August. By mid-September an embassy from Cleves and Saxony had arrived to recommence the marriage negotiations.

The problem that confronted the negotiators was Anne's supposed engagement to another. Not all of the documents had been found, or had been produced, but the ambassadors brought extracts purporting to explain the type of vows taken. These proved to be enough. Everyone was in a rush, and the manifold details regarding dowry and transportation, inheritance and widowhood were settled in the space of three weeks (not settled until February, however, was the defense pact between the two states). The marriage contract was signed on October 5, and the ambassadors left at once to provide escort for the wedding entourage.

That left Lady Mary. William would not accept her, so another suitor had to be found. English emissaries in Germany turned up the name of Philip of Bavaria of the powerful Wittelsbach family. Philip fit perfectly Henry's description of a desirable consort: he was Catholic, yet antipapal; he was close to the emperor (a member of the Order of the Golden Fleece), yet embittered by recent disappointments (reimbursements not paid for losses incurred, and permission not granted to marry the duchess of Milan); and he commanded modest forces available for loan as auxiliaries. He also was eager, betaking himself to London in December to negotiate the deal. Negotiations proved tricky, however: Mary was damaged goods; England was doctrinally mercurial; and Catholic Europe was talking war. Even so, the parties, in time, managed to agree. By the terms of the contract, Philip was to accept Mary 'as is', bastard child of the king, but was to receive a handsome dowry in lieu of her re-legitimation; and he was to supply specified numbers of cavalry and infantry, but he was not required to deploy them against his liege master, the emperor. Philip departed in late January, confident that his family would approve the alliance. They did not, and the venture collapsed.

Henry and Anne

A ship from the Netherlands to London would have been the quickest way to convey Anne to Henry. But the quickest way was not the safest way (the hazards of ocean sailing in winter months), nor the healthiest way (fears that Anne's constitution and complexion would suffer from the voyage). So overland travel through Imperial territories to Calais was decided on, once the necessary permits were obtained. It took the Cleves party a month to reach Calais, after which time another sixteen days passed before the party could sail for England, as bad weather made a Channel crossing impractical. While waiting, Anne was entertained by William Fitzwilliam, earl of Southampton, who endeavored to teach Anne Henry's favourite game of cards.

Anne arrived in Deal on December 27, recuperated there a day, then journeyed to Canterbury, where the archbishop greeted her on behalf of the king and the Lord Privy Seal. Cromwell wanted to make a good first impression, so he had Cranmer bestow a personal gift of fifty sovereigns on Anne. From Canterbury she traveled to Rochester, meeting with Norfolk who served as her host. Henry was at Greenwich, due to receive Anne on January 3. But anticipation so overcame him (or protocol simply required of him – as some scholars believe) that he rode to Rochester on New Year's Day to surprise his intended and to 'nourish love'. An account of the meeting, written by a member of the king's party, told how Anne was viewing a bear-baiting in the courtyard outside her window, when Henry, in disguise, embraced her, kissed her, and extended to her the king's New Year's gift. Startled, Anne responded politely but coolly to this masked stranger and returned to watching the contest below. Henry was taken aback; he left the chamber, replaced his costume with the royal purple, and reappeared as himself; whereupon the assembled lords, and Anne in imitation, bowed humbly to his grace. The account concluded with Henry and Anne lost in 'loving' conversation throughout the night and into the next day.

But after-the-fact accounts, some by Cromwell in prison, reported a different reaction altogether. Henry, by these accounts, was at once put off by the sight, the sound, and the dress of his bride-to-be. He failed to present the gift of furs he had brought for her and had it delivered by another the next day along with a curt note. On the return journey, he expressed his disappointment with Anne to Anthony Browne, his master of horse: 'I see nothing in this woman as men report of her; and I marvel that wise men would make such report as they have done.' Back at Greenwich he complained to Cromwell that had he 'known as much before as [he] then knew, she should not have come within this realm'. He repeated his initial harsh judgement, slightly amended, the following day: 'She is nothing so fair as she has been reported, howbeit she is well and seemly.' Seeing a chance to soften the king's opinion, Cromwell meekly added that he thought 'she had a queenly manner'.

Notwithstanding Henry's disenchantment, the reception of Anne and her retinue at Greenwich went on as planned. Few knew of the trouble that was brewing. The French ambassador did not, for he wrote that the king received Anne 'very graciously and conducted her into his house at Greenwich to the chamber prepared for her'. His impression of the queen, however, tracked closely Henry's own: older looking than her twenty-four years and of 'medium beauty' – an assessment which, when related by other emissaries, transmogrified into 'old and ugly.' But while the Greenwich reception came off on schedule, the wedding ceremony was delayed two days as Henry and his Council scratched their heads in desperate agitation searching for a way out of the engagement. Two matters, which still needed clarifying with the Germans, offered promise of escape: the status of the friendship covenant awaiting ratification by Cleves; and the validity of the 1527 marriage contract between Anne and Francis, son of the duke of Lorraine. The ambassadors conceded that they were not empowered to finalise terms of the political alliance, and they confessed that the documentary proof of Anne's freedom to marry had not been brought with them. The ambassadors seemed unprepared for questioning in these areas and asked for a day's adjournment. When pressed the next day on the second point in particular, they avowed that the precontract had been renounced; but having no paperwork to support their claim, they offered their persons as hostages until copies of the renunciation order and of the ratified treaty had been received. As an additional surety, Anne was prepared (and obliged) to swear before councilors and notaries that she was free from all contracts.

Strangely though, Henry did not seize upon the foot-dragging and broken promises of these German negotiators as his excuse for terminating the engagement. He rather lashed out at his councilors, charging that he had 'not been well handled' by them, while asking helplessly, 'Is there none other remedy but that I must needs against my will put my neck in the yoke?' It seemed that the muddle made of the marriage negotiations was not enough to provide Henry his sought-after release. For reasons small and great, he still felt himself trapped:

> If it were not that she is come so far into my realm and the great
> preparations that my states and people have made for her; [and if
> it were not] for fear of making a ruffle in the world that is to mean
> to drive her brother into the hands of the emperor and the French
> king's hands, being now well together, I would never have nor
> marry her.

'Being now well together' was to be taken literally. For at the very moment when Henry was entertaining Anne at Greenwich, Francis was feting Charles at Paris. The long procession of the Imperial court across France did occur in December (concurrent with Anne's journey to Calais). The monarchs met at Loches in mid-month, whence they proceeded northward in celebratory fashion, arriving on New Year's Day in Paris, where Charles and his courtiers were lodged at the Louvre. For eight days in early January Francis and Charles toasted each other's grandeur and pledged their undying friendship and loyalty.

England was thus vulnerable again, perhaps as much so as this time the year before. Cleves was its only ally; and a last-minute rejection of Anne would likely have turned Cleves into an enemy. If that had happened, Cleves perforce would have made peace with the emperor by relinquishing its claims to Gelderland, leaving the emperor free, aside from the Ghent disturbance, to direct his armies elsewhere. And England, isolated diplomatically, would have been one place for those armies to go – an appetizing morsel for the 'choppers' of Imperial power. Faced with this predicament, Henry VIII, on January 6, took Anne of Cleves to be his wedded wife. His troth he plighted with this touching vow of lasting love: 'If it were not to satisfy the world and my realm, I would not do that I must do this day for none earthly thing' (in truth, words spoken not to Anne at the altar, but to Cromwell as they departed the groom's chamber for the altar).

10

The Fall of Thomas Cromwell

The honeymoon did nothing to improve Henry's appreciation of Anne. Her lack of English was a complicating factor, as was Henry's taste in women. Cromwell made the mistake, after a day or two of wedded bliss, of asking how the royal couple was getting on. Henry barked out his disappointment and disgust: 'I liked her not well before, but now I like her much worse'; and he impugned Anne's figure and maidenhood: 'By her breasts and belly she should be no maid; which when I felt them struck me so to the heart that I had neither the will nor courage to the rest.' Henry slept with Anne often enough, but he would not – could not – consummate the marriage. Anne failed to excite him, her remarks to her chambermaids suggesting that she was innocent of feminine wiles and ignorant about carnal love. As far as she knew, sleeping with her husband meant merely that – sleeping – along with the exchange of pleasantries before dozing off and after waking up. Accordingly, the marriage for her was blissful, although the talk around court was of divorce.

Cromwell was answerable for this disaster of a marriage. He conducted the long-distance negotiations with Cleves. Correspondence passed through him and his office without ever receiving comment by Henry. The honour of the king required that he not be seen begging for a mate, so underlings had to woo in his stead. That was one reason for Cromwell's taking the lead; but so too was the objective of a German alliance, which Cromwell pursued more avidly than any other. Thus as Henry soured on his new wife and despaired of begetting additional heirs, he looked around for someone to blame; and who better than the Lord Privy Seal, who first reported on Anne's preeminent beauty, relaying the Mont *communiqué* that Anne of Cleves outshone Christina of Milan. Also Norfolk and Gardiner were at court, speaking libel in Henry's ear.

But Cromwell's grip on power depended less on the marital satisfaction of the king than on the continuing utility of the Cleves alliance. Henry married Anne, after all, for reasons of state, and for as long as those reasons remained valid, Cromwell was secure.

Mischief-Making at Royal Courts

January was a busy month. Besides receiving Philip of Bavaria (see 'The Cleves Alliance' in chapter 9), an embassy of Schmalkaldeners was in town, some as part of the queen's entourage; and English embassies went forth to Scotland and to Paris. The Schmalkaldeners, again led by Burkhardt and Baumbach, had come to register their objections to the *Act of Six Articles*, to urge England to embrace the true faith of Lutheranism, and to offer partnership with the League once a religious understanding had been reached. Such an alliance might superannuate the alliance with Cleves – an idea much relished by the king – but it would require up-front concessions on points of doctrine – an idea much to the king's disliking. Cromwell was instructed, when meeting with Burkhardt and Baumbach on the 12th, to press for a political alliance now and to offer assurances about a religious concordance to come. That he did, with apologies, saying that as the world stood, he could do no other than hold to his master's belief. The Germans refused his terms and left England on the 21st.

Meanwhile Ralph Sadler, a Cromwell secretary and longtime associate, was sent to Scotland to extend courtesies to King James and to discredit David Beaton, using – and misrepresenting – captured letters from a 1539 shipwreck which detailed papal instructions to the cardinal. The hope was to detach Scotland from France by dangling the possibility of James' one day succeeding to the English throne. James seemed receptive, as he proposed a meeting between Henry and himself; but as Francis was to be invited too, James seemed unwilling to conspire against a trusted ally. Still, Cromwell judged the mission a success and talked of a grand conference sometime in the future.

More important than the Sadler embassy to Scotland was the Thomas Wyatt and Edmund Bonner embassy to Paris. If Sadler was deputed to make nice, Wyatt (the poet) and Bonner (the bishop of London) were deputed to make trouble. Henry trusted that the permanent interests of France and the Empire would work against the occasional good will felt by Francis and Charles – given enough time and, if necessary, given meddling from without. Wyatt and Bonner were sent to meddle.

Among the exiles attainted in 1539 was Robert Brancestor, a colleague of Reginald Pole (and an ocean explorer). Brancestor was in France at this time as part of the emperor's train. Henry wanted him back in England to stand trial, and Wyatt and Bonner were charged with asking Francis to agree to his extradition. Francis did agree, not realizing that Brancestor was the emperor's subject, or claiming to be. Charles, when apprised of the matter, stood by Brancestor, extolling the services he had performed over ten or more years, disputing the validity of the charges against him, and objecting to his arrest and forced return home. For a brief moment it looked as if the two monarchs could be provoked into a fight. But Francis withdrew his consent, and the monarchs instead drew closer together. Their amity only strengthened when Bonner violated diplomatic protocol by remonstrating with the French king, who, indignant, demanded that Bonner be recalled. In the end it was Bonner, not Brancestor, who returned to England, and John Wallop (a Cromwell enemy) was sent in his place.

The embassy of real consequence though was that led by Norfolk, also to the French court. His mission was the same as Wyatt's and Bonner's, to cause a rift in Franco–Imperial relations. Norfolk arrived on February 14. Charles by then had left for Flanders, and Francis, unoccupied, received Norfolk promptly and cordially. Norfolk's instructions from Henry were to explain why Francis was being used by Charles (e.g., his need to put German affairs in order before renewing hostilities with France) and to inform Francis of a telling remark Charles had spoken recently to Wyatt. It seemed that when Wyatt complained to the emperor about his interference in the Brancestor case, citing treaty obligations and charging ingratitude (Henry had extradited a traitor wanted by Spain), the emperor fired back that he was no ingrate, for the superior could not be ungrateful to the inferior. Ingratitude was the vice of inferiors, of vassal states like England, and was hardly applicable to a liege lord like the emperor, who as temporal head of Christendom was everyone's temporal superior. Norfolk repeated the emperor's remark, translated into French so as to imply that France was compassed by it; and he suggested that the unbounded hubris of the emperor would preclude his returning Milan to French control. Norfolk reported that Francis was visibly disturbed and that he voiced his suspicions of the emperor's motives. This doubt, which Norfolk had sown, was validated later that month when Charles backed away from his promise to install Francis' son as duke of Milan.

The uprising in Ghent was put down in February by the emperor. Gelderland was his next objective, and he communicated to Duke William his demand for its surrender. The alliance with Cleves was intended to provide Henry with German auxiliaries in the event of an Imperial invasion of England. But by that same treaty Henry might now be called upon to supply troops to William in defense of Cleves. This unexpected development, on top of the manacling of Henry to a detested wife, caused Cromwell's stock at court to decline. At the same time, the perceived decoupling of Francis and Charles caused Norfolk's stock to rise.

Sectarian Follies

Cromwell was troubled along another front as well. One of his lieutenants, Robert Barnes, embroiled himself in a religious dispute with Stephen Gardiner, bishop of Winchester. Just back from Germany and the Low Countries where he had served as emissary to Protestant princes, Barnes was alarmed by the rightward turn of religious policy in England. He resolved to plant a flag and arrest the drift at a Lenten sermon delivered at Paul's Cross in March. Gardiner got wind of Barnes' plans and contrived to speak two weeks before him from the same pulpit. (Gardiner had been removed from Council in October 1539 for objecting to the appointment of Barnes.) A preacher's duel thus ensued in which Gardiner denounced Lutheran heresy in general and Barnes' version of it in particular, and Barnes insulted Gardiner and blasphemed against orthodoxy and the *Six Articles*. Gardiner complained to the king, who summoned both men before him and the Council. Henry's sympathies were plainly with the bishop, principal author of the *Six Articles*, and so Barnes found himself pressured to submit to Gardiner's instruction. Reluctantly Barnes agreed, and grudgingly Gardiner provided him a pension as reward for his humility. But it was not long before Barnes' radicalism burst forth again. When it did, just days later, a public recantation was demanded. Again Barnes retreated; but his abjuration was so measly and half-hearted that Henry ordered his arrest and the arrest of two of his followers. Cromwell wisely stayed out of the quarrel and extended no help in saving Barnes from imprisonment in the Tower. But Cromwell was not free of his friend's mess, since he was Barnes' longtime sponsor and had recently elevated Barnes to the prebend of Lambedye. Prudence demanded, therefore, that Cromwell too make peace offerings to the opposition.

On the same day that Barnes and company were arrested, Cromwell and Gardiner dined together at Cromwell's Bermondsey residence (March 30). The dinner lasted four hours, during which the two adversaries 'opened their hearts', forgave past wrongs, and pledged true friendship between themselves and their supporters. Neither of course intended true friendship, but a temporary truce was mutually beneficial, if only to quiet the rumours at court and reassure the king. Gardiner held the stronger hand, having been restored to the Council and to the king's favour, while Cromwell laboured under the triple disgrace of having procured a bad wife, negotiated a bad treaty, and associated with bad companions. But April brought a ray of sunshine in the form of French fortifications around Ardres, in the vicinity of and threatening to Calais. Renewed fears of a Franco–Imperial invasion, aggravated by an 'I'll fortify where I please' explanation from Francis, cast the Cleves alliance and its architect in a favourable light. On the other hand, a sumptuous party thrown by Gardiner at Winchester palace pushed Cromwell deep into the shadows, as Gardiner arranged to have paraded before Henry the duke of Norfolk's attractive young niece, Catherine Howard. A nubile teenager experienced in love, Catherine was everything erotic that dowdy old Anne, the 'Flanders mare', was not. Catherine also was Catholic and so a danger to Cromwell now entirely linked to Protestant reform.

The 1540 Session of Parliament

Cromwell had played his marriage card and come up empty. But he could still prove his worth as a lawmaker and manager of parliament. Parliament reconvened on April 12, having been prorogued at the 1539 session and having missed two previous start dates. Its task was to raise revenues and fix problems of varying description, such as the over-regulation of horse-bread baking and the theft of hawks' eggs. Cromwell, a member of Lords since 1536, addressed that body on its opening day with a Latin oration urging religious moderation. Cromwell's plan for a religious settlement was (and had always been) to split the difference between so-called papist corruption and superstition on the one hand, and so-called heretical radicalism and license on the other. His speech praised the king's attempts to bring Scripture to the people, but it lamented the scandal of quarreling sectaries (e.g., Gardiner and Barnes) and the discord caused by them. The king, the speech avouched, aimed for a golden mean, Cromwell's *via media*, not favouring either confessional extreme. As described by Cromwell, however, that mean seemed decidedly Protestant, insofar as the Word was the king's sure center around which orbited forms, rites, and traditions, permitted or not depending on judgements of their reasonableness and utility. The speech then called for the creation of two commissions to review the *Bishops' Book* of 1537/8, one to examine matters of doctrine, the other to examine matters of ceremony. Surprisingly, the clerics nominated to the doctrinal committee weighed heavily on the conservative side. This concession to orthodoxy did more than just rectify the rhetorical imbalance of the speech, for its practical effect was to cede control of the formulary to the Catholics – another sign that Cromwell held the weaker hand.

Cromwell could strengthen his hand by finding new money for Henry to spend. The monasteries had all been closed (the last one a month earlier), but overlooked in the dissolution was the order of the Knights of Malta, originally known as the Knights Hospitalers of St John of Jerusalem, and more recently as the Knights of Rhodes. This twelfth-century religious order was established to succor crusaders, Holy Land pilgrims, and the infirm. It hired crusaders to serve as bodyguards and in time incorporated them into the order, becoming thereby a religious and martial order combined. When expelled from the Holy Land (1187) and later from North Africa (1291), it regrouped on the island of Rhodes; and when expelled from Rhodes (1522), Charles V granted it rule over Malta (1530). In England at this time, the order owned forty-three wealthy houses, or commanderies, that had heretofore escaped suppression because of the history and reputation of the order and the ongoing charitable works of the knights – or because of oversight by the government. But an excuse to dissolve and expropriate was soon found. A handful of Mediterranean knights had recognised the supremacy of the English king, for which offense they were censored by the order's grand master (who, after all, was under Charles' protection). Henry was duly indignant, when notified of the fact by Cromwell. Legislation was thus drafted in Chancery and presented to parliament declaring the houses dissolved and their property forfeit on grounds that they acknowledged the authority of the pope and violated annates laws by sending tithed monies out of the realm.

A second infusion of cash came into the royal coffers by way of one lay and two clerical subsidy bills. The shires, cities, towns, and boroughs of England were to be taxed four fifteenths and tenths in loving gratitude for the peace, plenty, and enlightenment provided by the crown; more specifically, for the liberation of the realm from papal thralldom, the suppression of rebellion in Lincolnshire and the north country, the extension of law and justice to the Marches, the defense of the coastline and the augmentation of the navy, and the occupation and governance of Ireland. At the same time, the clergy were to pay additional taxes under the *First Fruits and Tenths Act* of 1534, with a special new tax laid upon the clergy of Canterbury. By some estimates, the amount collected by these several levies, plus the St John confiscations, came to £3,000,000, a sum far larger than the monies obtained from seizing the monasteries. Whatever the precise figure, the king was flush again, and the Lord Privy Seal was the magician who had conjured this bounty.

Henry was appreciative. He elevated Cromwell to the earldom of Essex and allowed the secretaryship which Cromwell then resigned to be bestowed on two of his loyal aides, Thomas Wriothesley and Ralph Sadler (both of whom took seats on the Council). Next, Henry appointed Cromwell Lord Great Chamberlain. Plainly Cromwell was back in favour, and the rumour-mill at court reflected his change in status. The French ambassador, who had only days earlier predicted Cromwell's imminent demise ('Cromwell is tottering'), reversed himself and reported to Francis that Cromwell was 'in as much credit with his master as ever he was, from which he was near being shaken by the bishop of Winchester and others'. German assessments were similarly unsteady, with some predicting a pogrom against Protestant believers and others declaring Cromwell effective king of the realm, dedicated to eviscerating the *Six Articles.*

Tipping the Scales

Cromwell elected to exploit his momentary advantage. He moved against two Gardiner allies, Richard Sampson, bishop of Chichester, and Nicholas Wilson, chaplain to the king (and lone survivor of the Fisher–More purge). These were charged with papist propensities and sent to the Tower. Five other bishops were thought to be under suspicion, causing a general panic inside the conservative camp. Lord Lisle, governor of Calais (and another Plantagenet), was ordered home to stand trial for conspiring with Reginald Pole. By the start of June, Cromwell's attack was in full swing. Attainders were passed in parliament against three Catholic priests: Thomas Abell (courier of messages from Catherine to the emperor, and in jail for six years), Richard Featherstone (tutor of Lady Mary), and Edward Powell (outspoken opponent of Luther and Latimer). Several others were likewise attainted at this time. Also, rumours circulated that Robert Barnes was about to be released from prison and that Hugh Latimer was about to be restored to his Worcester bishopric. Surveying the factional chessboard, the French ambassador gave the advantage to Cromwell: 'Things are brought to such a pass when either Cromwell's party or that of the bishop of Winchester must succumb. Although both are in great authority and favour of the king their master, still the course of things seems to incline to Cromwell's side.'

Parliamentary success and the titles betokening royal gratitude masked a fundamental weakness in Cromwell's position, however. The Cleves alliance was again becoming more bane than boon. The French had ceased their menacing of Calais, while the emperor had continued his menacing of Gelderland. Henry met with the Cleves ambassador at the end of May, and even though told that the emperor 'seemed to desire to be once in possession of Gelders', the response of Henry, this 'perfect friend' of Cleves, was to complain of the tardiness of communications and to profess uncertainty regarding the general state of the duke's affairs. Henry was stalling, in advance of retreating, and his advice to the duke was to work something out with the emperor. Earlier in the month (May 11), Henry directed Cromwell to write to Richard Pate, England's ambassador to the Imperial court (then in Ghent). Pate was to inform the emperor of the presence in Calais of two rebels seeking protection from Imperial summons and of Henry's willingness to hand them over for punishment. In light of the face-off over Brancestor just three months earlier, Henry's offer to extradite was less a gesture of goodwill (though presented that way in an elaborate cover-story concocted by Cromwell) than an admission of impotence and a plea for peace. 'The whole of Christendom hangs yet in balance,' said the letter to Pate, as if to emphasise the desperate urgency of current affairs. It seemed that Henry and some of his Council (having met two days earlier, May 9) were prepared to make amends to the emperor and to forgo support from all German allies. A conciliatory letter arrived from the elector of Saxony in April and was undiplomatically ignored, this being an early sign that Cromwell's German policy was about to be abandoned.

And then there was Anne. Bad enough was she (to Henry) when taken on her own; but doubly unsatisfying did she appear when compared with the delectable Catherine Howard. Henry wanted a divorce, and he expected Cromwell to provide it for him. The legal problem was easily resolved: the marriage was unconsummated and so no marriage at all; let the archbishop declare an annulment. Were that the whole of it, Cromwell could have set the divorce machinery in motion. But he had not given up on alliance with the Germans (first with Cleves, then with Schmalkalden). And he was loath to dispose of Anne, for a Cleves divorce leading to a Howard marriage would have been harmful to Cromwell personally, as his arch-foe, the duke of Norfolk, would then have become the uncle of the queen; also the Reformation would have suffered further setbacks from a Howard ascendancy at court. Cromwell's challenge was then similar to Wolsey's in 1529: namely, satisfying the marital needs of the king without undermining the political needs of the minister. Indeed, Cromwell's position may even have been the more precarious of the two: for Wolsey was no worse than lukewarm about Henry's second marriage, whereas Cromwell was secretly hostile to Henry's fifth and in public able to appear no better than lukewarm about the divorce from Anne. Thus when Thomas Wriosthesley visited Cromwell at his Bermondsey house (June 7), Cromwell gave the impression of desultoriness and indisposition when the subject of the divorce was mooted. Wriothesley conjectured that 'the king loves not the queen, nor ever has from the beginning, insomuch as I think assuredly she is yet as good a maid as when she came to England'; and he pleaded with Cromwell to 'devise how his Grace may be relieved one way or the other'. Cromwell acknowledged the problem but could provide no solution: 'Yes, but what and how,' he answered, and then nonchalantly set the matter aside. The scene was repeated the next evening, but with even greater urgency on Wriothesley's part: 'If he [the king] remain in this grief and trouble,' Wriothesley worried, 'we shall all one day smart for it'; on the other hand, he continued, 'if his Grace be quiet, we shall all have our parts with him.' To this appeal, Cromwell would say no more than 'it is a great matter'. When word of Cromwell's seeming indifference was reported to Henry (Wriothesley was then reassessing his loyalties), further cause was given for believing that the Lord Privy Seal was working against the king's own true interests.

It took only two days for the axe to fall. On June 10 at an afternoon meeting of the Privy Council, Norfolk rose to denounce Cromwell: 'My Lord Essex, I arrest you of high treason.' The constable of the Tower was on site to effect the arrest. Norfolk's coup had been in the works for months, but only now had the king come on board, persuaded that Cromwell had conspired with Germans to foist heresy on England and – as stated in a Council letter to ambassador John Wallop – that Cromwell had professed himself willing to 'fight in the field in his own person, with his sword in his hand against him [the king] and all other … if the king and all his realm would turn and vary from his [Cromwell's] opinions'.

Cromwell was caught completely unawares. He had been confident that the factional struggle was breaking his way and that the purge of his adversaries had solidified his hold on power.

But instantly did he realise his loss of the king's favour, and so instantly did he yield to the finality of Norfolk's command. He threw down his cap, asking plaintively if 'this be the reward for his services' and appealing 'to their consciences as to whether he was a traitor'; but being 'treated thus, he renounced all pardon, as he had never thought to have offended, and only asked the king not to make him languish long'. Some Privy councilors added their voices to the condemnation, rejoicing that the treason laws which had claimed so many lives would now take Cromwell's. Whereupon Norfolk tore away the order of St George worn around the traitor's neck (Cromwell's induction came in 1537), while Fitzwilliam, earl of Southampton, and one-time friend, untied the garter. Cromwell was hustled down a back stairs and out a postern gate to a waiting barge which delivered him to the Tower before Londoners could quite realise that the Lord Privy Seal had been degraded. The tip-off came a few hours later when Sir Thomas Cheney and the king's archers arrived at Cromwell's house at Austin Friars to inventory property and remove it to the treasury. Among the confiscated papers were letters to and from the German Lutherans, correspondence which so enraged the king and confirmed him in his ill opinion that the lone and mocking title he permitted Cromwell was 'shearman', all others being withdrawn and reassigned. Cromwell was again a commoner.

Immediately Henry explained himself to the French ambassador, Marillac, who communicated the explanation home. It supported the rationale provided by the Council – a Lutheran sectary and a traitor to the king:

The substance was that the king, wishing by all possible means to lead back religion to the way of truth, Cromwell, as attached to the German Lutherans, had always favoured the doctors who preached such erroneous opinions and hindered those who preached the contrary, and that recently, warned by some of his principal servants to reflect that he was working against the intention of the king and of the acts of parliament, he had betrayed himself and said he hoped to suppress the old preachers and have only the new, adding that the affair would soon be brought to such a pass that the king with all his power could not prevent it, but rather his own party would be so strong that he would make the king descend to the new doctrines even if he had to take arms against him.

Parliament, still in session, addressed the matter of Cromwell's fall a week later with consideration, and eventual passage, of a bill of attainder. Cromwell was granted no trial at which to defend himself – either for fear that his defense would expose the flimsiness of the charges against him, or as payback for the victims who had gone to their deaths by attainder without trial under Cromwell's ministry. The attainder indictment stipulated (though not exactly in this order): (1) abuse of temporal power, in the form of obstruction of justice, bribery and extortion, and usurpation of royal prerogatives; (2) abuse of spiritual power, in the form of licensing of heretical preachers, peremptory release of accused heretics, and cooperation in the spread of heresy; (3) violation of anti-heresy legislation, in the form of importation, translation, and endorsement of erroneous books; and (4) treason, specifically threats of rebellion against the king and injury to the nobles. Evidence consisted mostly of depositions by persons with their fingers in the air (among them Thomas Wriothesley, Richard Rich, and George Throckmorton).

The first charge was certainly true, though its offenses (e.g., interfering with the prosecution of accused traitors, selling licenses, appointing commissioners, issuing passports, and presuming to speak for the king) were unexceptional behaviours among the high officialdom, overlooked or excused when ministers were in favour. The second was a straight-up example of winner's justice, as the same charge, in opposite circumstances, could have been made by Cromwell against his enemies. The third meant to catch Cromwell sailing against the shifting currents of theological correctness, his purported approbation of lay distribution of the Eucharist being a case in point; but it too was an example of winner's justice. The fourth, and the most serious, was preposterous on its face, even though twice made before. Cromwell would never have defied his king for sectarian reasons; after all, he had told the Schmalkaldeners in January that his faith was the king's faith.

Either Henry had been manipulated by a court faction into believing that his trusted minister was a heretic and a traitor (the view of most scholars); or Henry had himself misrepresented the convictions and actions of his minister in order to sacrifice him for better relations with France and/or the Empire (the view of some revisionists).

In the Tower and on the Block

While parliament debated, Cromwell sat in a Tower cell subject to examination and commanded by the king to respond in writing to the as yet unfocused charge of treason. Cromwell answered in a letter dated June 12. He threw himself on the mercy of the king but refrained from confessing guilt as such. Neither did he plead innocence, exactly, though innocence he did imply:

> I have been accused to your Majesty of treason; to that I say I never in all my life thought willingly to do that thing that might or should displease your Majesty, and much less to do or say that thing which of itself is so high and abominable offense, as God knows, who I doubt not shall reveal the truth to your Highness. Mine accusers your Grace knows; God forgive them.

A later reference to the falsely accused Susanna of the Old Testament continued the suggestion of Cromwell's innocence. More straightforward was Cromwell in declaring his love for the king and in citing as proof his many 'labors, pains, and travails' undertaken in his Majesty's service. One fault to which Cromwell did confess was slackness in the detection, exposure, and punishment of lawbreakers (though, in truth, he performed this police work with zeal and aplomb, unless by lawbreakers Lutherans were meant). A second fault was meddling in royal affairs – 'so many matters under your Highness that I am not able to answer them all'; but he attributed this meddling to the nature of his job – 'hard it is for me or any other ... to live under your Grace and your laws but we must daily offend'. Three counts of indiscretion were laid against him, all apparently having to do with revelations about the queen. The first he denied; the second he conceded, but denied that secrecy was then expected or that discussion was actually harmful – on the contrary, it had proven useful to talk to Anne, her lord chamberlain, and her maids about how she might better please the king; the third he also conceded, but reminded Henry that it was undertaken on his request. Finally, the examiners of Cromwell had accused him of keeping retainers in violation of the laws. He explained that his retainers were all household servants and charity wards. The letter concluded with stock sentiments of the day: a general admission of sinfulness, combined with an appeal for divine and royal forgiveness; a firm denial of any intention to do wrong; and good wishes to the king and his heirs, coupled with curses upon their enemies.

This was not a letter of despair. It answered deftly the sundry charges that had surfaced so far. But the prosecution's case was still in the making. Wallop on the continent was asked to track down the four-year-old rumour that Cromwell had once expressed the intention of marrying Lady Mary and succeeding as king. The rumour proved to have originated with a Portuguese ambassador who had misunderstood a comment by Chapuys in one of his dispatches home. Again in circulation, and briefly credited, was the similarly outlandish accusation that Cromwell had boasted to Chapuys that 'the emperor will go to Constantinople and will give me a kingdom'. But making Cromwell out to be an agent of Charles, paladin of the Catholic faith, did not fit with the theme that Cromwell was a Protestant heretic, and so the latter crimination was dropped. Indeed, the heresy charge was advancing beyond ordinary Protestantism, intermittently embraced by the realm, to Lambert-style Sacramentarianism, eschewed by Henry and the Lutherans alike. Included in the attainder bill, now moving between houses of parliament, was the accusation that Cromwell had licensed the importation and translation of books which disputed the authenticity of the sacrament of the altar and which denied the distinction between the clergy and the laity. The indictment further alleged that Cromwell, upon reviewing these same books himself, proclaimed the material therein good and faultless.

In confinement Cromwell was visited by Norfolk, Southampton, and Lord Chancellor Audley on or about June 29, the day when the attainder bill passed in parliament. Equipped with a detailed list of questions, the trio examined the prisoner about the preliminaries of the king's marriage to Anne. It was expected that Cromwell would corroborate Henry's story of non-consummation and then commit his testimony to writing. That Cromwell did in two similar letters written on June 30. By then the verdict was in, and Cromwell was condemned to die. How he would die was left to the king's discretion; accordingly, Cromwell had cause to give the king what he wanted. Such a circumstance casts doubt on the veracity of Cromwell's account, but most scholars trust it nonetheless (noting, for example, that Cromwell's admissions of uncertainty and forgetfulness are inexplicable on the premise that the whole statement was a fabrication). The second letter contained a denial of the Sacramentarian charge.

Cromwell lingered in prison for another month, during which time the marriage to Anne was annulled by Convocation (July 10) and given statutory effect by parliament (July 14). Anne went quietly, stipulating in public and in a letter to her brother that the marriage to Henry had never been consummated. As a reward, she was granted a generous pension and two estates; she was thereafter referred to as 'sister' of the king and was sometimes invited to court. Many at court and across the land were overjoyed by news of Cromwell's fall (only Cranmer defended him); thus many were made anxious by his continuing hold on life. The king of France was among the critics who eagerly anticipated the day of doom. To hasten matters along, he informed Henry that Cromwell had corruptly adjudicated a dispute involving prizes captured by the ships of the governor of Picardy. Cromwell was obliged to respond to the charge, which he did, matter-of-factly, in his last letter written: 'but that ever I had any part of that prize or that I were promised any part thereof, my lords assure yourselves I was not, as God shall and may help me'.

Execution day was July 28. Henry had decided to extend mercy, in the sense that simple beheading was the allowed manner of death. But the execution was at Tyburn, where commoners endured every barbarity of the age, not on Tower Hill, reserved for finer folk. On the scaffold Cromwell delivered a confession in which he admitted some theological waywardness ('the devil is ready to seduce us, and I have been seduced'), but affirmed his return to orthodoxy at this his moment of death: 'I die in the Catholic faith, not doubting in any article of my faith, no nor doubting in any sacrament of the church.' Three accounts survive of the confession, all saying essentially the same thing, though eye-witness testimony, reported second-hand by Cardinal Pole, gave a much different impression. But whatever were the actual words spoken, it is unknowable whether they expressed Cromwell's true convictions, or were contrived by Cromwell to spare further injury to his son, or were even dictated by the king as the price exacted for a merciful death.

In the event, the death was not that merciful. The regular executioner was busy at Tower Hill that day and so a novice had to be enlisted to accomplish the beheading. According the Hall, he was a 'ragged and butcherly miser, which very ungoodly performed the office'. Three strokes of the axe were needed to send Cromwell from this world.

11
Cromwell, the Man and the Record

Character

Cromwell's life was a struggle. While he rose high, his accomplishments were resented, not applauded. He was a commoner, who presumed to give counsel to royalty. The emergence of this newcomer at court compromised the position of the peers, and they never forgave him his success and his talent. Other new men had preceded Cromwell in office; but aside from Thomas More, they had all been prelates supported by the power and prestige of the church. More, for his part, had education, family connections, and the love of the king working to smooth the way. Cromwell had only his native abilities: an analytical mind, a capacious memory, and an inexhaustible store of energy. He also had the courage and composure to live among enemies. The Hans Holbein portrait depicts a bull of a man, broad-faced with narrow eyes looking askance and quite through whatever object they are focused upon; a calculating and inquisitive man, plotting strategy, perhaps, or divining the secret thoughts of others; also a man seated before the tools of his trade – quill pen, bound book, papers of state – lost in a moment of reflection before returning to work.

Though the hazards of court life were quite enough to make a courtier tight-lipped and careful, Cromwell was a buoyant conversationalist, a wit, and a wordsmith. His stolid visage turned animate and jovial when clever thoughts were gestating and about to be born – so reported the Imperial ambassador, an opponent who became an admirer. Cromwell had a knack for putting people at ease and off their guard, for building trust and for extracting information from associates and adversaries alike. He was agreeable, when not terrifying, and he had friends to whom he was loyal. As he rose, so too did his friends, many of whom were associates from the Wolsey days.

But he could be terrifying, and on his own authority he issued arrest warrants and summons and sent instructions for the trials – and perhaps convictions – of supposed offenders. A group of miscreants once received this unnerving missive from the minister:

> And these shall be to advertise you that the king's pleasure is that you immediately upon the sight of these my letters shall repair hither to answer unto such things as then shall be levied and objected to you on the king our said sovereign lord's behalf. Fail you not thus to do, as you will avoid further peril and inconvenience.

Cromwell was not vindictive, however; killing was business for the good of the state, not sport for the gratification of private blood-lust. He used cruelty well, in conformity with Machiavellian doctrine, and generally he respected his victims, such as Thomas More. Where possible he mitigated their suffering.

On the personal front, Cromwell enjoyed hawking, hunting, gambling, and bowls; he raised greyhounds, played games, listened to music, and read avidly. A widower for his last dozen or so years, he nevertheless maintained an orderly household and entertained frequently. The small dinner party was his favourite form of recreation and a device for keeping abreast of ideas and events. From his houses alms and foodstuffs were distributed to the London poor, some two hundred of whom were daily supported by the minister's generosity.

Cromwell was then a man of means. He owned multiple houses in and around London and enjoyed the use of another as a perquisite of office. On a much reduced scale, he followed the king and the cardinal in renovating the properties he acquired; and in pale imitation of them both, he was, or could be, a bully about his affairs. There is the story, related by a descendant of the aggrieved, of how Cromwell, without notice or permission, took down a fence, removed a building, and walled in twenty-two feet of neighbours' ground in order to expand the garden of his own Austin Friars residence. While late to the nobility, Cromwell was quick to absorb its arrogance. In small ways and in large he began to live like a nobleman, daring to marry his son to a queen's sister. He appreciated well-crafted goods and from time to time paid premium prices to acquire a chest, a table, a globe, or a book. But in the main, and relative to others, Cromwell had simple tastes and moderate appetites. Wolsey furnished his palaces with paintings, tapestries, and carpets from all over the world; Cromwell was satisfied with the usual appointment of plate, goblets, and household wares. Cromwell earned vast sums of money during his years in office – enough to support the lifestyle of the earl he became – but when his domiciles were ransacked at the time of his fall, there was less accumulation than had been expected.

Politics was Cromwell's passion. He was a master of court intrigue, of the Machiavellian game of acquiring influence and power. Eventually conspiracy did him in, but numerous rivals went down before him, and as Lord Privy Seal he was all but indomitable. He delighted in the politics of diplomacy, and when allowed to try his hand, he did well for a low-born minister. Diplomacy at that time was the province of kings and nobles, for whom parlaying with a commoner (or a parvenu lord) was about as palatable as marrying a daughter to one. Cromwell was untrained and inexperienced, and his German policy collapsed around his ears. That policy, however, might have succeeded were it not for the intransigence of the king; moreover, that policy made sense, unless it is thought that twenty miles of Channel water forever guaranteed England's security. Some do think this, but then attack by the Spanish Armada gives reason for pause. Politics also meant the drafting of legislation, the management of parliament, and the execution of law, tasks which Cromwell performed with consummate skill. First and foremost, Cromwell was a public man – engaged in affairs, reform-minded, determined to make a difference.

Ideas mattered as well to Cromwell; and if it is too much to say that Cromwell was an intellectual, he certainly was a patron of intellectuals and a steady consumer of their produce. In Cromwell's employ were Thomas Starkey, mastermind of the 'middle way' faith of the Anglican church; Richard Taverner, translator of Melanchthon; and Richard Morison, populariser of Machiavelli and propagandist against the Pilgrimage of Grace. Many others hung about the periphery hoping for the chance to join the inner circle of Cromwell secretaries; for it was well understood that Cromwell maintained a 'think-tank' of scholars comparable in size and quality to the Reginald Pole household in Padua (indeed, several of Cromwell's writers were former house-guests of Pole – much to the embarrassment of all). Cromwell promoted education reform and continued the incorporation of 'new learning' subjects into the curriculum of the universities. He lacked formal education himself, but he was self-taught in languages (Italian, French, and Latin, with smatterings of German and Greek), politics, history, law (maybe), and religion.

About Cromwell's religious convictions, there is little that is known with certainty, much that is conjectural. Recent scholarship is of the opinion that Cromwell was a Lutheran, or at least an Erasmian. His commitment to such Protestant causes as vernacular translations of the Bible, lay control of the clergy, and iconoclastic demolition of the Catholic past counts as evidence for this position. To be sure, Cromwell harbored no affection for monks and their monasteries, and prideful prelates he viewed with contempt. He also winked at the import of heretical books and was lax in his enforcement of the *Six Articles* and of royal proclamations commanding religious orthodoxy. Protestant sectaries at home and abroad looked to him for protection and advancement. For their satisfaction and for the propaganda purposes served, he sanctioned and sometimes presided over the destruction of idols and images. But if Cromwell himself were an icon-smashing zealot, incensed at the simple piety of traditionalist Christians and resolved to destroy all instruments of the miraculous, he would not have given Queen Margaret of Scotland a present of cramp-rings, believed to have curative powers traceable to Edward the Confessor. (Cromwell demurred as to the value of the rings [whether monetary or medicinal value he did not explain], but he respected that the queen might regard them as valuable and asked that she accept the gift as a token of his good will.) Most telling though is Cromwell's admission to the ambassadors from the League of Schmalkalden that worldly realities required of him submission to his master's (forever shifting) beliefs. Religion, with its eye on salvation in the next world, did not supersede politics, fully focused on success in this world. He allowed that his own beliefs tilted in a Protestant direction, but that inclination may have been the result of Protestantism's tilt toward secular supremacy – with Bible translations, clerical disempowerment, and dismantling of monasteries all embraced because they contributed to that overriding goal. And if the thesis is accepted that Cromwell was a Machiavelli disciple, then it is quite unthinkable that Cromwell also was a true-believing Protestant, or even much of a Christian.

Reputation

Since Cromwell died a traitor's death, opinion of him in the immediate aftermath was far from sympathetic. But the resurgence of Protestantism in the reigns of Edward and Elizabeth prepared the ground for a change of view. That change came with the publication of John Foxe's *Book of Martyrs* in the 1560s. By including Cromwell among the martyrs of the true faith, Foxe transformed Cromwell from treasonous heretic to servant of the Gospel. The Puritans lauded his heroism, the Anglicans adopted his moderation, and historians for generations gave him favourable reviews. A competing and earlier account, originating with Reginald Pole, portrayed Cromwell as an unscrupulous adventurer and corrupter of a well-meaning king. But Pole the ex-patriot lacked credibility with Englishmen awash in nationalistic pride. Thomas More, the papist, suffered the same dismissive rebuke. Opinion shifted in the nineteenth century as some high-church Anglicans sought to reunite with Rome and as the campaign got underway for the canonization of More (St Thomas More it is, as of 1935). With the reputation of Catholicism on the rise, the reputation of those who quashed it went into decline, allowing the rendering of Cromwell by Pole to gain purchase at last. At the start of the twentieth century, Cromwell was seen as either a devil or a toady.

The first complete biography of Cromwell was by R. B. Merriman (1902). It accompanied the publication of Cromwell's letters. The Cromwell presented by Merriman was a self-seeking utilitarian, a secularist indifferent to the religious controversies of his day, and a statist determined to augment the power and the wealth of the monarchy. Indeed, the regime which he served and laboured to create was a Tudor despotism. Parliament was reduced to a shadow of its medieval precursor and remained an insubstantial body for the duration of the Tudor dynasty.

Merriman's depiction was seconded by Peter Wilding three decades later (1935), and Theodore Maynard offered it a third time at mid century (1950). Maynard credited Cromwell with being a first-rate administrator and an able statesman; with keeping the peace notwithstanding the warlike ambitions of his king; and with protecting and promoting the country's commercial economy. But Maynard would not forgive Cromwell his irreligiousness, his bribe-taking, his perfidy, his ends-justify-means morality; nor would he forgive him his destruction of the monasteries and his creation of a 'sultanate'. To Maynard the Reformation was an English calamity, unjust in its implementation and ruinous in its consequences.

A few years later the turnaround began with the publication of G. R. Elton's *The Tudor Revolution in Government* (1953). According to Elton, Cromwell, not Henry, was the star of the play, the revolutionary figure who launched a newly outfitted ship of state–united, independent, and constitutionally grounded. With executive power centralised in the monarchy, and with the monarchy assisted by a professional bureaucracy and yoked to the parliament, England was set for success in the modern world.

Elton's new view was quickly endorsed by the leading Reformation historian of the period, A. G. Dickens, who at decade's end brought forth a biography mostly laudatory of Cromwell (1959). In Dickens's account Cromwell accomplished the religious and political revolution which Elton attributed to him; in addition, Cromwell was privately a decent man, honest and brave in his service to Wolsey, generous in his treatment of the poor, sincere in his (changing) religious beliefs, a genuine Protestant sympathiser. Yes, Cromwell took bribes, but no more than was common for the day; and yes, he dissolved the monasteries, but the social benefits that were forthcoming more than compensated for the loss.

The last biography to date, by B. W. Beckingsale (1978), followed Elton and Dickens in its choice of Cromwell over Henry as the engine of reform; but Beckingsale disputed the thesis that what Cromwell wrought amounted to a revolution. No political revolution was attempted to make the state secular, bureaucratic, and modern; no social and economic revolution was envisaged to shift resources from the crown to the commonwealth; and no class warfare was prosecuted by an ambitious commoner resentful of his social betters – so concluded Beckingsale.

Scholarship over the last quarter century has continued along this line, with Elton's Cromwell serving as the target and with historians (many of whom are Elton students) either taking aim or providing defensive cover. The critics seem to be in the majority, and their labours have diminished somewhat the importance of Cromwell and the importance of the 1530s. As a rule, these critics prefer the paradigm of evolution to revolution and the causality of factional groups to that of heroic individuals. They argue that the age represented no dramatic break from the medieval past; that actors besides Cromwell had a hand in its shaping; and that the reforms attributed to Cromwell fell short of a revolution in government. For these reforms were, say the critics: manifestations of personal not institutional administration; unplanned responses to political emergencies; modest adjustments of established patterns unrelated to the innovations of a later time; or short-lived experiments not surviving Cromwell's own destruction. In reply, Elton has modified some positions and reinforced others. He grants, for example, that Household administration was more enduring and past parliamentary activity more vigorous than previously thought; and that *ad hoc* problem-solving was driving the agenda as much as principled reform. But he insists that Cromwell's personal control over elements of the bureaucracy – acknowledged but accounted for as a concomitant of founding – did not derogate from the institutional character of the revenue courts, newly founded; and that the evolutionary appearance of change was a conscious creation meant to project continuity while disguising transformation (Machiavelli's prescription exactly – *Dis*, I.25). The debate continues, and for as long as it does, Cromwell will remain a primary topic of early Tudor historiography.

Legacy

What did Cromwell accomplish in the main, and did his accomplishments endure? Merriman offers an assessment which will serve as a useful counterpoint for our own. Merriman regards Cromwell as a successful statesman in the short-run, but a failure in the long-run. Cromwell nourished three ambitions, says Merriman, all of which he achieved on the moment and all of which turned to dust in later years. First, Cromwell promised and delivered Henry a divorce from his wife Catherine, when Cardinal Wosley had failed at the same. The divorce required a homegrown agent to grant it, since the Roman pontiff, fearing the emperor's retaliation, declined to be of help. The empowerment and instruction of that agent – the English church with the Canterbury archbishop as its primate – mandated separation from Rome and subordination of church to state, or temporal supremacy. Once done, the king was conjugally free and politically omnipotent. Minister Cromwell had therefore achieved his objective. But religious independence produced a vacuum into which was drawn the Lutheran heresy from abroad. Henry was no Lutheran, and Cromwell the secularist was not aiming to trade one form of religious meddling for another. But such meddling occurred nonetheless. Henry's irritation over the course of reform cost Cromwell his life, and the course of reform – back and forth (Henry), then sideways (Elizabeth), and then straight ahead (Puritans) – cost England a civil war and the monarchy its supremacy. Hence the end result was failure, though taking more than a century to unfold.

The second ambition was to enrich the crown by dispossessing the monasteries. In the space of four years nearly a thousand religious houses in England, Wales, and Ireland were shut down, their wealth transferred to the royal treasury. Henry became a wealthy monarch, just as Cromwell had ensured he would. But the wealth did not remain with Henry; much he squandered, and much he circulated through the upper-tiers of society, increasing the size and importance of the aristocracy and landed gentry. In the following century, these classes challenged the monarchy, replacing an absolute despotism with a constitutional kingship, or with a king-in-parliament mixed regime. Since Cromwell served the cause of absolutism, wanting the country's greatness which only a despot could supply (he thought), once again Cromwell's early success turned into eventual failure.

The instrument of this absolutist state was parliament, ironically, a body which Cromwell kept almost continuously in session. Wolsey summoned parliament rarely, fearing its obstreperousness. Cromwell, himself a parliamentarian, had less to fear since by force and by fraud he had made parliament pliable. Rather than fight with its king, the Cromwellian parliament passed laws that legitimated his tyranny. Cromwell's third ambition was then the corruption of parliament and its conversion into a lap dog of the crown. But as with his other objectives, the passage of time and the passage of the Tudors allowed this ill-used institution to reclaim its original purpose and join in the struggle against royal absolutism. Thus religious, social, and political forces, which

Cromwell for a time had tamed and employed, turned on their court masters and took control of England.

Merriman's assessment, an application of the Whig theory of history, it might be noted, marks Cromwell out as a villain in the short-term and a loser in the long-term. But Cromwell shows a different face when seen in the light of different assumptions about his purpose. If Cromwell invited some degree of Lutheran influence, either because he himself was evangelical or was using the faith for secular ends, then the Reformation was not a whirligig that spun terribly out of control; it rather was a block in the foundation on which English sovereignty was erected. The false universalism of papacy and Empire required that the states of Europe embrace their particularity and assert their independence. In the accomplishment of this task, religious reform assisted political reform by helping with the construction of national identity. Secondly, if Cromwell aimed for greatness, he would not have sought it through despotism alone – not if Cromwell were a careful reader of Machiavelli. For he then would have known that the vitality of the state depended on participation by the classes as much as it depended on the might of the prince; in which case the disbursement of spoils to nobles and gentry was less a bribe for buying their immediate support than a power-sharing strategy for broadening the base. And if Cromwell saw secular supremacy as involving the parliament, then the reemergence of parliament in the next century was not a reversal of policy and defeat for the minister, but an anticipated evolution needed for the protection of liberty and the development of strength. On the basis of these assumptions then, Cromwell deserves recognition as one of England's leading statesmen whose accomplishments reached well beyond his own time.

Contrary to Merriman, the near-term, not the long-term, proved the greater enemy of Cromwell's policies. For it was in the near-term that a willful, but inconstant, monarch destroyed the minister who served him. Soon after, Henry expressed regret for what he had done, or had been goaded into doing, calling Cromwell 'the most faithful servant he ever had'. But no new minister, or successor Vicegerent, was appointed to carry on the Cromwell agenda. Decision-making in consequence depended increasingly on the personal rule of the king, which the moods of the king and the factions at court increasingly shaped. Cromwell, conversely, sought to rest lawmaking on the consent of parliament and administration on the offices of state. In the matter of religious reform, a retreat from Protestantism was already underway; and in the matter of social reform, such as poor relief and price controls, the king lost interest in the 1540s, returning to the militarism of his youth. Likewise the vast wealth supplied the crown was quickly spent. Cromwell was not a prince, but an adviser to a prince; and until that prince had concluded his reign, the adviser's plan for constitutional monarchy and English greatness fell short of realization.

Glossary of Terms

Affinity: a canon law impediment prohibiting marriage between in-laws (Catherine was Henry's sister-in-law), as well as marriage with the relatives of sexual partners, down to the sixth or seventh cousin (Mary Boleyn, sister to Anne, was Henry's former mistress)

Albigensians: a neo-Manichean sect preaching the eternal opposition of good (spirit) and evil (matter) forces; flourished in southern France in the twelfth century; suppressed in the thirteenth by the Albigensian Crusade launched by Pope Innocent III; name taken from the town of Albi

Anabaptism: an anarchist branch of the Reformation whose adherents rejected infant baptism or required the re-baptism of adults (*ana* meaning 'again' in Greek); private property and class distinctions also rejected

Annates and/or First Fruits: a one-time payment to Rome of the entire annual revenues of ecclesiastical benefices by new incumbents

Aragonese: Catherine of Aragon's defenders; more generally, the conservative opposition to the Reformation

Attainder: the penalty for treason and other high crimes, encompassing death, outlawry, loss of titles and estates, and corruption of blood (i.e., the exclusion of descendants from their inheritance); called a bill or act of attainder when initiated by parliament in lieu of a trial or when a previous legal judgement is confirmed by parliament

Babylonian Captivity: the removal of the papacy from Rome to Avignon during the years 1309–78; marked by a succession of French popes taking orders from French kings; named after the seventy-year captivity of the Hebrew people in Babylon (586–516 BC)

Bear-Baiting: a common entertainment in Tudor London; arenas for this and bull-baiting sat on or near the site of the future Globe theater in Southwark, along the south bank of the Thames

Benefice: an ecclesiastical office providing a salary to its incumbent (e.g., a bishopric); also a feudal land grant, or fief

Benefit of Clergy: the right of clergy and their associates to be tried by ecclesiastical courts; clerical exemption from the jurisdiction of secular courts

Black Death: the bubonic plague which ravaged Europe between 1347 and 1350, reducing its population by one third

Borgia: an Italian–Spanish family notorious for its ruthless pursuit of power; significant members included Pope Callistus III (1455–8), Pope Alexander VI (1492–1503), Cesare, the warlord-adventurer lionised by Machiavelli in *The Prince*, and Lucrezia, the poisoner

Bourbon: a family line of French kings from Henry IV to Charles X (1589–1830); interrupted by the French Revolution and Napoleon (1793–1814)

Caesaropapism: the belief that the emperor, like his Christianised Roman predecessors, is the head of the church

Canon Law: the body of laws and ordinances adopted by the Catholic church; from the Greek *kanon*, meaning 'rule' or 'direction'

Capetian: a family line of French kings running from Hugh Capet to Charles IV (987–1328)

Carolingian: a family line of French kings running from Pepin the Short to Louis the Sluggard (750–987)

Catholic Reformation: Catholicism's attempt to reform itself in partial response to the Protestant Reformation begun over a quarter-century earlier; the work of the Council of Trent (1545–7, 1551–2, 1562–3) and of the Jesuit Order (founded 1534)

Chancery Court: the court of the Lord Chancellor, using principles of equity instead of common-law precedent to adjudicate cases

College of Cardinals: selected archbishops and bishops serving as papal assistants, with the election of popes as the body's primary responsibility

Confirmation: a sacrament administered to young adults in confirmation of baptism administered to infants

Consanguinity: a canon law impediment prohibiting marriage between blood relations (incest) down to the sixth or seventh cousin (Jane and Henry were distant cousins)

Consistory: Roman cardinals convened as a senate

Convocation: the legislative assembly of the English church; a body independent of the king's parliament, with jurisdiction over wills, burials, marriages, morals, heresy, etc.; divided regionally into the Convocation of Canterbury (south) and the Convocation of York (north), with each assembly further divided into upper and lower chambers; upper chamber prelates (archbishops, bishops, abbots, priors) also *ex officio* members of the House of Lords

Copyhold: customary manorial land parcels held by will of the lord

Council of the North: one of the regional governments that administered crown policy in the provinces; established by

Richard III; reorganised by Henry VIII after the suppression of the Pilgrimage of Grace

Court of Arches: the oldest and most important court in the Canterbury jurisdiction, taking its name from its original London location at the Church of St Mary le Bow; archdiocesan appellate court

Cramp-rings: gold and silver rings good for curing cramp, palsy, and epilepsy; these blessed by English monarchs on Good Friday and distributed as gifts

Curia: the papal court and all of its functionaries

Dauphin: the first-born son of the French king and heir-presumptive

Disablement: a legal incapacitation from the inheritance of property, the exercise of rights, the performance of acts, or the holding of office; a non-capital form of attainder

Edict of Nantes: the 1598 grant of private worship to all Huguenot Protestants and of public worship to Huguenot nobles and to specified places historically Protestant; also full civil liberties, special courts and schools, and garrisoned cities paid for by the crown

Edict of Worms: an Imperial proclamation declaring Luther an outlaw and banning his books; the result of the 1521 Diet of Worms where Luther was interrogated and asked to recant his heresy

Enclosure: the fencing off for sheep-grazing of lands formerly used by tenant farmers for crop production, with the consequent dislocation of rural peoples and their reduction to vagabondage; legislation prohibiting the practice

Engrossing: large-scale buying aimed at establishing a monopoly of supply; the buying of farmlands and the neglect or abandonment of their farm buildings

Episcopal: of or pertaining to bishops, or the church government by bishops

Excusator: a state official sent to tender a formal excuse or apology

Extreme Unction: a sacrament of last rites administered to the dying and the seriously ill, in which the organs of the five senses are anointed with oil and sins are remitted

Faggot: a tied bundle of sticks used for fuel; particular association with the burning of heretics; small-bundle facsimiles carried around town by abjuring heretics as punishment

Field of Cloth of Gold: the 1520 meeting of Henry VIII and Francis I near Calais; the most ostentatious diplomatic conclave of the period; name taken from the gold-cloth tents that covered the field

Fifteenth and Tenth: an old form of taxation, originally assessed on movable goods in the amount of a fifteenth or a tenth of their value (sums collected respectively from rural and urban inhabitants), but converted in the fourteenth century into a fixed sum assessed on villages and boroughs

Freeholder: a person whose estate is owned absolutely and for life with the freedom to use and bequeath as the holder sees fit

Gray's Inn: a solicitors' society, or 'inn of court' (i.e., law school/law firm); one of four in London, the others being Inner Temple, Middle Temple, and Lincoln

Great Matter: the six-year campaign (1527–33) waged by Henry VIII to divorce his wife Catherine, out of which emerged the English Reformation

Great Seal: a large silver seal, held by the Lord Chancellor, used to stamp and validate documents from the sovereign

Groom of the Stool: the king's personal attendant during visits to the privy; a prestigious office in the Privy Chamber, giving its occupant daily and private access to the king

Hanseatic League: a mercantile alliance of the cities of

northern Germany and the Baltic region founded in the twelfth century, with Lübeck at the center

Holy Offices: the daily prayers of the Roman breviary

Holy Roman Empire: a millennium-long institution (beginning with Charlemagne and ending with Napoleon) that made the emperor the secular patron of the church and the highest ranked ruler in feudal Christendom; also a territory roughly coterminous with the Netherlands, Germany, and northwestern Italy

Household: a name for the king's court; in medieval times the seat of government

Huguenots: the name for French followers of John Calvin; derived perhaps from Besançon Hughes, leader of the Geneva Confederate Party, in combination with *eidgenot*, the French corruption of the German word for 'confederate'

Humanists: Renaissance writers whose focus was more on human nature than divine nature and more on this life than the next

Hundred Years' War (1337–1453): a military adventure of five English kings (Edward III to Henry VI) designed to seize and annex portions of French territory, with Henry V's victory at Agincourt representing the high point of success (1415); tide of war shifting with the appearance of Joan of Arc (1429–31)

Indulgences: church-distributed reprieves from purgatorial suffering in the afterlife, earned by such virtuous behaviors as alms-giving, shrine visitations, pilgrimages to Rome, and donations; the sale of indulgences being the immediate cause of Luther's revolt

Infante: any younger son of a Portuguese or Spanish king, not next in line to inherit the throne; 'infanta' for any daughter

Interdiction: a papal ban on the distribution of the sacraments; used to turn public opinion against offending monarchs

Justification: the state of being saved; for Luther, the product of faith alone; for Catholics, the product of faith plus good works

King-in-Parliament: an expression describing the legislative power of the British government in which royal proposals require the separate consent of the houses of Lords and Commons and in which parliamentary bills are subject to royal veto

King's Bench: a king's court, located in Westminster Hall, with jurisdiction over cases involving subjects and the king; also an ordinary criminal and civil court; like the court of Common Pleas in stressing common-law precedents

Livery: an identifying badge, suit, or uniform worn by a master's servants or retainers

Lord Chancellor: a ministerial office dating back to the Norman Conquest; usually held by an ecclesiastic who served also as king's chaplain; keeper of the great seal; judge; presiding officer over the House of Lords; importance of office determined by the occupant's status (almost the whole government during Wolsey's tenure)

Lord Great Chamberlain: one of the six great offices of state with special responsibility for Westminster palace and the House of Lords; more ceremonial than substantive; typically held by hereditary right by the de Vere family as earl of Oxford; made briefly a crown office with lifetime appointment during the latter half of Henry VIII's reign

Lord Privy Seal: a ministerial post charged with the keeping of the king's private seal, used to authorise expenditures from the Exchequer and to notarise minor documents

Magna Carta: the 1215 document limiting the powers of the king in relation to the clergy and the nobility

Marches: land on a country's frontier, with special reference to the English–Welsh and English–Scottish borders

Matins: morning prayers, specifically midnight or daybreak canonical office

Misprision: complicity in the commission of a crime or neglect in preventing or reporting a crime

Mortmain: ecclesiastical or corporate land held inalienably

Natural Law: the theory, originating with Stoicism and adopted by Christianity, that law embodies permanent moral standards arising out of human nature (e.g., self-preservation and the consequent wrong of murder), physical nature (e.g., gravity), or the created cosmos

New Learning: Renaissance humanism, with a focus in northern Europe on early Christianity, its history and texts

New Men: the term used to describe royal advisers and government ministers who were lacking in noble birth and its prescriptive claims on office

Order of the Garter: a brotherhood of knights formed in the thirteenth century with King Arthur and the Roundtable as their inspiration, with St George as their patron, and with Windsor Castle as their home; membership consisting of the king and the prince of Wales, plus twelve companions each

Order of the Golden Fleece: founded in 1430 by Philip the Good, duke of Burgundy; a confraternity of knights consisting of the grand duke and twenty-three others (later fifty-one) and dedicated to the defense of the Catholic faith and the code of chivalry; taken over by the Habsburgs in 1477 upon the marriage of Mary of Burgundy and Maximilian of Austria

Oyer and Terminer: Anglo–French for 'to hear and determine'; a commission charged with investigating all treasons, felonies, and misdemeanors in a given locality

Papal Legate: a prelate empowered to represent the pope; *a latere* (by the side) being the highest order of legate, whose acts are treated as though they were the pope's own (Wolsey's title – given temporarily in 1518 and for life in 1524)

Papal Nuncio: an ambassador or messenger of the pope

Paul's Cross: an open-air pulpit in the churchyard of St Paul's cathedral; a thirteenth-century creation remade in the fifteenth with stone steps, lead roof, low wall, and space to hold several persons; destroyed in 1643 by iconoclastic Puritans

Peasants' Revolt: an uprising of German peasants in response to longstanding grievances and recent hopes of liberation caused by Martin Luther's religious reformation; opposed by Luther and suppressed by German princes, with much slaughter on both sides (1524–5)

Plantagenet: a family line of English kings from Henry II to Richard III (1154–1485); from *planta genesta*, meaning broom flower; chosen as the Anjevin dynastic emblem by Geoffrey of Anjou, father of Henry II

Plentitude of Power: the claim by the medieval church that all power, spiritual and temporal, inhered in the papacy

Pluralism: the practice of holding multiple benefices and collecting multiple incomes

Politiques: a group of sixteenth-century French writers who, tired of the chaos caused by the religious wars, argued that monarchical power is absolute and (as with some authors) by a divine right equal to that of popes; opposed by the Monarchomachs, who argued for resistance to royal absolutism and (as with some authors) tyrannicide

Praemunire: Latin for 'forewarn'; the opening words of a writ of summons, *Praemunire facias* – 'cause to be forewarned'; fourteenth-century statutes forbidding wrongful prosecution of cases in church courts (rarely invoked and imprecise as to its meaning); more generally, ecclesiastical submission to the pope

Prebend: the endowed stipend paid to a clergyman, or the

clergyman receiving the stipend

Prelate: any high-ranking church official, most commonly a bishop

Prerogative Court: an archbishop's court for the probate of wills

Privy Chamber: part of the royal household or court; that small band of companions and confidants of the king with access to the king's private quarters or privy chamber; a product of palace architecture – i.e., private apartments situated behind the throne room, called the presence chamber, itself situated behind the great hall, called the watching chamber

Privy Council: the king's cabinet, composed initially of titled lords, but with membership extended in Henry's day to talented commoners called 'new men'; inside of which the Lord Chancellor, Lord Treasurer, Lord Privy Seal, and king's first secretary made up an *ex officio* secretariat

Proctor: a proxy, attorney, or agent employed to manage the affairs of another

Progresses: movements of the court from palace to palace

Protestant Reformation: the sixteenth-century schism within the western Catholic church started by Martin Luther, who objected first to church practices and then to church doctrines

Provincial: the head of an ecclesiastical province

Provisors: 'provisions', usually papal, entitling the holder to a benefice upon its becoming vacant; a practice outlawed by statutes of provisors

Public Honesty: a canon law impediment prohibiting marriage by those already married (bigamy), as well as by those merely betrothed (Anne Boleyn was thought to have been engaged to Henry Percy; and Catherine of Aragon was married at the altar to Arthur even if that marriage was never consummated, as she claimed)

Purgatory: in Catholic doctrine the place where souls of the dead go to expiate their sins in preparation for entry into paradise

Puritan: a term of abuse meant to describe late sixteenth- and seventeenth-century English Calvinists unsatisfied with the reforms and compromises of the Anglican church

Raison-d'Etat: French for 'reason of state'; a realistic diplomacy which puts the interests of country ahead of the requirements of morality

Regnum and Sacerdotium: state and church recognised as the two powers, or 'two swords', ruling over the post-Roman western world and competing for ascendancy

Regrating: buying commodities for resale at a higher price, usually in the same market

Rota: the supreme ecclesiastical tribunal hearing cases appealed to the Holy See

Royal Prerogative: the historic power of a sovereign king to act outside the boundaries of custom and law; applicable especially in diplomatic and military affairs

Sacramentarianism: the belief that the Eucharist is only metaphorically the body and blood of Christ; a Protestant sect associated with Ulrich Zwingli and Johannes Oecolampadius

St Bartholomew's Day Massacre: the slaughter of thousands of Huguenots assembled in Paris for the marriage of Henry of Navarre (August 1572); killings ordered by Catholic King Charles IX, on the urging of his mother Catherine de'Medici, who feared a Huguenot coup

Schmalkaldic League: a defensive alliance of Protestant German princes against the Catholic Holy Roman emperor Charles V; founded in 1531 in the town of Schmalkalden in Thuringia, with an eventual membership of fourteen cities

Simony: the practice of buying and selling ecclesiastical offices

Spanish Inquisition: an ecclesiastical court founded by Ferdinand and Isabella and answerable to the Spanish crown; designed for the suppression of heresy and the uncovering of false converts in the Spanish dominions; in existence until the nineteenth century

Star Chamber: the court of the Privy Council, relying on equity more than on precedent in arbitrating disputes; like Chancery in its procedures

Stuart: a family line of Scottish kings/queens of England from James I to Anne (1603–1714)

Sweating Sickness: an unidentified disease, perhaps a virulent strain of influenza, typhus, or prickly heat; first appeared in England in 1485, with serious subsequent outbreaks in 1508, 1517, and 1528; last appearance in 1551; usually fatal, taking the life of its victim in three or four days

Temporalities: the temporal possessions of ecclesiastical persons, offices, and corporate bodies

Transubstantiation: the conversion of the bread and wine of communion into the body and blood of Christ, in imitation of the Last Supper

Tudor: a family line of English kings/queens from Henry VII to Elizabeth I (1485–1603)

United Kingdom: the union with England of Wales (1536), Scotland (1603, 1707), and Ireland (1801 – then only Northern Ireland, 1922), plus outlying islands and overseas territories

Uses: a trust reposed in a person or body for the holding of property; a distinction in property rights between the owner and the user, employed to escape estate taxes upon the owner's death by transferring use of property to another; a practice regulated or curtailed by statutes of uses

Valois: a family line of French kings from Philip VI to Henry III (1328–1589)

Vulgate: the Latin translation of the Bible from the Hebrew and the Aramaic made by St Jerome around 400 AD; the standard translation until the Reformation

Walloon: The French-speaking people of southern Belgium, or Wallonia; combined as countrymen with the German-speaking Flemish of northern Belgium, or Flanders

Wars of the Roses: England's fifteenth-century civil wars (1455–85), pitting the House of Lancaster (Red Rose; descendants of John of Gaunt, duke of Lancaster and third son of Edward III) against the House of York (White Rose; descendants of Edmund, duke of York and fourth son of Edward III [r. 1327–77])

Whig Theory of History: a progressive view of history associated with the nineteenth-century British historian Thomas Macaulay, but named by the twentieth-century British historian Herbert Butterfield; emphasis on politics and individuals with the past seen as a march toward the present

Wolds: moors; unforested, rolling plains in northeastern Lincolnshire and southeastern Yorkshire counties

York Place: the London residence of the archbishop of York; confiscated by the king in 1529 and renamed Whitehall (the current seat of government)

Glossary of Persons

Anne of Cleves (1515–47): fourth wife of Henry (January 1540–July 1540), with the marriage annulled on grounds of nonconsummation; daughter of John III, duke of Cleves

Robert Aske (1500–37): Yorkshire gentleman and London lawyer; co-leader of the Pilgrimage of Grace rebellion; executed for treason

Thomas Audley (1488–1544): Speaker of the House of Commons (1529–32); later, Lord Chancellor (1532–44)

Francis Bigod (1507–37): Yorkshire knight; co-leader of the Pilgrimage of Grace rebellion; executed for treason

Anne Boleyn (1501/1507–36): Henry's second wife (1533–6); executed for treasonous adultery

Thomas Boleyn, Earl of Wiltshire and Ormonde (1477–1539): father of Anne; Lord Privy Seal and a member of the Privy Council

Charles Brandon, Duke of Suffolk (1484–1545): youthful companion of Henry and husband of his sister, Mary Tudor; Privy Council co-president

John Calvin (1509–64): follower of Luther; author of *Institutes of the Christian Religion*, emphasizing justification by faith and predestination; founder of the religious government of Geneva, a Protestant stronghold

Lorenzo Campeggio (1472–1539): cardinal and papal envoy to

England (1528–35); member of Lords as bishop of Salisbury

Nicholas Carew (1496–1539): Privy Chamber member and Aragon sympathiser; executed for participation in the Exeter Conspiracy

Catherine of Aragon (1485–1536): wife of Henry's brother, Arthur (1501–2), then wife of Henry (1509–33); aunt of Charles V

Eustace Chapuys (1489–1556): emperor's ambassador to England (1529–46); leading member of the Catherine of Aragon faction

Charles V (1500–56): king of Spain (1516) and Holy Roman Emperor (1519); crowned emperor by pope in 1530

Clement VII (1475–1534): Giuilo de Medici; pope (1523–34)

Robert Constable (1478–1537): Yorkshire knight; co-leader of the Pilgrimage of Grace rebellion; executed for treason

Henry Courtenay, Marquess of Exeter and Earl of Devon (1497–1538): cousin of King Henry and grandson of Edward IV; member of the king's Privy Council and Privy Chamber; implicated in the Exeter Conspiracy and executed for treason

Thomas Cranmer (1489–1556): archbishop of Canterbury (1533–53); chief instrument of Henry's divorce

Thomas Cromwell (1485?–1540): secretary to Wolsey; member of Commons; member of the Privy Council; elevated to peerage as baron Okeham (1536) and earl of Essex (1540); Henry's principal minister after More and the driving force behind the English Reformation; executed for treason and heresy

Thomas Darcy, Baron (1467–1537): Yorkshire lord of the Aragon faction; constable of Pontefract castle, surrendering it to the rebels at the outbreak of the Pilgrimage of Grace uprising; executed for treason

Edward (1537–53): son of Henry and Jane Seymour; king 1547–53

Elizabeth (1533–1603): daughter of Henry and Anne Boleyn; queen 1558–1603

Desiderius Erasmus (1466–1536): Dutch humanist; author of *The Praise of Folly, Colloquies, Education of a Christian Prince, Enchiridion*; friend of More

Simon Fish (?–1531): anticlerical pamphleteer; author of *A Supplication for the Beggars*

John Fisher (1469–1535): bishop of Rochester (1504–35); chancellor of Cambridge University (1509–35); executed for refusing to take the oath of succession

Thomas Fitzgerald, Earl of Kildare (1513–37): leader of the Geraldine rebellion in Ireland (1534–5); executed for treason

Henry Fitzroy, Duke of Richmond (1519–36): Henry's illegitimate son by Elizabeth Blount

Edward Foxe (mid-1490s–1538): diplomat and bishop of Hereford (1535–8); co-author of *Collectanea satis copiosa* which made the case for Henry's divorce; principal author of the *Bishops' Book*

Francis I (1494–1547): king of France (1515–47)

Stephen Gardiner (1483–1555): bishop of Winchester (1531–50, 1553–5) and a leading Privy Council member after the fall of Wolsey; Cromwell opponent; Lord Chancellor under Queen Mary

John Hallam (?–1537): Yorkshire farmer and agitator; co-leader of the Pilgrimage of Grace rebellion; executed for treason

Henry VIII (1491–1547): king of England (1509–47)

Hans Holbein, the Younger (1497?–1543): German artist at the court of Henry VIII, specializing in portraiture; famous paintings of Henry, his wives, More, Cromwell, and members of the nobility

Catherine Howard (1522/1523–42): niece of Thomas Howard and fifth wife of Henry VIII (q. 1540–2); executed for treasonous adultery

Thomas Howard, Duke of Norfolk (1473–1554): supreme peer; uncle of Anne Boleyn; Privy Council co-president; Lord Treasurer (1524–47); Cromwell opponent

John Hussey, Baron (1465/1466–1537): Lincolnshire lord; Aragon conspirator in collusion with the emperor and the pope; attainted for treason and executed after failure of the Pilgrimage of Grace

John Knox (1505/1515–72): Scottish preacher and rabble-rouser who led the fight to convert Scotland to Calvinism

Hugh Latimer (1485?–1555): unorthodox preacher patronised by Anne Boleyn; bishop of Worcester (1535–9); executed for heresy during Mary's reign

Edward Lee (1482–1544): archbishop of York succeeding Wolsey (1531–44); member of the Privy Council and moderate supporter of Henry

John Longland (1473–1547): bishop of Lincoln (1521–47); chancellor of Oxford succeeding Warham (1532–47); royal confessor and moderate supporter of Henry

Martin Luther (1483–1546): Augustinian monk who in protest over the sale of indulgences initiated the Protestant Reformation; author of over five hundred works

Niccolò Machiavelli (1469–1527): Florentine civil servant, poet and playwright, and author of the seminal political books, *The Prince* and the *Discourses on Livy*

Mary (1516–58): daughter of Henry and Catherine of Aragon; queen 1553–8; returned England temporarily to the Catholic religion; nicknamed by her opponents 'Bloody Mary'

Thomas More (1478–1535): author of *Utopia* (1516); Privy Council member (1517–32); knight and under-treasurer of Exchequer (1521–5); Lord Chancellor (1529–32); imprisoned (April 1534) then executed (July 1535) for refusing to take the oath of succession

Paul III (1468–1549): Alessandro Farnese; pope (1534–49)

Philip II (1527–98): son of Charles V; king of Spain (1556–98); also ruler of the Netherlands, Naples, Sicily, Portugal, and Chile

Reginald Pole (1500–56): Henry's cousin; cardinal (1536–56); enemy of Cromwell; author of *Pro Unitatis Ecclesiasticae Defensione*, a book attacking Henry and the Reformation; archbishop of Canterbury during Mary's reign

Richard Rich (1496–1567): lawyer; chancellor of Augmentations; Lord Chancellor in later years

Richard Sampson (1470?–1554): bishop of Chichester (1536–43), later of Coventry and Lichfield (1543–54); author of *Oratio* (1533), a book defending the royal supremacy; on the conservative side of the Henry bishops

Jane Seymour (1508–37): Henry's third wife (1536–7) and the mother of Henry's only legitimate son, Edward

John Stokesley (1475–1539): bishop of London (1530–39); on the conservative side of the Henry bishops

George Talbot, Earl of Shrewsbury (1468–1538): old nobility; member of the king's Privy Council; closet Aragonese but faithful servant of the king; active in suppressing the Pilgrimage of Grace uprising

George Throckmorton (1489?–1552): knight and member of parliament representing Warwickshire; outspoken Aragon supporter and frequent subject of treason investigations

Margaret Tudor (1489–1541): older sister of Henry; queen of Scotland (1502–13)

Mary Tudor (1496–1533): younger sister of Henry; queen of France (1515); duchess of Suffolk (1515–33)

Cuthbert Tunstall (1474–1559): bishop of London (1523–30); then bishop of Durham (1530–52, 1554–9); friend of More and Catherine

William Tyndale (1494–1536): leading English follower of Luther; translator of the New Testament; exile living in Antwerp; condemned for heresy and executed while abroad

William Warham (1450–1532): Lord Chancellor (1504–15); archbishop of Canterbury (1504–32); chancellor of Oxford University (1506–32)

Thomas Wolsey (1475?–1530): archbishop of York (1514–30) (and holder of lesser episcopates); cardinal, Lord Chancellor, and keeper of the great seal (1515–29); papal legate (1518–29); Henry's chief minister until removed from office on charges of praemunire (1529); arrested the following year, on charges of treason, but died before being imprisoned in the Tower of London

Bibliographical Note

Primary Documents and Contemporary Accounts

The official records of the reign of Henry VIII exist mainly in two multi-volume sets. The first, compiled between 1830 and 1852, is the *State Papers of the Reign of Henry VIII*, an eleven-volume edition consisting of selected letters printed in their entirety. The second, compiled between 1862 and 1932, is *The Calendar of Letters and Papers, Foreign and Domestic, Henry VIII*, a twenty-one-volume edition consisting of entries from the *State Papers* intermixed with lengthy abstracts of period documents found in the British Museum, the Vatican, and foreign capitals. In addition, the correspondence of some foreign ambassadors has been compiled in the *Calendar of State Papers, Spain, 1509-1547* (14 vols., 1866–1947) and in the *Calendar of State Papers, Venice, 1509-1547* (4 vols., 1867–73).

Statutes of the Realm, vol. III (Dawsons of Pall Mall, 1963) contains complete transcripts of all of the laws passed by parliament during Henry VIII's reign. *Tudor Royal Proclamations*, vol. I (Paul Hughes and James Larkin, eds., Yale, 1964) contains complete texts of the proclamations of three Tudor kings, Henry VII, Henry VIII, and Edward VI. Other collections of Tudor documents are: Joseph Tanner, ed., *Tudor Constitutional Documents, A.D. 1485-1603*, 2nd ed.

(Cambridge, 1930); Carl Stephenson and Frederick Marcham, eds., *Sources of English Constitutional History* (Harper and Row, 1972); and G. R. Elton, ed., *The Tudor Constitution: Documents and Commentary* (Cambridge, 1960). Assorted records of the English Reformation are printed in Gilbert Burnet, ed., *The History of the Reformation of the Church of England*, 7 vols. (Oxford, 1865, 1969); and Henry Gee and William John Hardy, eds., *Documents Illustrative of English Church History* (Macmillan, 1896).

Edward Hall was a burgess for Wenlock in Shropshire during the Reformation Parliament. A king's man and friend of Cromwell, Hall wrote a history of the reign called *The Triumphant Reigne of Kyng Henry VIII* as part of a larger work called *Chronicles* (2 vols.; T. C. and E. C. Jack, 1904). The title of the Henry volume indicates well enough the point of view. Some particulars of the period, some of them touching on Cromwell, have Hall as their only source. The same is true for George Cavendish, a Wolsey steward who wrote a biography of the cardinal a quarter-century or so after Wolsey's death. The biography is called *The Life and Death of Cardinal Wolsey* (Oxford, 1959). Cromwell appears in several places, drawn sympathetically as a true friend of the cardinal and effective servant of the king. A third period book of consequence is John Foxe's *Acts and Monuments*, (AMS Press, 1965), also known as *The Book of Martyrs*, an eight-volume memorial to Christian martyrs, especially martyrs for the Reformation. Cromwell is portrayed as an early Protestant hero. At the end of the century, the antiquarian John Stow described Elizabethan London in his *Survey of London* (Dent, 1945), a book which looks back to London's beginnings and in passing provides important information related to Cromwell, namely his practice of supporting the poor and his confiscation of property adjacent to his home.

General Studies

Tudor England has been the subject of numerous histories over the years. The melodramas of Henry and his six wives, and of Elizabeth, the virgin queen, have proven irresistible to historians and their publics. A good introduction to the Tudor period is still G. R. Elton's, *England under the Tudors*, 3rd ed. (Methuen, 1991). The book is not new; indeed, its first iteration is a half-century old; but as Elton is a lightning rod attracting controversy wherever he goes, his book continues to be read, cited, and commented on. More recent studies are John Guy's *Tudor England* (Oxford, 1988)–a full-blown narrative that incorporates all of the then-current scholarship; Susan Brigden's *London and the Reformation* (Clarendon, 1989), and *New Worlds, Lost Worlds: The Rule of the Tudors, 1485–1603* (Viking, 2000), both works treating of the lives led and the religious choices made by people, but with the second situating England's Renaissance and Reformation in a larger, British Isles, context; and Richard Rex's *The Tudors* (Tempus, 2002), featuring readable biographies of the public lives of the five Tudor monarchs. An edited volume worthy of note is Robert Tittler and Norman Jones, eds., *A Companion to Tudor Britain* (Blackwell, 2004).

Cromwell

Cromwell has hardly been neglected by historians, as he is the subject of at least six biographies written in the twentieth century, and of three in the twenty-first.

Biographies critical of Cromwell are: R. B. Merriman, *Life and Letters of Thomas Cromwell*, 2 vols. (Clarendon, 1902); Peter Wilding, *Thomas Cromwell* (Heinemann, 1935); Theodore Maynard, *The Crown and the Cross: A Biography of Thomas Cromwell* (McGraw Hill, 1950); and Philip W. Sergeant, *Rogues and Scoundrels* (Brentano, 1927), which includes a chapter on Cromwell.

More positive renderings are given by: A. G. Dickens, *Thomas Cromwell and the English Reformation* (English Universities, 1959); B. W. Beckingsale, *Thomas Cromwell, Tudor Minister* (Rowman and Littlefield, 1978). Robert Hutchinson, *Thomas Cromwell: The*

Rise and Fall of Henry VIII's Most Notorious Minister (Thomas Dunn Books, 2009); and John Schofield, *The Rise and Fall of Thomas Cromwell: Henry VIII's Most Faithful Servant* (The History Press, 2011). Cromwell shares space with Wolsey in a dual biography by Neville Williams, *The Cardinal and the Secretary: Thomas Wolsey and Thomas Cromwell* (Macmillan, 1976) – a clear, well conceived study, though somewhat spotty in its coverage. And a chapter is devoted to Cromwell in Paul Van Dyke's *Renascence Portraits* (Charles Scribner's Sons, 1905).

Refurbishing the reputation of Thomas Cromwell has been the central focus of Elton's scholarly career. Elton's chief works, about more than just Cromwell, are:

The Tudor Revolution in Government (Cambridge, 1953)
England under the Tudors (Methuen, 1955, 1974, 1991)
Policy and Police: The Enforcement of the Reformation in the Age of Thomas Cromwell (Cambridge, 1972)
Reform and Renewal: Thomas Cromwell and the Common Weal (Cambridge, 1973)
Reform and Reformation: England, 1509-1558 (Harvard, 1977)
Studies in Tudor and Stuart Politics and Government, 4 vols. (Cambridge, 1974, 1983, 1992)

Elton's aggressive promotion of Cromwell has produced a predictable push-back reaction, first in the 1960s, in a running controversy in the journal *Past and Present*; then in the general histories of the Tudor period published in the 1970s (e.g., Penry Williams, *The Tudor Regime* [Clarendon, 1979], 457–58), as well as in a 1979 article by Brendan Bradshaw ('The Tudor Commonwealth: Reform and Revision', *Historical Journal*, 22); then in a collection of essays edited by Christopher Coleman and David Starkey: *Revolution Reassessed: Revisions in the History of Tudor Government and Administration* (Clarendon, 1986).

G. W. Bernard stated his misgivings in 'Elton's Cromwell', a (previously published) chapter of a book titled *Power and Politics in Tudor England* (Ashgate, 2000); this critique he continued in his seven-hundred–page *The King's Reformation: Henry VIII and the Remaking of the English Church* (Yale, 2005); as suggested by the title, Bernard credits Henry with nearly everything.

Machiavelli is thought to have lent theoretical heft to Cromwell's practice of statecraft. Two older scholars who acknowledge Machiavellian influences on Cromwell are W. Gordon Zeeveld, *Foundations of Tudor Policy* (Harvard, 1948), 184–89 – a study of intellectuals working for Wolsey, Pole, and Cromwell; and T. M. Parker, 'Was Thomas Cromwell a Machiavellian?', *Journal of Ecclesiastical History*, 1 (1950). A recent scholar who espouses the same view is K. R. Bartlett, 'Morley, Machiavelli, and the Pilgrimage of Grace', in *'Triumphs of English': Henry Parker, Lord Morley, Translator to the Tudor Court, New Essays in Interpretation*, Marie Axton and James Carley, eds. (British Library, 2000); included in the book is the complete text of Morley's letter to Cromwell.

Scholars holding the opposite opinion are, besides Van Dyke: Arnold Weissberger, 'Machiavelli and Tudor England', *Political Science Quarterly*, 42 (1927); G. R. Elton, e.g., *Reform and Reformation*, 171; A. G. Dickens, *Thomas Cromwell and the English Reformation*, 39, 58; J. J. Scarisbrick, *Henry VIII* (California, 1968), 303; and B. W. Beckingsale, *Thomas Cromwell, Tudor Minister*, 104. In some cases scholars are simply repeating Elton's conclusion.

Henry VIII, His Court and His Queens

A. F. Pollard's *Henry VIII* (Longmans, 1905; Green, 1951) held sway for over half a century. Since then the seminal biography, by consensus opinion, is J. J. Scarisbrick's *Henry VIII* (reprinted by Yale, 1997). With Pollard, and to some degree with Scarisbrick, the central question has been Henry's command over policy – nearly total for

Pollard; for Scarisbrick, feeling the weight of Elton, not that much, but still a lot, especially in regards to the supremacy. These are both big books. A good, brief 'biography,' which does not exactly focus on its titled subject, is David Starkey, *The Reign of Henry VIII: Personalities and Politics* (Franklin Watts, 1986).

Starkey's theme is court faction. This he has investigated in a host of book chapters and journal articles, with special attention paid to the Privy Chamber. His adversary, who minimises the existence and import of faction, is G. W. Bernard. Bernard's Henry is a grand puppeteer, and faction at court suggests a monarch not fully in control. In addition to Bernard's *Power and Politics in Tudor England* and *The King's Reformation*, there is 'The Making of Religious Policy, 1533–1546: Henry VIII and the Search for the Middle Way', *Historical Journal*, 41 (1998). Outside of this 'king or faction' debate, and serving as a general introduction, is David Loades' *The Tudor Court* (Barnes and Noble, 1987). Neville Williams' *Henry VIII and His Court* (Weidenfeld and Nicolson, 1971) is a richly illustrated book that interweaves pageantry and politics. A longer and more gossipy version of the same is Alison Weir's *Henry VIII, the King and His Court* (Ballantine, 2001).

David Starkey is again useful for study of Henry's queens; his *Six Wives: The Queens of Henry VIII* (Harper Collins, 2003) is the new standard work. Regarding particular monographs, Garrett Mattingly's *Catherine of Aragon* (Little Brown, 1941), though dated and decidedly friendly toward its subject, provides a fascinating account of the intrigue that swirled about Catherine. Anne Boleyn is understandably the queen most doted on by historians. Paul Friedmann's *Anne Boleyn*, 2 vols. (Macmillan, 1884) is still helpful for its wide setting and attention to chronology; Retha Warnike's *The Rise and Fall of Anne Boleyn* (Cambridge, 1989) is still valuable for its contrarian theses; and E. W. Ives' *Anne Boleyn* (Basil Blackwell, 1986) is still the standard text. Warnicke is also the author of a recent study of Henry's fourth wife, titled *The Marrying of Anne of Cleves:*

Royal Protocol in Early Modern England (Cambridge, 2000); the subtitle identifies the focus. Margaret C. Barnes' *My Lady of Cleves* (Macrae-Smith, 1946) is better as straightforward narrative.

Government

A good introduction to the study of Tudor government, one which takes a wide view and is steeped in historiographical controversy, is S. J. Gunn's *Early Tudor Government, 1485–1558* (St Martins, 1995). The architecture of Tudor government is well laid out in David Loades' *Tudor Government* (Blackwell, 1997). Three edited volumes deserve mention regarding the politics of the time: Claire Cross, David Loades, and J. J. Scarisbrick, eds., *Law and Government under the Tudors* (Cambridge, 1988); Diarmaid MacCulloch, *The Reign of Henry VIII: Politics, Policy and Piety* (Macmillan, 1995); and John Guy, ed., *The Tudor Monarchy* (Arnold, 1997).

The history, structure, and workings of Tudor parliaments can be studied in Michael R. Graves' *The Tudor Parliaments: Crown, Lords, and Commons, 1485–1603* (Longman, 1985); and in Jennifer Loach's *Parliament under the Tudors* (Clarendon, 1991). Stanford Lehmberg has provided the two most comprehensive examinations of Henrician parliaments: *The Reformation Parliament, 1529–1536* (Cambridge, 1970); and *The Later Parliaments of Henry VIII, 1539–1547* (Cambridge, 1977).

Church and Religion

The English Reformation, by A. G. Dickens, has long been the standard text on church and religion in Tudor England (Schocken, 1964; Pennsylvania State, 1989). Its more recent, and like-named, competitors are: Christopher Haigh, *English Reformations: Religion, Politics, and Society under the Tudors* (Oxford, 1993); and Norman Jones, *The English Reformation: Religion and Cultural Adaptation* (Blackwell, 2002). A solid introduction to the subject is Richard Rex's *Henry VIII and the English Reformation* (St Martin's, 1993). Reformation historiography (through the mid 1980s) can be reviewed in Rosemary O'Day's *The Debate on the English Reformation* (Methuen, 1986).

Protestant radicals and their Catholic persecutors is the subject of William Clebsch's *England's Earliest Protestants, 1520–1535* (Yale, 1964). The reception given the Reformation at the popular and local level is examined in J. J. Scarisbrick's *The Reformation and the English People* (Basil Blackwell, 1984); more recent contributions are Eamon Duffy's *The Voices of Morebath: Reformation and Rebellion in an English Village* (Yale, 2000); and Alec Ryrie's *The Gospel and Henry VIII: Evangelicals in the Early English Reformation* (Cambridge, 2003). The dissolution of the monasteries received its classic statement in David Knowles' *The Religious Orders in England,* vol. 3 (Cambridge, 1959). The subject is sympathetically handled in Eamon Duffy's *The Stripping of the Altars: Traditional Religion in England, c.1400–c.1580* (Yale, 1992).

Opposition

The fourth chapter of Anthony Fletcher's *Tudor Rebellions,* 3rd ed. (Longman, 1983) provides a brief overview of the Pilgrimage of Grace rebellion. The most exhaustive study of this and the Exeter conspiracy is the two-volume tome by Madeleine Hope Dodds and Ruth Dodds, called *The Pilgrimage of Grace and the Exeter Conspiracy* (Frank Cass, 1971; originally published in 1915). Their study takes the side of Robert Aske and the rebels. The present-day scholar whose name is most associated with the northern rebellions is Michael Bush, author of numerous articles and of two books: *The Pilgrimage of Grace: A Study of the Rebel Armies of October 1536* (Manchester, 1996); and, with David Bownes, *The Defeat of the Pilgrimage of Grace: A Study of the Postpardon Revolts of December 1536 to March 1537 and Their Effects* (Hull, 1999). G. R. Elton, in 'Politics and the Pilgrimage of Grace' (*Studies,* vol. 3), argues that the rebellion was gentry-led by London courtiers who had lost out to Cromwell after the fall of Anne Boleyn. R. W. Hoyle returns to the standard interpretation of a popularly based uprising in his *The Pilgrimage of Grace and the Politics of the 1530s*

(Oxford, 2001). A page-turning narrative of the event is provided by Geoffrey Moorhouse, *The Pilgrimage of Grace: The Rebellion that Shook Henry VIII's Throne* (Weidenfeld and Nicolson, 2002).

The Geraldine revolt can be studied in Brendan Bradshaw's 'Cromwellian Reform and the Origins of the Kildare Rebellion', *Royal Historical Society Transactions*, 5th series, 27 (1977), and in Bradshaw's *The Irish Constitutional Revolution of the Sixteenth Century* (Cambridge, 1979); part 2. Chapter 7 of Steven Ellis' *Tudor Frontiers and Noble Power: The Making of the British State* (Clarendon, 1995) is likewise devoted to the Irish campaign.

War and Diplomacy

Henry's first martial adventure is the subject of Charles Cruickshank's *Henry VIII and the Invasion of France* (St Martin's, 1990). R. B. Werham's *Before the Armada: The Emergence of the English Nation, 1485–1588* (Harcourt, Brace, and World, 1966) is a commonly cited text on international relations in the sixteenth century; likewise P. S. Crowson's *Tudor Foreign Policy* (St Martin's, 1973). The standard work is Garrett Mattingly's *Renaissance Diplomacy* (Jonathan Cape, 1962). Rory McEntegart's *Henry VIII, the League of Schmalkalden and the English Reformation* (Boydell Press, 2002) challenges the conventional view that Anglo-German relations carried little religious significance (at least for the English) and were used as a pawn on the larger chessboard of great-power politics.

Appendix 1: Domestic & Foreign Relations

Dates plus Coronations and Elections	Anti-French/ Scottish Actions	Anti-Papal Actions	Peace-Making, Neutrality	Anti-Spanish/ Imperial Actions	Anti-English Actions
1509 Henry VIII, King of England			Marriage of Henry to Catherine of Aragon		
1511	Holy League: Papacy, England, Spain (joining in 1513)				
1512	Anglo-Spanish operations against Navarre (successful)			Battle of Ravenna: French victory, but loss of commander	
1513 Pope Leo X	Battle of Novara: Swiss victory; French abandonment of Italy Anglo-German operations against Thérouanne, Tournai; Battle of Spurs (successful) Battle of Flodden Field: English victory over Scotland; James IV killed				
1514			Separate peace with France by Spain and Germany Anglo-French treaty: marriage of King Louis XII and Mary Tudor		
1515 Francis I, King of France	Anglo-Spanish treaty			Battle of Marignano: French victory over Swiss mercenaries of Holy League; capture of Milan	French claim to protectorship during minority of Scotland's King James Return to Scotland of (anti-English) Duke of Albany
1516 Charles, King of Spain	English-Spanish-Papal-Swiss alliance Siege of Milan English-German-Swiss alliance				Treaty of Noyon: Franco-Spanish alliance
1517		Luther begins Protestant Reformation			Germany joins Treaty of Noyon
1518			Treaty of London: continental peace based on collective security		
1519 Charles V, Holy Roman Emperor					
1520 Suleiman the Magnificent, Turkish Sultan			Field of Cloth of Gold: Anglo-French summit Anglo-Imperial summits at Gravelines and Calais		

31. 1509–29 shows the war-and-peace relations among European powers during the first twenty years of Henry's reign. Prior to Charles' election as emperor in 1519, Imperial affairs are labeled 'German'; after Charles' election, Spanish affairs are labeled 'Imperial.'

1521	French driven out of Milan *Treaty of Bruges*: Anglo-Imperial plans for 1523 invasion of France		*Calais conference*: arbitration of French violations London treaty		Duke of Albany again in Scotland
1522 Pope Adrian VI	Anglo-Imperial war planning				English-Scottish skirmishing
1523 Pope Clement VII	English invasion of France (inconclusive)				
1524	Siege of Marseilles by Charles, Duke of Bourbon			French recapture of Milan	
1525	*Battle of Pavia*: Imperial victory; capture of Francis English plans for dismemberment of France (rejected by Emperor)			*Treaty of the More*: Anglo-French alliance	
1526			*Treaty of Madrid*: Franco-Imperial peace; release of Francis; surrender of French claims to Italy Marriage of Charles to Isabella of Portugal English attempts to broker continental peace	*League of Cognac*: France, Papacy, Milan, Venice, Florence	
1527		Sack of Rome by Imperial forces; imprisonment of Clement VII Escape of Clement VII to Orvieto	English attempts to broker continental peace, with Wolsey to serve as acting pope	*Treaty of Westminster*: French alliance French military successes in Italy	
1528	Imperial military successes in Italy		English peace proposal: Charles anointed emperor by pope, sons of Francis released from captivity		
1529	*Battle of Landriano*: Imperial victory	Treaty of Barcelona: Papacy yields to Empire	*Treaty of Cambrai ("Ladies Peace")*: Imperial hegemony in Italy acknowledged		

Dates	English Affairs	Imperial Affairs	French Affairs	German Affairs	Papal Affairs
1529	Fall of Wolsey Thomas More named Lord Chancellor Anticlerical legislation			Second Diet of Speyer: protesting princes named "Protestants"	Nullity suit revoked to Rome
1530	Death of Wolsey	Coronation of Charles HRE by Clement VII Knights of Rhodes moved to Malta	Marriage of Francis I to Eleanor of Portugal, sister of Charles	Augsberg Confession	Henry cited to appear at Rome
1531	Praemunire charges Conditional Supremacy			League of Schmalkalden formed	
1532	Conditional Restraint of Annates Supplication against Ordinaries Submission of Clergy Anne Boleyn named Marquess of Pembroke		Divorce support promised by Francis at Franco-English summit		
1533	Thomas Cranmer named Archbishop of Canterbury Restraint of Appeals Divorce of Catherine of Aragon Marriage of Henry to Anne Boleyn Birth of Elizabeth	Marseilles conference: Francis mediating with pope			Provisional excommunication #1 of Henry
1534	Submission of Clergy Absolute Restraint of Annates Succession Execution of the "Maid of Kent" and collaborators				Henry-Catherine marriage ruled valid Death of Clement VII Coronation of Paul III Jesuit Order founded
1535	Imprisonment of Fisher and More Supremacy Oath of Succession Treasons Visitation of monasteries; Valor Ecclesiasticus Execution of Fisher, More, and others	Capture of Tunis Occupation of Milan (following death of Sforza)	Matrimonial negotiations with England	Lübeck-Denmark war, with English involvement Wittenburg conference: Lutheran princes and English envoys	Provisional excommunication #2 of Henry
1536	Dissolution of Monasteries Court of Augmentations Union with Wales				

32. 1529–36.

Dates	English Domestic Affairs	Anglo-German Relations	Anglo-French-Imperial Relations	Franco-Imperial Relations	Imperial-German Relations	Papal-et al Relations
1536 Winter	Death of Catherine; Parliament in session; Coverdale Bible					
Spring	Parliament in session; Execution of Anne; Marriage of Henry and Jane					
Summer	Parliament in session; Ten Articles; Injunctions #1			War		
Fall	Pilgrimage of Grace			War		
1537 Winter	Pilgrimage of Grace			War		Reginald Pole in Flanders
Spring	Dissolution of monasteries (till 1540)					
Summer	Bishops' Book; Matthew Bible; Injunctions #2			War		
Fall	Birth of Edward; death of Jane			War		General Council scheduled, but delayed
1538 Winter			Henry + French brides	War		
Spring			Henry + Imperial bride	War		
Summer		Schmalkaldic emissaries in London	Henry + more French brides	Truce of Nice; Aigues Mortes summit		
Fall	Exeter Conspiracy; Lambert trial					Excommunication of Henry
1539 Winter		Negotiations with Cleves	Recall of ambassadors	Treaty of Toledo: peace between France and Empire		Pole sent to Imperial and French courts; David Beaton in Scotland
Spring	Parliament in session; Great Bible	Schmalkaldic emissaries in London	Return of ambassadors		Frankfort accords; Ghent rebellion	
Summer	Six Articles		Henry + Imperial bride			
Fall		Cleve emissaries in London; Philip of Bavaria in London		Passage of Imperial court through France		
1540 Winter		Marriage of Henry and Anne of Cleves		Charles fêted in Paris		

33. 1536–40.

Appendix 2:
What Did Thomas Cromwell Know About Machiavelli?

Machiavelli came into England by way of Thomas Cromwell—maybe. The source is Reginald Pole, cousin to Henry, cardinal of the church, and archbishop of Canterbury under Queen Mary. Pole reported a conversation he had with Cromwell in which the then-Wolsey minister dilated on the responsibilities of the courtier-adviser. In response to Pole's contention that the adviser should counsel the prince to adhere to Christian principles, Cromwell countered that the adviser should eschew ethics and take as his guide the prince's desires, however unholy or illicit they maybe. The good adviser, he added, knows the prince's mind, executes the prince's will, and represents the prince's policies as the product of pure virtue. Cromwell complained of advisers, fresh from the schools, who tried applying moral theory to political practice and of those writers, starting with Plato, who created imaginary republics unfit for use in this world. But he recommended the work of a contemporary author, unnamed, whom he praised for his deft interweaving of experience and learning. Cromwell promised to lend Pole the recommended book. When the book never came, Pole investigated (like a general seeking out 'the dispatches of an enemy to know his plans') and concluded that *The Prince* was the book and that Niccolò Machiavelli was the author.

The date of the conversation was about 1528, the recollection of it in 1539 (in *Apologia Reginaldi Poli ad Carolum Quintum Caesarem*, a belated preface to Pole's 1536 book *Pro Unitatis Ecclesiasticae Defensione*, abbreviated *De Unitate*). Machiavelli's *Prince* was written in 1513, and while it was not published until 1532, it circulated in manuscript form since the time of its composition, and a plagiarised redaction was published in Latin in 1523. Cromwell could have procured a copy during a visit to Italy, or an associate could have acquired one for him.

But scholars today are inclined to discount Pole's reminiscence. They base themselves on a century-old article by Paul Van Dyke, written as an appendix to his *Renascence Portraits*. In this meticulous examination of the content and publication history of Pole's preface, Van Dyke argues that Pole searched out the title and author of the recommended book not immediately (Pole said 'afterwards') but a decade or so later; that the book in question was more likely *The Book of the Courtier* by Baldesar Castiglione; and that Cromwell probably did not own a copy of *The Prince* until a friend gave him one in 1539. Van Dyke marshals a wealth of evidence in support of these judgements; but never is the evidence quite enough to turn plausible conjecture into certain fact.

In the *Apologia* Cromwell was described as the emissary of Satan responsible for the horrors perpetrated by Henry; and Machiavelli's *Prince* was identified as the source of Cromwell's satanic advice. But Pole, reasons Van Dyke, could not have formed this ill opinion of Cromwell until the late 1530s, since Pole's occasional correspondence with Cromwell in the mid 1530s was friendly and polite. And when that ill opinion was once formed, Van Dyke surmises, the unnamed book was then—and only then—sought out and identified, with Machiavelli then—and only then— fingered as the person at fault for all that had gone wrong in England.

There are though grounds for doubt. Van Dyke assumes that Pole was sincere in his expressions of good will, even though Pole was sometimes operating as a papal envoy, charged with concealing intentions and misleading adversaries; and even though Pole knew that Henry and Cromwell, who referred to him as 'detestable traitor,' were plotting his arrest or assassination; or that Pole, who in his *De Unitate* had poured invective upon Henry, believed assurances from Cromwell that the king still regarded Pole with favour; or that Pole, who was himself plotting the overthrow of the crown and was supplying rebels with arms and funds, genuinely meant his offer of continued service to Henry (all remarks contained in the correspondence of the period). It was not uncommon in the sixteenth century (or in any century since) for diplomats to say one thing and intend another, or for fulsome professions of friendship to be less than sincere.

Van Dyke adduces two reasons for preferring the *Courtier* by Castiglione to *The Prince* by Machiavelli. The *Courtier* was printed in 1528, whereas *The Prince*, as mentioned, was first published in 1532; the *Courtier* speaks directly to the issue of the Pole-Cromwell conversation—the job of the adviser—whereas *The Prince* is silent about the subject.

The first point is not dispositive, as Van Dyke acknowledges. The fact that the *Courtier* was easy to come by (and known to have been in Cromwell's library as of 1530) does not mean that *The Prince* was impossible to acquire in advance of its publication. The second point is supported by a passage quoted from the *Courtier* in which the adviser is told to adjust his counsel to the character of the prince. Cromwell apparently said the same to Pole, and so Cromwell apparently recommended the book that backed up his advice. But in the very passage cited by Van Dyke, the stated purpose of the adviser's trimming and tack is to 'lead him [the prince] to virtue.' This practical counsel, traced to Plato and Aristotle and consistent with More, is hardly the immoralism which Pole remembered Cromwell to have uttered. In fact, the *Courtier* in content is nearer to being a book which the pious Pole would have recommended to Cromwell than a book which the satanic Cromwell would have recommended to Pole.

It is said that *The Prince* does not address the subject of the courtier-adviser. That statement, often repeated, is not exactly true, as four chapters of *The Prince* (9, 20, 22, 23) explain how the prince should choose, utilize, and relate to his advisers; and two chapters of the *Discourses on Livy* (III.35, 41) explain how the adviser should deliver counsel to the prince. But more importantly, the entire political corpus of Machiavelli is in one sense an examination of the role of the adviser, since in writing these books Machiavelli put himself in the position of adviser to princes and potential princes across the centuries.

Central to the case is a Cromwell associate named lord Morley (Henry Parker), who sent Cromwell a copy of Machiavelli's *Florentine Histories* in February 1539. Delighted by the narrative of a city-state sometimes at war with Rome and scornful of its curses, Morley thought, and stated in an accompanying letter, that the history of Florence would make pleasant reading for the king. He also recommended *The Prince* as 'a very special good thing' for Cromwell 'to look upon,' implying that Cromwell had not before seen the book. From this one comment (plus its companion: 'as I suppose you yourself shall judge when you have seen the same'), in this one letter, scholars infer that 1539, not 1528 (or earlier), was the date when Cromwell first acquired a copy of *The Prince*.

But is this inference incontestable, or for that matter even warranted? First of all, from mid decade on, Machiavelli was constantly appearing in the writings and state propaganda of a Cromwell secretary named Richard Morison. It is difficult to believe that Cromwell could have sponsored Morison (whose manifestoes were published on the king's press) and known nothing of Morison's Italian exemplar. Morley's supposition that Cromwell was unfamiliar with Machiavelli may therefore have stemmed from Morley's own excitement in reading the *Histories* and his desire to share his discoveries with others. Morley enthused about the parallels he had seen between the current-day English and the Florentines of yesteryear, and he urged the king's attention directed to passages about the 'bishop of Rome,' passages conveniently marked by Morley in the book's margins. Morley, it appears, wanted to be helpful and so needed fresh information to bring to Cromwell and the king. Or, as one scholar speculates, Morley, a conservative lord, anxious to reassure the government of his loyalty in the aftermath of a northern uprising, was providing the crown with a ready-made set of Machiavellian excuses for its own Machiavellian conduct in putting down the rebellion—excuses which would have been all the more appreciated, if Cromwell and Henry were hearing them for the first time. Morley himself offered some bit of confirmation when he asserted, following a sketch of papal usurpations gleaned from the *Histories*, 'I do know very well your lordship will affirm to have read no such thing'— i.e., you will admit to having learned of these enormities from no other source. Morley was, or hoped to be, the bearer of a heretofore unknown indictment of the papacy contained in the pages of the heretofore unread *Histories*. On the other hand, Morley's implicit claim to detailed knowledge of Cromwell's reading material is difficult to countenance, since Morley was more a client than a confidant of the Lord Privy Seal.

In sum, Morley's above phrases describing the novelty of his gift are hardly enough to push back to 1539 the date of Cromwell's first encounter with Machiavelli. After all, in 1538 Pole remarked to a young companion, one John Leigh, whom Pole was hoping to steer away from Machiavelli, that Machiavelli had 'already poisoned England and would poison all of Christendom.' If by 1538 England (meaning its government) had already been poisoned, Cromwell, the source of the poison, as judged by Pole, must himself have been poisoned (i.e., exposed to Machiavelli) many years prior. As for Morley's gift of *The Prince* (likely bound with the *Florentine Histories* in a 1532 edition), it in no way proves that a manuscript copy was not already in Cromwell's possession. Some recent, and not so recent, scholarship believe that it was, and believe that the date of the gift and of the letter was 1537 (Van Dyke's argument in part requires that the date be 1539).

This rather tedious business of pinning down dates of book acquisitions and the contents of private libraries is important to a large body of scholars determined to show that Cromwell was no disciple of Machiavelli. G. R. Elton is the dean of this school. He argues the Cromwell was actually an Aristotelian, as demonstrated by the fact that Cromwell requested an explication of Aristotle from one of his secretaries and by the fact that Cromwell himself studied the reputed Aristotelian, Marsilius of Padua. But interest in Marsilius is not interest in Aristotle, since Marsilius, was hardly a faithful follower of Aristotle's thought. Another scholar certain that Cromwell was no Machiavellian is A. G. Dickens, who dismisses claims that Cromwell turned to Machiavelli for guidance. Dickens' confidence, though, is a little strained, given that Dickens uses concepts taken straight from Machiavelli to describe Cromwell. Here Cromwell is the Machiavellian fox and virtuous new prince capable of changing his appearance at will (*Prince*, 6, 15–19):

> In the courts of princes the smooth surfaces of formal address masked rampant jealousy and treachery; for all the bows and titles, men fought like animals for preeminence, privilege and wealth. Even those born near the summit had to be cunning, cautious, adaptable. How much more so the rare man who had risen from the bottom and had been entrusted with the least popular tasks of government! Life became infinitely calculating; he must learn when to be humble, when to be hard, when to be sociable, when to take advantage of an opponent's weakness (*Thomas Cromwell and the English Reformation*, 36).

And here Cromwell is a practitioner of 'cruelty well-used' (*Prince*, 8) and a new prince whose wickedness eliminates problems once and for all, unlike a good prince whose guilt-ridden half-measures exacerbate problems and who himself should stay out of the politics of founding and reform (*Dis*, I.26):

> And if he could return to argue his case in retrospect, Cromwell would doubtless point out the fact that a major historical crisis was surmounted with little bloodshed precisely because, at the earliest sign of trouble, his government struck ruthlessly at the heart of the resistance. Weak and vacillating rulers, he would perhaps urge, ended by causing large-scale revolution, repression and slaughter. . . . The dilemma of power will remain as long as politics exists: it is the factor which must exclude men of sensibility from joining the unclean game in troubled times (135).

It is important for these scholars to put distance between Cromwell and Machiavelli, because these scholars largely accept Pole's estimate of Machiavelli as Satan's messenger; and because they seem to assume that Pole's account of the conversation with Cromwell, if allowed to stand, would represent the whole of Cromwell's understanding of Machiavelli. There is satanic wisdom in Machiavelli, without doubt; but present as well are concern for the common good, for power-sharing, and for the rule of law. And while the Cromwell of the conversation with Pole was a low-order Machiavellian adviser, Cromwell over time may have learned more from Machiavelli than narrow selfishness and obsequiousness to the prince.

List of Illustrations

1. © Ripon Cathedral.
2. © Elizabeth Norton.
3. © Amberley Archive.
4. © David Baldwin.
5. © Elizabeth Norton.
6. © Stephen Porter.
7. © Elizabeth Norton.
8. © Jonathan Reeve JR1009b66fp181 15501600.
9. © Jonathan Reeve JR1160b4p600 15001550.
10. © Ripon Cathedral.
11. © Jonathan Reeve JR1169b2p7 15001550.
12. © Elizabeth Norton.
13. © Elizabeth Norton.
14. © Elizabeth Norton.
15. © Elizabeth Norton.
16. © Elizabeth Norton.
17. © Jonathan Reeve JR1882b46fp186 14501500.
18. © Jonathan Reeve JRCD33b20p1025 15501600.
19. © Jonathan Reeve JRCD2b20p769 15501600.
20. © Jonathan Reeve JR1872b46fp16 13001350.
21. © Jonathan Reeve JR1884b46fp192 15001550.
22. © Elizabeth Norton and the Amberley Archive.
23. © Jonathan Reeve JR1189b67plixB 16001650.
24. © Jonathan Reeve JR1171b2p45 15001550.
25. © Jonathan Reeve JRCD3b20p913 15001550.
26. © Jonathan Reeve JRCD2b20p929 15001550.
27. Europe *circa* 1530s.
28. The map shows England divided into counties. County representation in the House of Commons was by knights of the shire; enfranchised cities and towns were represented by burgesses.
29. The Pilgrimage of Grace 1536–7.
30. Germany *circa* 1540.
31. 1509–29.
32. 1529–36.
33. 1536–40.

Also available from Amberley Publishing

The complete letters, dispatches and chronicles that tell the real story of Anne Boleyn

Through the chronicles, letters and dispatches written by both Anne and her contemporaries, it is possible to see her life and thoughts as she struggled to become queen of England, ultimately ending her life on the scaffold. Only through the original sources is it truly possible to evaluate the real Anne. George Wyatt's *Life of Queen Anne* provided the first detailed account of the queen, based on the testimony of those that knew her. The poems of Anne's supposed lover, Thomas Wyatt, as well as accounts such as Cavendish's *Life of Wolsey* also give details of her life, as do the hostile dispatches of the Imperial Ambassador, Eustace Chapuys and the later works of the slanderous Nicholas Slander and Nicholas Harpsfield. Henry VIII's love letters and many of Anne's own letters survive, providing an insight into the love affair that changed England forever. The reports on Anne's conduct in the Tower of London show the queen's shock and despair when she realised that she was to die. Collected together for the first time, these and other sources make it possible to view the real Anne Boleyn through her own words and those of her contemporaries.

£25 Hardback
45 illustrations
352 pages
978-1-4456-0043-7

Available from all good bookshops or to order direct
Please call **01453-847-800**
www.amberleybooks.com

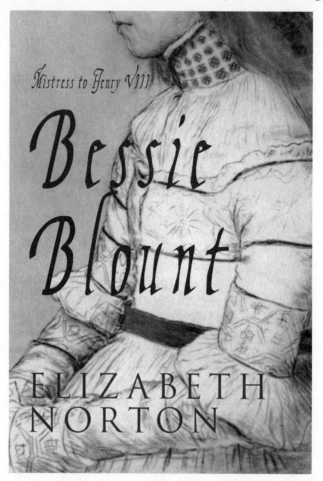

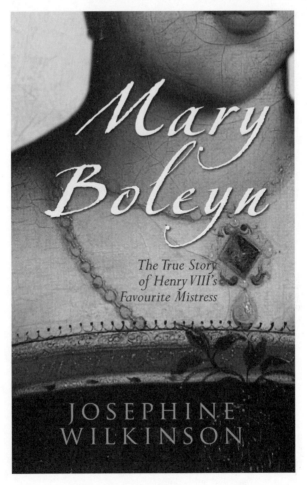

Also available from Amberley Publishing

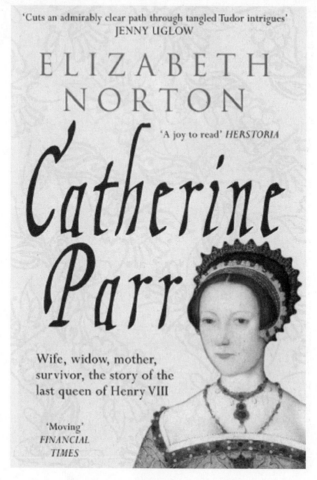

'Cuts an admirably clear path through tangled Tudor intrigues'
JENNY UGLOW

ELIZABETH NORTON

'A joy to read' HERSTORIA

Catherine Parr

Wife, widow, mother, survivor, the story of the last queen of Henry VIII

'Moving'
FINANCIAL TIMES

Wife, widow, mother, survivor, the story of the last queen of Henry VIII

'Scintillating' THE FINANCIAL TIMES
'Norton cuts an admirably clear path through the tangled Tudor intrigues' JENNY UGLOW
'Wonderful, an excellent book, a joy to read' HERSTORIA

The sixth wife of Henry VIII was also the most married queen of England, outliving three husbands before finally marrying for love. Catherine Parr was enjoying her freedom after her first two arranged marriages when she caught the attention of the elderly Henry VIII. She was the most reluctant of all Henry's wives, offering to become his mistress rather than submit herself to the dangers of becoming Henry's queen. This only served to increase Henry's enthusiasm for the young widow and Catherine was forced to abandon her lover for the decrepit king.

£9.99 Paperback
49 illustrations (39 colour)
304 pages
978-1-4456-0383-4

Available from all good bookshops or to order direct
Please call **01453-847-800**
www.amberleybooks.com

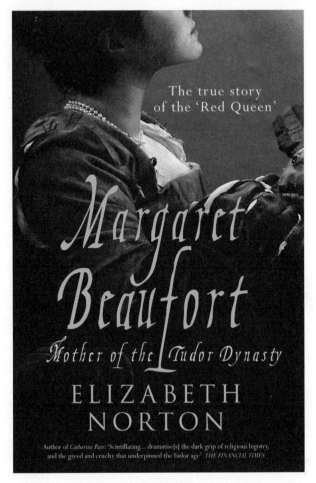

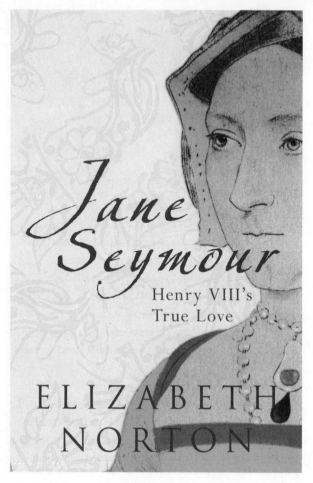

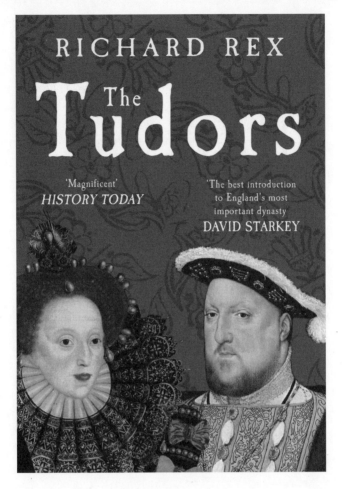

Also available from Amberley Publishing

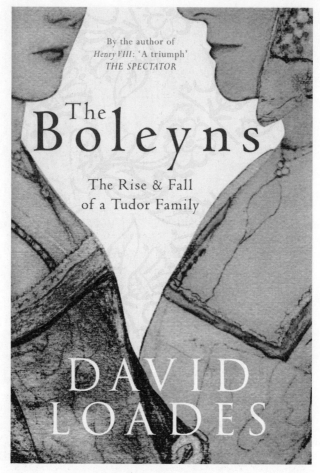

*A magnificent tale of family rivalry and intrigue set against
Henry VIII's court*

The fall of Anne Boleyn and her brother George is the classic drama of the Tudor era. The Boleyns had long been an influential English family. Sir Edward Boleyn had been Lord Mayor of London. His grandson, Sir Thomas had inherited wealth and position, and through the sexual adventures of his daughters, Mary and Anne, ascended to the peak of influence at court. The three Boleyn children formed a faction of their own, making many enemies: and when those enemies secured Henry VIII's ear, they brought down the entire family in blood and disgrace.

£20 Hardback
50 illustrations (25 colour)
352 pages
978-1-4456-0304-9

Also available from Amberley Publishing

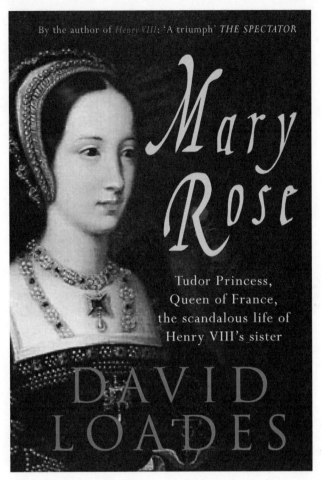

Tudor Princess, Queen of France, the scandalous life of Henry VIII's sister

'A paradise... tall, slender, grey-eyed, possessing an extreme pallor'. The contemporary view of Henry VIII's younger sister, Princess Mary Rose as one of the most beautiful princesses in Europe, was an arresting one. Glorious to behold, this Tudor Princess with her red hair flowing loose to her waist, was also impossible for Henry to control.

David Loades' biography, the first for almost 50 years brings the princess alive once more. Of all Tudor women, this queen of France and later Duchess of Suffolk remains an elusive, enigmatic figure.

£20 Hardback
40 illustrations (20 colour)
272 pages
978-1-4456-0622-4

Available from all good bookshops or to order direct
Please call **01453-847-800**
www.amberleybooks.com

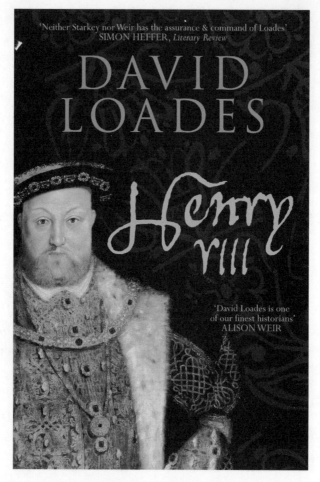